Women, Violence
and War

Women, Violence and War

WARTIME VICTIMIZATION OF REFUGEES IN THE BALKANS

edited by
VESNA NIKOLIĆ-RISTANOVIĆ

CEU PRESS

Central European University Press
Budapest

First published in Serbian as *Žene, nasilje i rat*
by the Institute for Criminological and Sociological Research,
Belgrade, 1995

English edition published in 2000 by
Central European University Press

Október 6 utca 12
H-1051 Budapest
Hungary

400 West 59th Street
New York, NY 10019
USA

Translated by Borislav Radović
English translation © by Borislav Radović, 1999

Distributed in the United Kingdom and Western Europe
by Plymbridge Distributors Ltd., Estover Road, Plymouth PL6 7PZ,
United Kingdom

ISBN 963-9116-59-9 Cloth
ISBN 963-9116-60-2 Paperback

Library of Congress Cataloging in Publication Data
A CIP catalog record for this book is available upon request

Printed in Hungary by Akaprint, Budapest

All these infinitely obscure lives remain to be recorded...the accumulation of unrecorded life, whether from the women at the street corners with their arms akimbo, and the rings embedded in their fat swollen fingers, talking with gesticulation like the swing of Shakespeare's words; or from the violet-sellers and match-sellers and old crones stationed under doorways; or from drifting girls whose faces, like waves in sun and cloud, signal the coming of men and women and the flickering lights of shop windows. All that you have to explore.

Virginia Woolf, *A Room of One's Own*

Table of contents

Preface

Presently, dominant Serbian public discourse about the 1991–95 war in the former Yugoslavia can be reduced to a simple formula—the war was inevitable, history keeps repeating itself and a sacrifice for higher national goals is not devoid of sense. Within such a discursive scheme, stories about individual victims and the suffering of ordinary people are only given a marginal place. The entry of Serbia into a new war (in Kosovo), its isolation (and self-isolation) from the international community, its false democratization and delayed transition towards a market economy make the arguments for such a narrative quite easy to find. Deeply set into a basically pessimistic historical script, Serbia became a self-fulfilling prophecy about isolation and sacrifice, excommunication and suffering. Although it is too early to speak about the causes of such a state of affairs and, perhaps, it may be impossible to reach a simple causal explanation, one thing seems certain; the meta-narration about the national project (failed or realized?) must be supplemented by those fragmented and chaotic yet important elements which relate to personal experiences. The choice between the macro-historical and micro-historical perspective is, of course, a matter of personal value orientation. Still, one could claim that advocating the micro-perspective of individual experience means advocating the authentically feminist perspective, which is, at the same time, humanistic and even pacifistic. Perhaps the most convincing way of criticizing war would be to document the suffering of "ordinary" people—those who were caught in the vortex of war, regardless of their intentions and without the possibility of deciding their own fate or even understanding what had happened to them. In that sense, the notorious feminist slogan that "the personal is the political" should be paraphrased to read "the historical is personal."

This book represents a step away from the meta-narrative about the national project. Within the context of contemporary Serbia, it should be seen as a first-class intellectual and political challenge. In fact, the documents gathered in this book deeply subvert the war narrative itself, even the political carriers of that narrative. The official political discourse in Serbia completely ignores individual suffering and sacrifice, as well as other "proofs" of the absurdity of the war and the high price the civilian population was made to pay. Individual testimonies about the war are allowed to enter the public discourse only for the sake of propaganda and the manipulation of public opinion. In that way human stories, if they are used at all, quickly become tools for the reinforcement of national homogeneity and the instigation of vindictive emotions. Thus, within the public space Serbs are again and again presented as victims. Unfortunately, similar methods have been present in the public discourse of other parties in the Yugoslav conflict, where violence against women in particular was manipulated for political goals.

One of the undeniable achievements of this study is that it approaches women as individual victims, regardless of their ethnic affiliations or the ethnic affiliations of the perpetrators of violence against women. In that way, this study clearly stands against the possible political abuse and manipulation of the problem. Reading this book, we do not discover how many women were exposed to violence from men of the "opposite" ethnic group(s), because the "numbers game" would instantly place us within the "male game of war." We cannot find any numbers here, but we are clearly given the message that even one case of such violence is too much. Widespread violence against women in Serbia is a social fact, deeply rooted in the war-oriented patriarchy and Serbian public opinion, which is far less sensitive to violence against women than is public opinion in developed countries where women's rights are deeply rooted. That is why violence against women in Serbian public opinion has quite different connotations than it has in Western societies, and that is precisely where the possibility lies for manipulation of this problem in international politics.

However, the publication of this book in English offers a possibility for the international intellectual community to acquaint itself with some overlooked aspects of the war in the former Yugoslavia. Unfortunately, within the public discourse of many foreign countries, and especially in the media, the problems of the war in the former Yugoslavia were approached exclusively from the historical and politicological macro-perspectives. Both perspectives have, explicitly or implicitly, legitimized collectivist ideas about collective rights, collective culpability and collective responsibility. This, however, has obscured the very essence of the war in the former Yugoslavia, which cannot be reduced to the dynamics of relations between ethnic collectivities; ethnic political élites were producers of the war and therefore are responsible for it.

The authors of this study have made use of the individual experiences of women victims of violence to deconstruct the meta-narrative about the national project. They have also performed a gender-inspired deconstruction of war, demonstrating clearly the opposition between the macro and micro level of analysis, history, everyday life and the male and female. However, it is not men and women as concrete social groups which are opposed here, but rather the ideal types of "masculinity" and "femininity" as they are constituted in a patriarchal society in the state of war. In that sense, this is not a book about women-victims and male-violators, because that would represent a one-dimensional reduction of the problem to an essentialist argumentation. This is a book that demonstrates the ways in which the archaic patriarchal matrices are activated in wartime. It is quite clear that women who have endured violence are dehumanized and reduced to the status of objects; still, there remains the open question of the desubjectivization of the perpetrators, who were not only individual actors but also agents of a collective patriarchal destruction.

The very method applied in this study contains the essence of feminist methodology, which can be reduced to the simple message that one should trust the victim. This is the simplest way of deconstructing androcentric knowledge about war, which manifests itself precisely in the politicological and historical discourse about war. The authors of this book do not pretend to hold *the* truth, nor do they hide the fact that objectivity is not the supreme goal of their research. On the contrary, the sense of this study is the painful writing of the narrated female experience, so rich and dense that it cannot be reduced or compared to some other similar experience. And, although it is individual, it is undoubtedly a part of the patriarchal tradition that always produces violence, especially in war.

The feminist methodology present in this study is also endowed with some therapeutic effects; the very process of transmitting the experience regenerates the victim and brings about catharsis. Also, the verbalization of the painful experiences through a communication process produces a certain cognitive and intellectual consolidation. The essence of trauma is very often bound up with the fact that the victim's experience cannot be communicated in (and cannot be reduced to) the terms of the dominant discourse. In its very process, the research performed in this book aimed to partially desensitize the victim by treating her as a self-reflexive subject and assisting her in her efforts to make her experience communicable and therefore understandable. The authors have succeeded in remaining unobtrusive and discreet yet emphatic and with a visible and firm value orientation. That is why this study has succeeded in penetrating deeply into the subjective, reminding us once again that only the subjective represents the real measure of justice and injustice, peace and war, happiness and unhappiness.

The book has several levels of possible readings and several potential codes of interpretation. On the meta-level, it is constituted as a narrative about good and evil, two values always present and especially active in wartime. On that level, the book poses a question about "the triggers of the evil," as well as about the responsibility for "letting the genie out of the bottle." Much more than merely stating that there are some "good guys" and "bad guys," it simply says that there is good and evil, two opposite principles. It also says that evil can be activated under certain conditions and that being civilized means making every effort to avoid and control those conditions. Therefore, it is not a question of the eradication of evil but about controlling the conditions that might activate it. In that sense, responsibility does not lie exclusively with those who did evil deeds, but also with those who have created favorable conditions for that evil to appear.

The second possible level of reading is at the macro-sociological level. During the war in the former Yugoslavia, the ubiquitous and never uprooted evil was made to grow to terrifying proportions. One could hear plenty of "outsiders" and "insiders" wondering "why" this war had happened, but this is not the question. Every "because" in this case represents a retrospective justification and attribution of sense. The real question should ask about the "how" of this war, since the mechanisms of the activation of evil were quite consciously and rationally structured by the ethnic political élites of the former Yugoslavia. The development of the deconstruction of the former Yugoslavia is a process that took decades to unfold entirely. Quite briefly, the essence of the war is that the states-to-be produced "their" societies through war. To become new states, first they had to have "their" societies. The absurdity and instability of the existing borders between the former Yugoslav republics, and their establishment by murder, rape, exodus and genocide, demonstrate clearly how painful this process was for the formerly well integrated and multicultural society of the former Yugoslavia. This book demonstrates to what extent violence was functional for the creation of a gap between those ethnic groups that, until the beginning of the bloody war (1991), demonstrated only the "antagonism of small differences."

The next level of this book is the level of gender relations. There is no doubt that the experiences of the interviewees largely reflect peacetime patriarchal patterns. The matrix of gender relations is reconfirmed also by male violence against women, by everyday female support to "their" men-warriors and by the modes of female life in refuge. The level of development of female subjectivity largely depends on their social and ethnic backgrounds and level of education. The ways of problem-solving in refuge, the ability to adapt to the new social environment and the development of rational coping strategies correlate significantly with pre-war female experiences. The women who, in the pre-war period, were more emancipated from traditional roles could better cope with the problems they encountered in war and refuge.

However, regardless of the many levels on which this study can be read, there remains the fact that it was written in a manner that leaves a lot of space for the reader to develop his/her own reflections. But this is an "open" book in yet another sense of the word; no definition, including the definition of "violence," is fixed. In a good feminist manner, women researchers have decided to "open up" definitions and let the women victims define for themselves what violence is, on the basis of their own self-reflection. Thus, surprisingly enough, we discovered that any interruption of the normal order of things or any interruption of the cyclical nature of everyday habits was experienced as violence. It turned out that the women interviewed in this study saw themselves as victims not only because they have experienced violence against their souls and bodies but also because their lives (and especially the lives of their children) were severely interrupted in such a way that any perspective was erased.

The intensity and variety of violence in war will shock every reader of this book. This book makes us realize that during the war there were basically three types of violence. The first one represents a simple extension of the peacetime patriarchal patterns of violence against women. The second type of violence is represented by the establishment of new forms of violence, characteristic of wartime. They are "innovative," recurrent and circulate between all parties in conflict. Finally, there is the violence that does not fit into any recognizable or intelligible pattern. This is pure, brutal and arbitrary violence. The general conclusion is that the more violence "fits" a socially constructed pattern the bigger the possibility for the victim to reconstruct her identity.

Although this differentiation undoubtedly exists, and although it may inspire future research, the main point of the book is that violence in war represents an extension of the patterns of patriarchal order. In that sense, violence in war is just an extreme form of the violence that exists in peacetime. In fact, war is the logic of patriarchy pushed to its extreme—the logic of power, hierarchy, absolute truth, the "final solutions of national questions," and absolute right embodied in conflict by only one party.

Patriarchy as the source of war violence against women, however, does not imply that there is some male collective guilt. On the contrary, "liberation" from patriarchy implies liberation from enforced group identities, female and male ones alike. The idea of collective culprits, whether ethnic or gender, only pushes us into helplessness and irresponsibility. On the other hand, sensitivity towards individual victims and individual resistance to war makes possible our individual approach to collectivities and metanarrations, and thus individual responsibility is made possible as well. There were many men who refused to participate in the war in the former Yugoslavia; still, women and civilians are the biggest victims of all wars. However, this statement needs to be refined, because women in war take on very different and very numerous roles. They are victims of war violence but they are also accomplices and warriors; they are peace activists but they are also members of the political élite, making decisions about war and peace. Throughout the course of history, women have been bribed in different ways by the patriarchal structures, sometimes even to the extent that they have been ready to sacrifice their own children. A multitude of roles produces a multitude of identities, and vice versa, so that claiming, in a general fashion, that only women were victims and that all males were violators would mean falling into the same old patriarchal exclusiveness that produces war in the first place. Women, therefore, are not the only victims and they are not only victims, but the absence of an organized large-scale male resistance to the war in the former Yugoslavia obscures this truth. The pacifistic movement in Serbia was predominantly female.

This book will be interesting and provoking to researchers and theorists from many different fields, including gender studies, sociology, criminology, law, history and philosophy. Aside from its documentary and analytical value, this book also has literary value. But first of all, for all of us who, one way or another, feel ourselves to be victims of the war in the former Yugoslavia, this book represents not a voice against war, but a scream.

Marina Blagojević

Acknowledgments

We would like to thank most sincerely all those who have helped us in our research about violence against women in war. Most of all, we would like to express our gratitude to the ones without whose understanding and cooperation this book would never have been written, the ones whose feelings and thoughts are interwoven in these pages: Snežana Minić, Smiljana Dragaš, Slavica Lokvančić, Radina Kosjerina, Sanja Lasica, Radmila Žarković, Radojka Višnjevac, Zora Jovović, Romana, Ines, Milka, B. M., B. V., N. and other women whom we talked to and who wished to remain anonymous.

We also feel deeply indebted to our female friends from the Autonomous Female Center against Sexual Violence, Women in Black (in Belgrade) and SOS Phone for Women and Children Victims of Violence (in Belgrade and Niš). We are especially indebted to the representatives of the Open Society Fund Yugoslavia, who assisted us in establishing contacts and conducting interviews with women refugees. Finally, we feel especially obliged towards Sonja Drljević, Dragan Marković, Svetlana Kijevčanin, Igor Tadić, Lepa Mlađenović, Ljiljana Gaković, Nadežda Ćetković and Zdravko Petrović.

The authors

Introduction to the Serbian edition

War is timeless, and it may be something that is rooted in us, in what it is to be a human being. If that is so, and if we are to survive, it is important to investigate the parts played by women in war, it is time to listen to what they have to say. Women have been encouraged culturally to keep silent, unless they are telling stories pacifistic in nature or intent. It is clear that we need to know much more about gender and war, and about why women have been excluded from war's discourse.

Sally Hayton-Keeva,
Valiant Women in War and Exile, p. VIII

This is a book about war, as it was seen, felt and interpreted by women. It was written by four women who have not experienced war themselves, but who lived with stories about violence in the territory of the former Yugoslavia for one year. During that time they listened to stories told by seventy women who did live through that war and the violence.

Each one of us had, deep down inside ourselves, a story we heard a long time ago—about a grandmother who was tortured in a camp because her son was a partisan, or about a mother who lost a brother or a son. Such stories have become a kind of oral tradition that a grandmother tells her granddaughter, or a mother tells her daughter. Written history, however, records something different. In it there are stories about victories and defeats, enemy losses, heroic battles and heroes, usually men, with only a few women mentioned here and there. Raped women, weeping mothers, women in black, orphans, the hardships of a life in exile—all that is quickly forgotten, considered a minor sacrifice which women are expected to offer as a price for the "protection" and defense of their "freedom." Lerner said, "Until the most recent past, these historians have been men, and what they have recorded is what men have done and experienced and found significant. They have called this History and claimed universality for it. What women have done and experienced has been left unrecorded, neglected, and ignored in interpretation" (Lerner, 1986, p. 4).

What were our motives in researching the experiences of women regarding violence in war? We are conscious that a bloody war is still being fought here in our immediate neighborhood, and just as it has always been, it is the women and children who suffer the most and have the most casualties. It is to them that we, as women criminologists and victimologists, are obliged to offer our modest contribution of making that suffering more sociably visible. It is a fact that women's voices are hardly heard, whether because of the terror they have lived through or are still facing, or because men's weapons are louder. Naturally, this is the case only until women's suffering becomes useful for the realization of some daily political or military goals.

We have also decided to approach war from the perspective of how women experience it because the influence of war on women implies its influence on all the members of a community exposed to violence, as well as to all the groups imperiled by war on the whole (El Bushra, Lopez, 1993). As Lerner wrote,

> Such war-induced conquest usually occurred over people already differentiated from the victors by race, ethnicity, or simple tribal difference. In its ultimate origin, "difference" as a distinguishing mark between the conquered and the conquerors was based on the first clearly observable difference, that between the sexes. Men had learned how to assert and exercise power over people slightly different from themselves in the primary exchange of women. In so doing, men acquired the knowledge necessary to elevate "difference" of whatever kind into a criterion for dominance. (Lerner, 1986, p. 214)

By deciding to do such an investigation, we have also tried to help women voice their own experiences in a way that does not hurt them, but helps them free themselves from the burden of accumulated fear and emotion. There was also an active component of the research, which mostly manifested itself in the different, mostly symbolic, forms of help given to the women who were interviewed. In addition, they were empowered through speaking about their and other women's experiences of war.

The women we talked to were refugees who had become foreigners in a country that had, until very recently, been their homeland. They had been uprooted from their environment, from their everyday life, they had lost their homes, friends and jobs. Many of them carry their homeland and their homes only in their memories. Many will never go back to where they belonged. Today many of these women live in rented lodgings, in collective accommodations, with their relatives, and friends—that is, with people who were ready to offer them help when they were in need. Some of them have in the meantime left the country and gone abroad.

We have encountered difficulties, mostly expected, during our research. Burdened by their experience during war and exile, we were greeted with a caution and restraint that revealed their fear and suspicion. Nevertheless, after the first encounters, in most cases they accepted us with trust and joy at finding someone with whom to talk and be friendly. We are especially grateful to our friends from the Soros Foundation, from The Autonomous Women's Center against Sexual Violence and the Women in Black for helping us to make contacts with the women refugees.

All the stories in this book are absolutely authentic, although the names of the women narrators have been changed to protect them from possible unpleasantness. Each one of them spoke about her own personal experience of violence in war. Along with their own story, most of them told one or two more stories about what other women experienced in the war territories. They had either witnessed the events themselves or had heard about them from other people. So the basic material for our analysis was 150 stories of women refugees talking about violence in war or connected with war. Thirty-nine stories deal with physical violence (not followed by sexual), forty-nine deal with sexual violence and sexual harassment, while pure psychological violence and fear are described in 113 cases. In most cases violence took place between members of different nationalities and only in two cases was there violence between the members of the same national group. Ten of the interviewed women became widows in this war, and twenty-two of them have lost children or other members of their family. Separation from a member of a family is described in ten cases, while banishment from home occurred in eight cases. Almost all of the women talked about the problems they faced in exile.

The war has not ended yet and the suffering of the innocent people continues. This book is just a contribution to the times we live in. It does not intend to give statistical generalizations, political assessments, or to measure the extent of guilt or human suffering. As was once written by Iran Mayor, "horror suffocates the scream of the victim." For this reason, we who are permitted by circumstances to do so must raise our voices.

Introduction to the English edition

The book, *Women, Violence and War*, was originally published in the Serbian language in August 1995. During the course of the research and the editing of the book the war in the former Yugoslavia was still ongoing. At the same time, our contacts with the world were rendered extremely difficult, chiefly because of the UN-imposed sanctions against the Federal Republic of Yugoslavia. Thus the bulk of foreign work about violence against women in war was out of our reach. That is why, while preparing the English edition, we have attempted to supplement the analysis of our research by a critical analysis of the writing of Western authors about violence against women during the war. Moreover, the time which has elapsed has enabled us to deepen and refine our analysis and approach violence against women from the standpoint of human rights, especially as those standards were applied in the work of the International Tribunal for the former Yugoslavia.

While carrying out our research and analyzing female experiences of violence in war, we placed women in the focus. Trying to make the female experience of war visible, we found it important to highlight similarities and differences in the experiences of women who differ among themselves by nationality, age, profession, and other considerations. Our respondents were mainly Serbian, not because we intentionally chose them to form the majority of our sample, but because they were the ones who were most accessible. Since we were equally interested in the experiences of women of other ethnic groups who came to Serbia, we tried hard to gather as much information about them as we could, either directly or through the oral accounts of our Serbian interviewees. Moreover, we tried to gather information not only on rape but also on any other experiences that our interviewees experienced as violence. We were rather surprised to discover that we have remained alone in this endeavor. That is why the publication of an English edition represents, among other things, an effort to draw attention to the wide scope of violence against women in war, as well as to shed some light on the violence that Serbian women endured during the war in the former Yugoslavia.

In addition, the English edition of this book has been supplemented by a brief history of Bosnia-Herzegovina in order to clarify the wider social and political context in which military conflicts and violence against women occurred.

CHAPTER 1

A brief history of the state of Bosnia-Herzegovina (from its origins to the 1995 Dayton peace accords)

NATAŠA MRVIĆ-PETROVIĆ

The first written sources about Bosnia date from the tenth century (A.D. 950). At that time, already populated by Slavs, it formed part of Serbia, which was ruled by Prince Časlav. From that period on, Bosnia gradually developed into a separate state. Because of its important geo-strategic position in the central Balkans, Bosnia has continually been coveted by its powerful neighbors. Its political fate always depended on the changing power relations between neighboring states, first Hungary and the Byzantine empire, then Hungary and Serbia, and Venice, Turkey and Russia still later on.

Hungary, Bosnia's northern neighbor, annexed Croatia in 1091, and was continually exerting considerable military and political pressure on Bosnia[1]. That is why Bosnian rulers (called bans), among whom the most important ones were Kulin (1180–1203) and Stjepan II Kotromanić (1322–1353), fought as vassals for the Hungarians, while occasionally trying to secede from the central authorities. One special characteristic of Bosnia, which was of the utmost importance for the independence of the Bosnian state, but which also served as the basis for the subsequent rapid islamization, was the acceptance of Patarinism, in the twelfth century, as the official religion. The Patarins (or Bogomils, as they were called in this part of Europe) had been ruthlessly persecuted in medieval Serbia and Hungary. They found refuge in Bosnia, where they established their own church. Because of this, Catholic Hungary led several crusades against Bosnia in the thirteenth century; these, nevertheless, failed to eradicate Patarinism.

The feudal Bosnian state reached its pinnacle in the fourteenth century, during the reign of King Tvrtko (1353–1391), who was still a vassal to Hungary. Profiting from disputes among Serbian feudal lords and the military impotency of Dubrovnik, Tvrtko I considerably enlarged Bosnian territory by taking what is known today as Herzegovina, Kotor Bay and regions adjacent to Serbia alongside the Drina river. In 1377, Tvrtko I proclaimed himself the heir of the Serbian dynasty of Nemanjići, therefore claiming the title King of Serbia and Bosnia. However, immediately after his death, a power struggle broke out which completely distracted the Bosnian nobles from the imminent danger of Turkish invasion. After several brief intrusions during the fourteenth and fifteenth centuries, the Turks finally, in 1435, forced the Bosnian King Tvrtko II to accept vassalage and payment of annual tribute to the sultan, while Bosnian cities were gradually turned into Turkish fortresses.

Profiting from the newly created situation, Sandalj Hranić, a local nobleman from what is now Herzegovina, enlarged his domain at the expense of neighboring Bosnia. In 1448, his heir, Stefan Vukčić Kosača, proclaimed himself the herzeg,[2] from which the very name "Herzegovina" sprung. Kosača's territorial conquest, made at the expense of Venice, Hungary and Serbia, included the Neretva valley, the Dubrovnik hinterland, some Adriatic islands and Zeta (today's Montenegrin coast).

Having finally defeated Serbia and Macedonia, the Turks, led by Sultan Mehmed II, destroyed the Bosnian state in only six weeks, in the spring of 1463, during their push towards central Europe. Herzegovina succumbed a couple of years later (1465–90). With their fall, the only remaining Christian states in the Balkans succumbed to the Turks. The newly conquered countries were incorporated into the Ottoman Empire. Due to their central position between Venice and Hungary, they were used as a base for further Turkish invasions towards Dalmatia, Croatia, Slavonia and Slovenia.

The Turkish conquest initiated the process of islamization. The domestic population, attracted by the privileges offered by the conquerors, converted gradually to Islam. The process was particularly strong amongst the younger Bosnian nobles who had been taken prisoner by the Turks and resettled in Bosnia thereafter.

The further spread of Turkish authority during the sixteenth century towards southern Croatia (Krajina), Dalmatia, Bosnian Posavina and Slavonia was effected through constant battles with Hungarian and Croatian feudal lords and their armies. During the sixteenth and seventeenth centuries, this broad area exposed to Turkish incursions was called Croato-Turkish Krajina. Both of the parties in the conflict often forcefully populated Krajina with Christian (mostly Serbian) subjects, who were granted certain privileges in exchange for permanent military service and border surveillance duties. This form of territorial organization was unknown in other parts of the Ottoman Empire. The systematic set-tlement of Serbs in the frontier regions of Hungary and Turkey produced a considerable mixing between all three religious groups and is responsible for the isolated existence of Serb settle-ments in various parts of Bosnia.

From the second part of the sixteenth century on, the Turkish feudal system began to manifest serious weaknesses, since it was based on forceful expropriation of land from the non-Moslem serfs, continuous extortion, mistreatment and even child kidnap-ping (the infamous "blood toll"). This made Bosnia the breeding ground for numerous rebellions against the Turkish authorities.

During the seventeenth and eighteenth centuries, Turkey suf-fered a series of defeats at the hands of Venice and the Austro-Hungarian Empire. Moreover, the Bosnian Moslem gentry began to oppose state reforms that had been introduced by Istanbul. Using the defense of Islam as pretext, the rebellious Bosnian nobles won to their side wide strata of the Moslem population, persuading them to take arms against the central authorities. It was only by the middle of the nineteenth century that Istanbul finally succeeded in crushing the disobedience of the local Moslem gentry.

At the same time, encouraged by successful rebellions in Serbia, Bosnian Serbs rose against Turkish domination several times (Mašićka buna, 1809; Bosansko-hercegovački ustanak, 1875–78). The main reasons for the rebellions were economic and political disfranchisement and national and religious inequality. However, due to the religious and national divisions within the population of Bosnia and because of the territorial dispersal of Bosnian Serbs, Serbian rebellions in Bosnia were not as successful as they were in Serbia. The most exploited rural Serbs acted as the spear of the re-bellion that broke out in the regions where they were in the major-ity (eastern Herzegovina, Bosnian Krajina and Bosnian Posavina). The ill-fated Bosansko-Hercegovački ustanak (1875–78) united the Bosnian Serb bourgeoisie as well, which gave the whole event the character of a national liberation movement. However, the inabil-ity of Turkey to quell the rebellion and the crisis that remained for several years inspired Austria to obtain agreement from all the ma-jor European powers to occupy Bosnia. The occupation, sanc-tioned by the Berlin Congress (1878), was carried out between July 13 and October 20, 1878, and was followed by a massive rebel-lion of Bosnian Moslems.

The period of Austrian rule (1878–1918) profoundly influ-enced the recent history of Bosnia. It remained under the military rule of Austria, which, in its internal policies, favored the Catholics

(Croats) at the expense of the Orthodox (Serbs) and the Moslems. This led to a series of local uprisings in eastern Herzegovina and Kotor Bay, with one of them (Hercegovačko-Bokeljski ustanak, 1882) uniting Serbs and Moslems for the first time in their history. The conflict was resolved through the establishment of ecclesiastical autonomy for Serbs (1905) and Moslems (1909).

However, the forced annexation of Bosnia by Austria in 1908, in spite of protests by the Entente powers (Great Britain and France) and neighboring states (Serbia and Montenegro), triggered a new international crisis which accelerated the outbreak of World War I. Within the new power structure, Moslem nobles (called beys) were granted a limited participation in power. Serbs remained politically marginalized and repressed, as they were continuing to fight for their civil emancipation, the liberation of Bosnia from Austrian rule and unification with Serbia. The assassination of the Austrian heir-apparent Archduke Francis Ferdinand by a Bosnian Serb, Gavrilo Princip, on June 28, 1914, was used as a pretext by Austria to declare war on Serbia, accelerating the outbreak of World War I. During the war years (1914–18) Bosnia served as a base for huge military operations against Serbia, while Bosnian Serbs were recruited and sent to fight for Austria on other fronts, such as northern Italy and Poland.

At the beginning of the hostilities, the Austrian authorities enforced a campaign of terror against Bosnian Serbs, with thousands being interned in concentration camps (in Arad, Žegar, Doboj, Komarno and Graz). Hundreds of Serbian intellectuals were court-martialed and sentenced to death. Immediately before the outbreak of the war, the *schutzkor*[3] committed numerous massacres of Serbs, followed by the looting of Serbian property and the forced expulsion of Serbs to Serbia and Montenegro.

The year 1918 brought the establishment of the first Yugoslavia (Kingdom of Serbs, Croats and Slovenes). Bosnia entered the new state, which lasted twenty-three years before breaking down at the beginning of World War II. After the capitulation of the Kingdom of Yugoslavia in June 1941, Bosnia (although divided into Italian and German spheres of interest) was included in the German-sponsored Independent State of Croatia. Aside from the regular authorities, Croatian fascists (called *ustaše*) quickly formed their own military units. One of them, the infamous Black Legion, was very active in Bosnia from the end of 1941 on.

Playing upon inherited religious and national animosities, *ustaše* and Germans, assisted by Catholic prelates, won over large portions of the Croat and Moslem population of Bosnia for the

World War II-era genocide against Serbs.[4] Croats and Moslems were encouraged to freely persecute Serbs and loot their property, while Croatian authorities prohibited all Serbian associations, introduced *ustaše* controllers in all Serb-owned firms, banned the use of the Cyrillic alphabet, and began the forced conversion of Serbs to Catholicism.[5] The forced expulsion of Bosnian Serbs to Serbia soon gave place to numerous individual crimes and massacres of Serbs (in Ružin Dol, at Opuzen in Herzegovina, in Bosanska Krupa, Ključ, Sanski Most, Glamoč, Prijedor, in the vicinity of Čapljina, and so on). In *ustaše* extermination camps (Jasenovac, Jadovno, Stara Gradiška, etc.) some 800,000 people were killed, the majority Serbs. *Ustaše* atrocities in eastern Herzegovina (in the municipalities of Nevesinje, Gacko, Stolac and Lubinje) triggered a Serbian armed rebellion in June 1941. In order to repress the rebellion, the *ustaše* also enforced terror against urban Serbs. Thus, in June 1941, thousands of individuals were killed, along with a considerable number of communists. That is why the first resistance movements against Germans and *ustaše* originated in the regions populated by Serbs (Drvar, Ozren, Bihać, Romanija, Bosanska Krajina, the area surrounding Sarajevo, in Bosnia and the regions of Lika, Banija and Kordun, in Croatia). At the beginning of the war, Serbs formed 90% of the partisan units that were active in the Independent State of Croatia.

During World War II, the territory of Bosnia-Herzegovina was the ground for grand battles of partisans with Germans, *ustaše* and chetniks[6] (with offensives on the Neretva, Sutjeska and in western Bosnia). After the capitulation of Italy (in 1943), Moslems and Croats began joining the partisan movement in larger numbers. After the second session of the Anti-Fascist Council for the National Liberation of Yugoslavia, in Jajce (November 29, 1943), Bosnia entered as an equal federal unit into the future Yugoslav commonwealth.

After World War II, Yugoslavia developed as a socialist community of equal nations and national minorities. Not only Serbs and Croats but the Bosnian Moslems were also granted the status of nation. A gradual decomposition of the Yugoslav political and economic system began with the Constitution of 1974, which granted the federal units (republics and provinces) the status of states. Political conflicts arose between the presidents of the republics, with rising nationalist antagonisms and desires for independence. These produced, at the end of the 1980s, the dissolution of the League of the Communists of Yugoslavia,[7] the creation of national parties, attacks on the officers and soldiers of the Yugoslav People's Army

(YPA) and the enlargement and reinforcement of the already existing home guards as the future armed forces of the newly created states. These processes were reinforced by the long-lasting crisis of the socialist economy in the 1980s[8]. The political crisis reached its peak when on June 25, 1991, Slovenia and Croatia unilaterally proclaimed their independence from Yugoslavia.[9] In multiethnic regions (such as Croatia and Bosnia-Herzegovina) it was impossible to effectuate independence without obtaining the consent of numerically important ethnic groups. The lack of a mutual agreement between Moslems, Croats and Serbs about their political future was a direct cause of the outbreak of civil war in Bosnia-Herzegovina.

The first armed conflicts were preceded by political crises, characterized by the fact that the representatives of Croats and Moslems in the highest political bodies of Bosnia constantly outvoted the representatives of Serbs. That is why Serbian representatives left both the National Assembly and the Presidency of Bosnia-Herzegovina. The representatives of the Moslems and Croats proclaimed the independence of Bosnia-Herzegovina on October 15, 1991, after the unilateral referendum.[10] The representatives of the Bosnian Serbs did not participate in this decision. Instead, they formed the Assembly of Serbs of Bosnia-Herzegovina on October 24, 1991, which, after the plebiscite of Bosnian Serbs, voted for a resolution to create the Serb Republic of Bosnia-Herzegovina on December 21, 1991. Since the European Community had recognized Bosnia-Herzegovina on April 6, 1992, the Assembly of Serbs of Bosnia-Herzegovina proclaimed the Serb Republic (Republika Srpska) on the following day. Thus the Serbs realized their right to self-determination. Soon after the Bosnian Serb proclamation, Bosnian Croats also proclaimed their own state, the Croatian Community of Herzeg-Bosna, the third independent state in the ex-Bosnia-Herzegovina.

Almost a year after the outbreak of hostilities between the newly created Croatian armed forces and the YPA, on March 1, 1992, Moslem irregulars shot at a wedding party in front of the Serbian Orthodox church in Sarajevo. This triggered armed conflicts in the territory of Bosnia-Herzegovina.[11] A couple of days later, Serbian irregulars set up barricades in Sarajevo. During April 4–5 (the celebration of Bairam, the most important Moslem holiday), street fighting began in Sarajevo between Serbs, on one side, and Moslems and Croats, on the other. The city itself was divided into two parts controlled by the two belligerent parties.[12] On April 12, 1992, the president of the incomplete Presidency of Bosnia-Herzegovina (incomplete since the Serb representatives had left),

Alija Izetbegović, issued an order for the headquarters of the Moslem home guard to launch an overall attack on the YPA barracks. Some time later (May 5), the Presidency of the Socialist Federal Republic of Yugoslavia decided to withdraw the YPA from Bosnia-Herzegovina, stating that YPA members of Bosnian nationality could remain in the country. Ex-members of the YPA (who were Bosnian citizens) and various armed units of Bosnian Serbs formed the Army of the Serb Republic, on May 12, 1992.

On May 2, 1992, Moslem armed units attacked the column of the YPA Command of the Sarajevo Region which was retreating from Sarajevo, in accordance with the previous agreement with the government of Bosnia-Herzegovina and the United Nations Command in Sarajevo. Nineteen YPA conscripts lost their lives. In the same way, a YPA column that was retreating from Tuzla, according to a previously concluded agreement, was attacked, and forty-nine soldiers and officers lost their lives.

Aside from the immediate deployment of peacekeeping forces, the international community had several times mediated in talks between the parties in conflict, but without having a clear picture of the future of Bosnia-Herzegovina. After initially supporting the unity and territorial integrity of Yugoslavia, declarations were made by the European Community, the OSCE and the UN which labeled Serbia and Montenegro as the key culprits for the violent breakup of Yugoslavia, and as such these states were subsequently made to suffer economic sanctions.[13]

Although they had demanded international arbitration, both Bosnian Serbs and the Federal Republic of Yugoslavia (Serbia and Montenegro) questioned the opinion of Badinther's commission, which took the stand that Serbs from Bosnia and Croatia should be granted the status of national minority. Thus, the political fate of one ethnic group, which prior to the civil war had the status of a constituent nation, was tied to the political will of two other ethnic groups (Moslems and Croats) with whom it theretofore had been equal but whose political interests had become completely opposite to its own.

At the beginning of the civil war in Bosnia, Moslems sided with the regular Croatian Army, while the Serbs enjoyed the logistic support of neighboring Serbia and Montenegro. Especially in 1992 and 1993, Moslems were generously assisted by the Organization of Islamic Conference, which includes some fifty states and is headed by Turkey. This help included weapons, foodstuffs, humanitarian material, money and even volunteer mujahedin combatants.

Continuous negotiations, momentous cease-fires, and abortive peace talks have deeply marked the Bosnian crisis. Several plans that were intended to bring peace to Bosnia have failed without finding a solution that would satisfy all sides (Lord Carrington's, Cutillero's, Vance's, Vance-Owen's, Owen-Stoltenberg's and the plan of the Contact Group). Moslems, for example, refused to sign the Lisbon agreement in May 1992. In their turn, Serbs refused to sign the Vance-Owen plan in November 1992, according to which Bosnia-Herzegovina should have been divided into seven to ten cantons. Instead, they offered a seven-point plan of their own which was rejected by the other two sides. The otherwise very successful Geneva Peace Conference was interrupted on January 22, 1993, after a Croatian army attack on Serbian Krajina. This attack occurred at the very moment when all sides had finally accepted the constitutional principles of the Vance-Owen plan.

The development of the military situation in the period 1992–1994 was to the advantage of Croats and Serbs. With the participation of the regular Croatian Army (sent from Croatia itself), in 1992 Croats took almost all of the region where they formed the ethnic majority. The region, called Herzeg-Bosna, makes up some 30% of the territory of the former Bosnia-Herzegovina. In the summer of 1992, fighting broke out in the Mostar area and in western Herzegovina as well. This happened first through Moslem and Croat attacks on the YPA and later on through the clashes between Serbs, on one side, and Croats and Moslems, on the other. During the fighting the Serbs withdrew from Mostar and the Neretva valley. On July 22, 1992, an agreement on friendship and cooperation was signed between Bosnia-Herzegovina and Croatia. The agreement, in effect, sanctioned the already existing military cooperation of Croats and Moslems against Serbs and legitimized the presence of the Croatian Army on Bosnian soil. In the region of Herzeg-Bosna the Croatian dinar became the official currency. Croatian laws were proclaimed as valid for the whole region, while Bosnian Croat boys began to be recruited into the Croatian Army.

By the middle of 1992, Serbian military forces took the city of Bijeljina, pushing Moslems from the region of Semberija and later on from the regions near the border with Serbia, along the Drina (the cities of Zvornik, Višegrad and Foča) and Sava rivers (Brčko). By the end of 1991, the Army of Republika Srpska had conquered the whole region of Podrinje (except the cities of Goražde and Žepa), some cities in central Bosnia (Jajce and Donji Vakuf) and Bosnian Posavina. This created a corridor along the Sava river which joined the Serb-controlled parts of Bosnia-Herzegovina to Serbia itself.

In the civil war in Bosnia-Herzegovina, which broke out after the declarations of independence of the new states, not only were there confrontations of Serbs with Moslems and Croats, but also Moslems with Croats, and even Moslems with Moslems (in the region of Bihać). At the beginning of September 1992, armed clashes broke out between the former allies, Moslems and Croats. Thus, at the beginning of November, the members of the British peace-keeping forces, to their great amazement, discovered the bodies of massacred Moslem civilians in the city of Prozor, killed by Croats in an operation of "ethnic cleansing."

As does every total war, the civil war in Bosnia mostly affected the civilians.[14] They were the principal victims of "ethnic cleansing" performed by all three warring parties against the members of other ethnic groups. Serbs did their "job" in the region of Brčko, Semberija and the parts along the Drina river (the cities of Višegrad and Foča). Moslems did the same in the cities under their control (Sarajevo, Tuzla and Zenica), while Croats were especially active in the regions of Bosanska Posavina, western Herzegovina and in the cities of Ključ and Prozor. Civilians were also victimized in the besieged cities, either during the military operations or by criminal gangs that had entered the hastily formed ethnic militias. Captured Serb civilians in the Moslem-controlled parts of Sarajevo were, just like the captured Moslem civilians in the Serb-controlled part of Sarajevo, used as a "living shield" or forced to dig trenches at the front. All warring parties soon set up detention camps; Serbs did it in Omarska and Manjača (a prison near the city of Banja Luka), Croats in the cities of Mostar and Čapljina, and Moslems in the camp of Čelebići and the Koševo football stadium in Sarajevo. For the sake of "higher national goals," armed members of all three ethnic groups pillaged, killed and raped the unprotected in the areas under their control. Neither cultural nor religious monuments were spared. Thus, Croatian units willfully destroyed the magnificent medieval Turkish bridge in Mostar, as well as the medieval Serbian monastery of Žitomislić, Orthodox churches in the cities of Čapljina and Mostar, and some monuments commemorating *ustaše* genocide against Serbs, Jews and Gypsies during Word War II (the ossuaries in Prebilovci and Čapljina). Serbs made their contribution by destroying some of the finest monuments of Islamic architecture in Bosnia-Herzegovina, including all of the mosques in the cities of Foča and Banja Luka, while Moslems destroyed the Franciscan monastery in Kreševo.

Continuously unsuccessful negotiations and the prolongation of the war finally led major powers (the United States, the United

Kingdom, France, Germany and Russia) to form the "Contact Group." Their explicit goal was to establish mutual cooperation and to create a unified approach towards a peaceful solution of the Bosnian crisis. The 1994 Contact Group plan offered a territorial partition of Bosnia-Herzegovina, which offered 49% of the territory to Bosnian Serbs and 51% to Bosnian Croats and Moslems, while obliging the two entities to unite into the future Union of Bosnia-Herzegovina. This peace proposal, however, was rejected by Republika Srpska (in spite of huge pressure by the Federal Republic of Yugoslavia). This eventually produced a breakdown of the mutual economic relationships between the two Serb-dominated states, contributing to the first Bosnian Serb military defeats (in the area of Kupres, Bosnian Krajina, Igman and Bjelašnica). The most successful military actions of the Croats and Moslems were achieved with the help of NATO air strikes against Serbian positions. Numerous civilian casualties among Bosnian Serbs were caused by the problem of separating military targets from the civilian environment, as well as the difficulties inherent in high altitude actions, with possible misidentifications of targets and marginal errors.

In March 1994, Bosnian Croats and Moslems concluded a general agreement establishing the Bosnian-Croat Federation, made up of the Republic of Bosnia-Herzegovina and Herzeg-Bosna. After significant political and military pressure on Republika Srpska during talks in Dayton, in the United States, peace accords were signed on November 21, 1995, between the Bosnian-Croat Federation, Republika Srpska, the Republic of Croatia and the Federal Republic of Yugoslavia. Thus the Republic of Bosnia-Herzegovina became a Union composed of the Bosnian-Croat Federation and Republika Srpska. The former acquired 51% and the latter 49% of the territory of the former Socialist Republic of Bosnia-Herzegovina. Within the Union, Republika Srpska enjoys the status of a state, or an entity which has the attributes of a state (separate territory, administration, police force, an army and the possibility of establishing special relationships with the Federal Republic of Yugoslavia). However, only on the surface has Dayton put an end to the Bosnian crisis.

The suffering of the victims in the war zone is just a part of the history of the war. The other one, much more subtle and shocking, is the fate of refugees. The neighboring countries, Serbia and Montenegro, immediately after the outbreak of the war accepted the majority of Serbian refugees.[15] Today, refugees make up 10% of the population of Montenegro and 6% of the population of Serbia. The vast majority of refugees (96.9%) have found some private accommodation, either on a commercial (landlords) or non-commercial (friends and relatives) basis. The Federal Republic of Yugoslavia is unable to take care of refugees; they are, therefore, obliged to turn to private citizens, who are themselves unable to do much, their economic power having been destroyed by the enduring economic crisis which was only aggravated by the UN-imposed sanctions against the Federal Republic of Yugoslavia (1992–95). Foreign aid, especially in 1994 and 1995, was seriously reduced so that for the time being it does not cover more than 9% of refugee needs. Radical impoverishment, unemployment, a lack of communal support, the hostility of the new social environment and the practical impossibility of obtaining citizenship make a new crown of thorns for the people who, having survived life-threatening danger and the loss of close ones, began to believe that they were finally rescued. Thus, the consequences of the war still unfold.

Notes

1 From 1138 onwards, Hungarian kings had the title of the King of Rama (an ancient Hungarian term for the southern region containing Bosnia), thus expressing their territorial pretensions to Bosnia.

2 The term was derived from the German term "Herzog," which means "duke." Therefore, "Herzegovina" means "the duchy."

3 A sort of home guard, organized by Austrian authorities and staffed by Bosnian Croats and Moslems.

4 Following a direct appeal of the Moslem party to Adolf Hitler, a special SS legion (called the "Handžar division") exclusively staffed by Moslems, was formed at the end of 1942. The division, under direct German command, participated in numerous offensives and punitive expeditions against the partisans and Bosnian Serbs.

5 Up until May 1943, a total of 243,000 Serbs from Croatia and western Bosnia were forcibly converted to Catholicism.

6 "A Serbian nationalist guerrilla force that formed during World War II, to resist the Axis invaders and Croatian collaborators but that primarily fought a civil war against the Yugoslav communist guerrillas, the Partisans," *Encyclopaedia Britannica '99*, CD 2.

7 The League of the Communists of Slovenia and the League of the Communists of Croatia separated from the League of the Communists of Yugoslavia in 1988.

8 During the 1980s, economic crises were also present in all Eastern-bloc countries. Similar phenomena also took place during the dissolution of the Soviet Union and Czechoslovakia, although without producing as serious consequences as a civil war.

9 They were recognized on January 15, 1992, and were admitted to the United Nations on May 22, 1992.

10 The Republic of Bosnia-Herzegovina was recognized on April 6, 1992, and was admitted to the United Nations on May 22, 1992.

11 The armed conflicts were preceded by the rejection of the Serb and Croat proposal to supplement the referendum question with the question of the sovereignty of Moslems, Croats and Serbs. The national parties of Croats and Serbs were in favor of the division of Bosnia-Herzegovina into cantons, with full sovereignty for all three ethnic groups on their respective ethnic territories. The leading Moslem party (the Party of Democratic Action) insisted on a unitary republic. On February 29, 1992, following a recommendation of the EC Arbitration Commission, a referendum was held for "a sovereign and independent Bosnia-Herzegovina." Croats and Moslems participated, while Serbs boycotted the event.

12 Before the war, in the city of Sarajevo itself (in the valley), the majority of inhabitants were Moslems, while Serbs predominantly lived in the hills and the suburbia. With the outbreak of the war the formerly mixed population began to split into ethnic getthoes.

When the war started in April 1992, the inhabitants of Sarajevo, regardless of their nationality, began leaving the city. They set out on roads leading either towards Belgrade (Serbia) or along the Neretva valley towards Split (Croatia). The former Yugoslav army kept continuously evacuating citizens of Sarajevo free of charge by the civilian and army air fleet. After April 30, 1992, when the official evacuation ceased private attempts to emigrate often failed and ended in death. At one point during the war, the Red Cross began organizing exchanges of individuals who wanted to change their area of residence. In total, some 138,000 Serbs have left the city during the war. The emigration of Moslem inhabitants of Sarajevo has also taken on gigantic proportions.

13 The efforts of the international community to peacefully resolve the Bosnian conflict were only a part of the overall efforts to resolve the Yugoslav crisis. The efforts resulted in the Hague International Conference on Yugoslavia, the creation of the Arbitration Commission (known as Badinther's commission), the Brussels Conference (May 1992), the London Conference (August 28, 1992) and the Geneva Peace Talks (January 10–12, 1993). On June 1, 1992, UN Resolution No. 757 imposed sanctions against the Federal Republic of Yugoslavia, reinforced later by Resolution 820.

14 The first civilian victims of the Bosnian war fell as early as March 27, 1992, when Croatian and Moslem military units massacred five Serbian families in the village of Sijekovac near Bosanski Brod, also setting on fire some fifty houses. This was only the beginning of a list of crimes that all three sides would commit against each other. Crimes against civilians and forced migrations have significantly altered the demographic and ethnic structure of Bosnia-Herzegovina. Before the war, the majority of Bosnian inhabitants lived in ethnically mixed areas. Of

all the former Yugoslav republics, Bosnia had the highest percentage of ethnically mixed marriages.

15 According to the 1996 *Census of Refugees and Other War-Affected Persons in the Federal Republic of Yugoslavia* (carried out jointly by the United Nations High Commissioner for Refugees and the Commissariat for Refugees of the Republic of Serbia), there were 566,375 refugees in the Federal Republic of Yugoslavia. Of this group, 537,937 were settled in Serbia and 28,388 in Montenegro. Refugees from Bosnia-Herzegovina amounted to 232,274.

CHAPTER 2

Definitions of violence in war and the experience of women: the subject of research

VESNA NIKOLIĆ-RISTANOVIĆ

Although different forms of violence can be observed in everyday life during peacetime, violence inflicted in wartime influences people in a drastic way because the whole community takes part in war. Its result is not just individual death and injury, but also the widespread destruction of property, homes, families and economic stability. War influences the lives of women and men in different ways; this happens regardless of women's attempts to continue a normal life in the war territories, to live in territories where there is no immediate war danger, or to attempt to escape into exile. In all forms of warfare, women are victims even if they are not wounded on the battlefield. They are victims in international and civil wars, whether the motive is religious, ethnic or nationalistic. Most civilian victims of modern forms of warfare are women (Chinkin, 1993, p. 204) and they suffer different forms of violence, most of which remain socially invisible.

Naturally, many men are also unwilling victims of war. They are killed, tortured, made to take part in the fighting, banished from their homes. Also, there are some women who take an active part in war. But there is an essential difference between men's and women's experience of violence in war. In an armed conflict there is a struggle for power, in which men and women take part in different ways, because the two sexes have different modes of access to power, depending on the social role of each sex. Bearing that in mind, an analysis that deals with gender contributes to the study of the relations of power by showing the ways in which power is manifested in the structural relations between men and women. In this way the analysis of the influence of war on women defines the conflict as a demonstration of power. Because physical power and the power of controlling material resources are traditionally connected with men, men are the ones who want to use it as a means of making others do what they want (El Bushra, Lopez, 1993, p. 62). As a result of this, men are the ones who, as a rule, have a more active part in war. They are the ones who are the victors or the defeated, and who prefer to be heroes rather than victims (Fischer, 1994, p. 166). Or, as Lerner said so well,

> Men and women live on a stage, on which they act out their assigned roles, equal in importance. The play cannot go on without both kinds of performers. Neither of them "contributes" more or less to the whole; neither is marginal or dispensable. But the stage set is conceived, painted, defined by men. Men have written the play, have directed the show, interpreted the meanings of the action. They have assigned themselves the most interesting, most heroic parts, giving women the supporting roles. (Lerner, 1986, p. 12)

War strengthens the already existing dominant marginalization of women. As a result, women tend to define themselves more often as the passive victims of war than as active strategists of survival in war and exile, although they are often more active than men in facing the new situation. War increases their feeling of helplessness more than it increases their power; attacking their physical and mental health, war makes them dependent on others as it strengthens the social views which tend to maintain or intensify their submissive role. In war women generally feel helpless rather than empowered.

Public attention is mainly focused on rape, so much so that it is often considered a synonym for violence against women in general, especially in war. As we will see later, this attitude influences women's own definitions of violence. This can be understood up to a point, because in rape, as El Bushra points out so well, sex, war and power are all concentrated in one, representing the domination of the strong over the weak. As such, rape can be considered a symbol of all conflicts in war (El Bushra, Lopez, 1993, p. 42). However, women in war are also subject to other kinds of sexual violence and sexual harassment; they are victims of torture, murder, malnutrition, psychological violence, fear, physical violence exercised by a husband (who is of another nationality, or back from the front). Women suffer—because they have lost or been separated from a child, husband, or other family members, because of different forms of discrimination and violence they are faced with in exile, and so on. Women are endangered directly or indirectly, if their children, husband or someone else close to them has suffered or been killed. Both are forms of victimization, because a woman can suffer great physiological consequences even when she is not physically hurt. As a Palestinian woman, Nuha Nafal, says, "when a soldier is killed, he is dead. But who continues to suffer? The Mother, the Sister, the Wife" (Hayton-Keeva, 1987, p. 57). As previous studies have shown, women experience stressful situations with greater difficulty. They take more intensive and greater care of the family, generally speaking. They feel more helpless and they have less time and opportunity to talk to other people (El Bushra, Lopez, 1993, p. 60). Considering all this, their whole physical and psychological health is endangered more than men's.

Starting with the personal experience of women, we considered that the best definition and meaning of violence, and thus, of the subject of our research, can be given by those who have survived this war. In accordance with the feminist approach, we considered that the women should be free to define themselves and their experience, instead of having it again defined for them by their culture and their men (Faludi, 1992, p. XXIII). Rigid definitions would, as they have so many times before, inevitably lead to the use of men's terminology, and make the inference that man was the center of the discourse (Lerner, 1986, p. 221). Certainly we are aware that such self-definition is possible only to the extent that women are capable of perceiving their experience of violence from their own perspective, after having been socialized in a strong patriarchal society and after seeing how much the fate of men and women in war is interdependent. But, as Lerner noticed, women must use a patriarchal language, even when they think in a language which is not a part of patriarchy. That language is also the language of women, in the same sense that civilization is theirs, although it is patriarchal. Women are the ones who should change, create again, and by doing so, transform thought and practice so that a new, joint language, free of sexual inequality can be created (Lerner, 1986, p. 229). While not ignoring the male experience of violence in war, we hope that an analysis of women's definitions and women's experiences with violence in war will contribute to attaining a more complete picture of war and will once again raise the issue which can never be analyzed enough: the meaning and absurdity of war.

In response to questions about their experience and the experience of their friends, most of the women we talked to, generally speaking, defined violence on two separate levels: in terms of chronology and in terms of content.

The first response of most women (fifty-four out of the interviewees) was to give an answer of the type: "I did not experience anything." The meaning of this, as we found out in further talks, as a rule was: "I was not a victim of rape." Also, when questioned about other women's experiences of violence, their first reaction was that they knew little or nothing about that.

It is obvious that the first association for most women, when violence against women in war was mentioned, was sexual violence and the physical violence that is inherent in it. So it seemed in the beginning that their definition of violence is linked with the most visible and most often mentioned form of violence. But in further talks it turned out that the equation of violence against women in war with rape and accompanying physical violence is linked to something other than the fundamental nature of this violence, the most specific and one of the most serious forms of violence done to women in general. Their association is also linked to the large media campaign which dealt with rape in war and which practically equated the notion of violence done to women with rape. By giving answers like "Nothing has happened to me," and "I haven't heard or seen anything," it seemed as if the women were trying to protect themselves from being accused of having had something happen to them. They seemed to be protecting themselves from a possible stigmatization with which all victims of rape are faced in patriarchal societies. It showed that the women did not trust us and it showed their fear of the possibly embarrassing consequences for families who remained in the territories where the war was still being fought.

Such responses were not unusual, and were given by women even if they had been victims, witnesses to violence, or had heard of cases of sexual or some other kind of violence in war. It is also well known that women who have survived rape talk about it very reluctantly and when they decide to talk they use the third person. Other studies, like the ones dealing with physical violence in marriages, for example, have shown that women tend to reject defining the violence they so clearly described. By doing so they are trying to protect themselves from stigmatization, from the characteristic attitudes of a patriarchal society which justifies the husband's violent behavior while at the same time finding fault with the wife (Nikolić-Ristanović, 1994a, p. 411). It is quite understandable that women who have already been singled out, who face a lot of unpleasantness because of their refugee status and who are burdened with the care of their families are afraid of speaking out. They worry that by speaking about violence done to other women they could be misunderstood, and thus put themselves and their families into an even more difficult situation.

After this first response, which was characteristic for most of the women we talked to and which could be described as a form of rejecting talk about violence against women in war, a change in attitude occurred. It usually occurred when they began to trust us and when they realized that we had the same goal. The change was manifested in their willingness to talk about their own experiences as well as the experiences of other women, and their attempts to explicitly and implicitly define violence against women in war. It is interesting to note that most women later on not only agreed to talk, but also tended to characterize a wide range of actions in which women are victims as "violence," much wider than we imagined at the onset.

A smaller number of them reacted in a different way. Ten women were ready to confirm that they considered themselves victims of violence done to women in war and that they knew other women who had also experienced violence. Having in mind their own experiences and those of other women, they defined what they thought violence against women in war was. Three of them were very persistent in defending their belief that violence against women included, besides sexual violence, other forms of harassment, as well as the fact that the life of women was forcibly changed. In the beginning, most other women talked primarily of their experience of life in exile, emphasizing that for them it now represented the worst form of violence. This was obviously something that had occurred in the time that lapsed between the violence they had experienced in war, and their preoccupation with their current experiences in exile.

Twenty-six women explicitly defined violence. The definitions of the other women are incorporated in the contents of their stories, although they have refrained from an explicit definition. There are similarities and differences in the way the women defined violence. All the women included in their definition the behavior that is generally considered violent, such as sexual and physical violence. Most often they added to this other forms of behavior which cause women to suffer, based on their own experiences or the experiences of other women. In some cases women could not separate violence done to women from violence done to men, so their definition was of a general character.

There is a visible difference in the approaches to defining violence. While some of them tended to give a more or less comprehensive definition, others emphasized certain forms of violence. They tended to single out a certain form of behavior that they considered violent, more serious than sexual or physical violence; they underlined a specific women's experience of war. Both types of definitions formed the subject of our study. Taken together, the definitions that dealt only with a certain aspect of violence completely justified the acceptance of general definitions as a basis for the final definition of the subject of the study. It is important to point out that the definitions given by women at the beginning of our study were decisive for us, because they answered our questions as to what influences of war on the life of women our study should consider. Their definitions showed us the way. Because we mainly heard about the most visible and direct forms of war violence, we were ready to accept the usual narrow definition, which only includes physical, sexual and psychological violence against women.

Analyzing the explicit definitions of violence given by the women we talked to, we begin with the most fragmented ones and end with the most comprehensive ones. According to the way women described their personal views and experiences of violence in war, the definitions can be grouped in the following way:

- Definitions made on the basis of personal experience, which strive to show the forms of violence, apart from sexual and physical, that women were exposed to in war;
- Definitions made by comparing different forms of violence;
- Definitions mostly based on current situations in exile;
- Definitions which have a tendency to define violence in abstract terms and are based on personal experience as well as the experience of other men and women;
- Definitions based on enumerating the forms of violence the women were exposed to in war, grounded in personal and other women's experience.

Definitions primarily based on personal experience

Women's personal experiences of violence are not necessarily reduced to cases of violence aimed directly against them. The general wartime atmosphere brings about countless compelling changes in a woman's life. This, coupled with the exceptional emotional and mental susceptibility that women typically possess, obviously affects women and causes suffering even when they are not directly involved. Svetlana's examples illustrate the fact that violence directed against all members of a national group, as well as changes in family life caused by war, can be experienced as violence, and gravely harm women.

> Mental harassment, aimed not only against women, but the derision of an entire culture, a people—that was more difficult for me to bear than the shortage of water and electricity and the shelling. The idea that Serbs are savages was inadmissible; it meant tampering with our entire history. I would have lost my mind if I had stayed there. That is what most alienated me from them. I am aware that Serbs also molested many Moslems. Later, I heard about all their atrocities. They were also shelling us continually, since we used to live in the Moslem part of Sarajevo. Having armed us, they withdrew into the surrounding hills and targeted us. Being separated from my children was harder for me than having to endure wartime conditions: the anxiety, the fear that something could happen to them. For me, these are all instances of violence I suffered during the war.

Young girls, like Jovana, see violence as an unexpected confrontation with the cruel reality of war, which, as she put it, "forced her to mature." As we will see, adult women who were helpless when surrounded by suffering took it as a particular form of violence, but the young ones, barely over the threshold of girlhood, were obviously much more deeply distressed. "Violence means being forced to witness the suffering of others, and even then being almost completely prevented from helping them. For me, the way I was thrust into adulthood by this war was an act of violence." She illustrated her definition of violence with a description of her "forced maturing." "I was a nurse on the front line. At night, I went up a hill and watched Pakrac. It was perishing in flames. Can you imagine the feeling when you watch the town where you spent your most beautiful moments disappear in front of your eyes? It is like losing part of yourself. While I was looking down on that scene, I realized that it was not just a nightmare but sheer reality. For me, it meant growing up. I grew up against my will."

Although they were not subjected to physical violence, Vida and Nadežda define their war experience as violence, having lost their next of kin, all their hard-won possessions, and their normal everyday lives.

VIDA: "My father was killed in the war, my house was destroyed, and for me those are acts of violence. We had been building that house for twelve years, we moved in in December 1992, and we had to desert it in May the very next year. The house was razed to the ground, pillaged and burnt down during the Moslem conquest of Trnovo. Also, the fact that I was banished from Trnovo, my lifetime's possessions being reduced to what a handbag could hold, is for me an act of violence."

NADEŽDA: "I suffered terribly when I found out that my brother had been killed in the war. He was in the Serbian Army and had gone to fetch water when he stepped on a mine. I lost several relatives in this war, but my brother's death was the hardest for me to bear. I left behind my flat and all the comfort I had, which I also see as great violence. Nobody assaulted me physically, but living in these conditions is extremely difficult for me and I take it as violence."

As Olga and Maja say, sexual and physical violence in wartime is coupled with uncertainty and the fear of high-handed authorities.

OLGA: "In my opinion, apart from sexual and physical violence, acts of violence directed against women during the war are groundless arrests, inflicting fear, threats, as well as the persecutions of others that I was forced to witness."

MAJA: "The inconvenience I was exposed to during the frequent searches conducted in our flats for me were acts of violence."

For Lepa, violence meant losing her freedom because of her national affiliation. "The moment you become a political prisoner and a prisoner of war, you are subjected to violence. Being confined to your place of residence, with limited freedom of movement and being constantly under surveillance, with your mail scrutinized and your visitors watched, actually means being deprived of your freedom just because you are a Serb. I went through all those things."

Jasminka and Senka point out that it is the women, together with their children, that are usually forcibly deprived of normal living conditions and victimized in massive ordeals in public places.

JASMINKA: "It is an act of violence to besiege a city for two and a half years, leaving the people short of food and water. It is mostly the women who go to fetch water and queue for it. And they take their children along. In many instances these places were shelled. Those are very long queues and many women and children were killed in them."

SENKA: "In my opinion, the siege of Sarajevo and abnormal living conditions, being unable to cater for your basic needs, represent the worst instances of violence. This is massive violence directed against innocent civilians, mostly women and children. That is why I fled from there. Because of my two children."

Definitions based on comparing various kinds of violence

The women who tried to define violence in war by singling out the forms that they consider to be the gravest (that is, forms worse than sexual and physical violence) mostly emphasized the violence that a woman suffers at the loss of her husband, children or some other close person. Although other interviewees also included these forms of violence in their definitions, this group of definitions is typical in that the women regarded violence against their children and other people they were close to as worse than violence directed at the women themselves. This attitude results from, of course, their love for their nearest and dearest; yet, in addition, it probably also results from socialization, a process by which they were taught to live "through others," to make sacrifices and achieve their identity primarily as mothers and wives.

The underlying feeling in this group of definitions is the fear a woman suffers during the war as a form of mental violence. Also emphasized are the specific experiences women have as opposed to the ones men have.

Anka and Sofija, for example, considered that the loss of children and other close persons is the worst form of violence inflicted upon women in a war. For Anka, rape is less horrible than the loss of a child.

ANKA: "The worst form of violence by far is having your child killed. Compared to that, rape is nothing. If I were told that my child was going to be killed, I would say 'Come on, rape me as much as you like, just leave my child alone.'"

SOFIJA: "There is no act of violence that can be compared to the loss of a dear one."

The woman sees the child as the most precious part of herself and she is ready to endure any form of sacrifice for him or her. As we will see further on, Olivera reasoned in a similar way when she claimed that she would rather be raped herself than see it happen to her daughters. To what lengths women are prepared to go can be heard from others, particularly from Olivera's daughter, who said that she would rather be killed than raped.

Gordana's speculations about the topic of violence against women in war dealt with differences between men's and women's experiences of violence related to the differences in power, that is, women's vulnerability to power, and about fear as a form of violence.

Women are naturally weaker than men. Like in times of peace, during a war, problematic people will sooner vent their fury on women than on other men. Women are exposed to different forms of violence, ranging from that prior to the war and wartime violence. The Croats used to turn away from me, and not from their work supervisors, although they, too, were Serbs. I suppose this was because the men would have sorted out that problem in a fight. They would have slapped them. It is true that men were also tortured in prisons, but after they were disarmed...Women are overpowered by fear for their children. A lot of women saved themselves, by saving the children. I was also one of them. Fear is a form of violence in a war. In my opinion, fear holds as much violence as real physical violence does.

Natalija related how the fear of death, as a form of mental violence, can be more difficult than any other form of violence. "Mental violence is the worst; when you feel absolutely helpless, and you constantly live in fear that a sniper might kill you or a bomb hit you. It is terrible when there is no food, and you cannot even prepare whatever you may have to eat."

Definitions primarily influenced by the present situation of refugees

Some women said that the violence they experienced during the war was overshadowed by the hardships of life as refugees, their concern for family members left behind in the war zone and the torment of being separated from them. These were mostly women who had been away from the war-affected areas for a long time. Borjana remarked,

You would probably like to hear something about violence against women in war, but I am not affected by that at the moment. Some other things affect me, a different form of violence that resulted from this war. It is violence exercised by the state against the man in the street. Doesn't manipulating women and children refugees mean violence? Doesn't queuing for milk, waiting for electricity to come back or freezing of cold mean violence? Or when you camp on the officials' doorsteps unable to do anything?

JELENA: "I barely had a break from being exposed to violence, being labeled a Serb, when other forms of harassment and mistreatment started in the refugee camp."

MERIMA: "What is happening to me is not rape, but it is a terrible mental harassment. In my opinion this is also a form of violence against people, the psychological burden we have to bear. Fear for those we have left behind; whether they will stay alive, whether we shall ever see each other again. And, in addition to that, there is the question of survival here, of keeping your courage up and bringing up your children decently, creating a normal situation for them although one of the parents is not here."

EMINA: "I consider being a refugee and being separated from my husband an act of violence against me."

VESNA: "I feel the urge to have someone with me here, to feel some protection and support, but I wonder how he would take that. Men get away with these things much more easily in times of peace, too. In my opinion this is also an instance of violence in not allowing ourselves to do what we want to do. Life without joy is the hardest to bear; when you turn in for the night with nothing to look forward to. I feel a tremendous need to be devoted to someone and to love him."

Definitions that tend to define violence in an abstract way

Two women, Mirjana and Ana, tried to find a common denominator for women's and men's experience of violence, and to generalize about it. As they see it, violence is a demonstration of power, particularly poignant in war and among refugees, and which affects both men and women equally, changing their lives against their will.

MIRJANA: "Violence assaults one's personality."

ANA: "Violence brings out what you do not want to be."

Underlying both definitions are, obviously, the sense of having lost control over one's life, bitterness for being cast off and compulsorily assimilated into a new environment. Ana's definition sounds more like a definition of power than a definition of violence, but for her, this demonstration of power means violence. This definition is interesting also because it reflects the utter helplessness that both men and women experience in a war; both are forced to lead a life they do not want to lead, and to "be what they do not want to be."

Definitions that list the forms of violence against women in war

Some of the women we interviewed attempted to summarize various forms of violence against women in war, based on their own experiences or those of other women. In addition to rape and physical violence, these definitions usually also involved violence against children and other close relatives, "violence against emotions," fear, and other forms of mental harassment (separation from children, forced expulsions, and other such experiences).

NADA: "It is physical violence to separate women from their children and take them away, killing children and other close relatives, even forcing women to watch the plight of complete strangers. The latter is, in my opinion, violence against emotions, and emotions are the most precious part of the woman, they surpass beauty or anything else."

BOSILJKA: "Violence—that means suffering, sorrow, rape, hunger, threats and fear."

SANDRA: "When your physical and mental integrity are put in jeopardy, and you are forced to leave your home and head for an uncertain future, the ill-treatment on leaving Sarajevo; all those are acts of violence."

OLIVERA: "Sexual violence and death, concern for the children, fear that something could happen to them, the hardship we endure for our children and other family members, separation from the children, means violence for me."

MILEVA: "Rape and killings during the war—that is violence."

On this subject Smiljka said, Women and children are those whose lives are being violated the most in the area of the former Yugoslavia. Rape is not the only form of violence against women. It is true that there were perpetrators on all three belligerent sides. But women are threatened not only physically, but also in many other ways. Violence against women in war involves rape, their children being killed, their families destroyed, struggling for survival, suffering mental damage, harassment and extortion as refugees, irrespective of their religion and things like that.

This group of definitions had a decisive influence on the final choice of the topic of our study. We could say that the interview with Smiljka was a turning point in that sense, since she convinced us of the need for a broader insight into women's wartime experiences; that is why her definition can be considered as the most precise determination of the object of our study. It illustrates the personal aspect of violence, caused by changes imposed on the lives of women. And the changes that are brought about by war are always violent. Our analyses were therefore applied to violence against women, as well as forms of violence directed at abstract victims or other people, and other violent changes that inflict suffering and give an intimate feeling of violence to the lives of women.

CHAPTER 3

The method and the sample— a contribution to the feminist critique of methodology

VESNA NIKOLIĆ-RISTANOVIĆ AND IVANA STEVANOVIĆ

On the method of research

Because of the many negative and restrictive features of traditional methods of research into women's problems, researchers of feminist orientation have tried to contribute to the improvement of research methodology. Feminist research is supposed to collect data on women's experiences in a way that overcomes the traditional hierarchical relations between the interviewer and the interviewee, and makes it possible for those interviewed to become the subject, and not the object of research (Gelsthorpe, Morris, 1990, p. 91). Therefore, feminist research requires the cooperation and active participation of the women who talk about their experience of violence. Their suggestions helped researchers decide which methods to apply, to define the object of their study, to identify the aims of the study, to interpret the results and put them to use by changing the existing practices. A very important feature of feminist research is that it is action research. Cooperation between the researcher and the interviewee is a good ground for confidence-building. Research becomes part of this process through maximal dialogues between the researchers and the women they are interviewing, so that they both become, as the feminist poet-singer Cris Williamson puts it, "the changer and the changed" (Lather, 1988, p. 570). In this way the main aim of feminist research is to change those who are being studied, those who are carrying out the study, and the social response to violence against women.

These axioms of the feminist critique of methodology have had a very powerful influence in the world recently. They were the starting point for our methodological approach to violence against women in war (Nikolić-Ristanović, 1994b and 1994c).

Research regarding violence against women in war was conducted throughout 1994, through interviews with sixty-nine
women refugees in the Federal Republic of Yugoslavia or in Ser-
bian-held territories in Bosnia-Herzegovina. Sixty-six women were
interviewed directly. In three instances, audio-taped interviews
conducted in the Autonomous Women's Center Against Sexual
Violence in Belgrade were used. Apart from interviews, letters that
one of our interviewees received from her sister, who had remained in the war zone, were also used. She was included in our
study as the seventieth woman. We also used letters we received
from interviewees when they returned to their places of residence
or left the country. In addition to this, data was collected through
informal conversations with women before and after the interviews, as well as from supplements to interviews that some of the
women sent us later. We must add that our interviewees approved
all the material we used, including their personal correspondence.

During the interviews a draft questionnaire consisting mostly of
open-ended questions was used so that women could freely express their own definitions, attitudes and personal experiences of
violence in war and against refugees. The draft questionnaire was
used essentially as a reminder to the researchers who conducted
the interviews. The women interviewed were encouraged to talk
about their experiences and give their own definitions of violence
in general and of war violence. The women we spoke to were encouraged to join our activities and interview others. One woman
accepted, interviewing two of her friends.

There were other ways in which our interviewees were involved in the process of research. Some of them helped us contact
other women. During the interviews, more than half of them
(thirty-six) expressed the desire to keep in touch with us. Thirty of
them wanted to see the final text in writing and to possibly make
some remarks. Together we discussed the object of our research
and the method of data collection. We took into consideration
their evaluation of both our analysis and our interpretation of their
statements. Also, our efforts as researchers were coupled with the
efforts we were making as members of autonomous feminist organizations to help women refugees, so that the research team
worked as a support group at the same time. We tried to facilitate
their contacts with institutions, to supply them with medicines,
food and hygiene products. We encouraged them to face their
problems in an active way or were just friendly and talked to them
for a long time. We suggested they cooperate with and actively join
feminist groups and feminist media activities, such as Women in

Black, SOS Hot Line for Women and Children Victims of Violence, the Autonomous Women's Center against Sexual Violence and the magazine *Feminist Notebooks*. During our research, we personally cooperated with these feminist groups, who helped us contact the women and encouraged them to join our research, and also participated in the interviews of ten women.

A very refined analysis of the material obtained from the interviews was carried out, and only a small number of general facts were statistically processed. In this way we tried to preserve the women's experiences to their full extent, both in terms of their content and the richness of their language.

General data on interviewed women and the sample group

The sample of seventy women who were involved in our study is by no means a representative one, but it is illustrative.

Most women were between 25 and 40 years of age (thirty of them). Eighteen women were between 40 and 55; twelve were over 55; and ten were between 17 and 25. Therefore, nearly three-quarters of the women interviewed (68.6%) were between 25 and 55 years of age, the time when women reach the peak of their activity and aptitude for work.

Forty women were married, out of whom eleven had husbands of a different nationality. Five women were children of mixed marriages, and four of them were married to people whose parents were of different nationalities. There were thirteen widows, ten of whom lost their husbands in this war. Two women were divorced.

As to their education level, most of our interviewees (thirty-three) had completed secondary education,[1] two had completed higher education of some sort, and sixteen women had completed university-level studies. Among the rest of them, ten had only completed elementary education and four were illiterate.[2] As is usually the case with women, their professions before the war were predominantly outside the sphere of the private economy: many were government officials or worked in the fields of public service, child-care and education (for example, as administrative and economic technicians, accountants, clerks, saleswomen, teachers, architects, lawyers, economists, doctors, pharmacists, dentists, social workers, nurses and so on).

More than three-quarters of the women (fifty-eight) were employed before the war started. Six of them had retired, having fulfilled legal requirements for a pension. Only nine of them were housewives. This pattern within our sample leads to the conclusion that most of the women were professionally independent and, therefore, used to the privileges that are associated with activities outside the home: a certain social status, a decent financial standard and the provision of a safe living for their families.

As to the ethnic pattern, our sample does not differ substantially from the official statistics on refugees in Serbia in 1994.[3] Most women declared themselves to be Serbs (fifty-three of them), whereas a few belonged to other nationalities: seven were Moslems, two Croats and one Slovene. Two women identified themselves as Montenegrins, and five as Yugoslavs.

Our interviewees lived in various parts of the former Yugoslavia till the onset of the civil war, mostly in Bosnia-Herzegovina. Most of them (thirty-five) came from Sarajevo, while the others were scattered in twenty-five different places throughout our former homeland: four came from Mostar (Bosnia), three from Zenica (Bosnia) and Konjic (Bosnia) respectively, and two each from Tuzla (Bosnia), Čapljina (Bosnia) and Brčko (Bosnia). There was one woman from each of the following places: Vojnić (Bosnia), Foča (Bosnia), Srbac (Bosnia), Otočac (Croatia), Kupres (Bosnia), Vukovar (Croatia), Međaši (Bosnia), Čemerno (Bosnia), Osijek (Croatia), Bradina (Bosnia), Tasovčići (Bosnia), Sijekovac (Croatia), Pakrac (Croatia), Hrasnica (Croatia), Karlovac (Croatia), Knin (Croatia), Zagreb (Croatia) and Ljubljana (Slovenia).

When each woman left her former residence varies, depending on the date of the onset of violence in a certain area. The first wave of refugees came in 1991, as a result of the war in Croatia. The first refugees from Croatia headed for the Danube Basin in Serbia as early as March 1991. Most of them settled in Apatin, Sombor, Bačka Palanka, Odžaci, Šid, Sremska Mitrovica and other towns in Vojvodina. Eight of our interviewees came to Yugoslavia in 1991. As the war spread, the number of refugees rose sharply. In 1992, forty-eight women from the sample fled to Serbia and Montenegro. Their arrival was connected with the outbreak of the war in Bosnia-Herzegovina. In 1993 and 1994 the flow of refugees decreased, and it reached its low point in 1993, the point at which two of the women we interviewed fled to Serbia and to Montenegro. The influx of refugees increased in 1994; that year, eight of our interviewees came to Serbia and Montenegro.

Most of the women we spoke to (forty-one) lived in refugee camps. A smaller number (twenty-nine) lived in private apartments or rented flats. The interviews were conducted in Belgrade, Niš, Bogovađa, Herceg Novi and in those parts of Sarajevo controlled by the Serbian authorities.

Notes

1 There were five students and a high-school senior among them.
2 Except for one girl who was mentally retarded, all in this group were women over 50 years of age, who were housewives living in rural areas.
3 According to data of September 1994, the ethnic spread of refugees in the territory of the Republic of Serbia was as follows: 77% of refugees were Serbs, 9% were Moslems, 2.6% were Croats, while 11.4% of refugees were of other nationalities (data obtained from the Commissariat for Refugees of the Republic of Serbia and the Red Cross of Serbia, and presented in the publication *Refugees in Serbia*, Belgrade, 1994, p. 29).

Chapter 4

Sexual violence

VESNA NIKOLIĆ-RISTANOVIĆ

Historically, men have always raped and in other ways sexually abused women in times of peace as well as in times of war. In wartime, men continue doing what they have been doing in peacetime, albeit more irrationally and less selectively, and their behavior receives more "understanding" and "indulgence" (Vickers, 1993, p. 16). Rape has accompanied all wars, be they religious, revolutionary, civil or international, and regardless of whether they are "just" or "unjust" (Brownmiller, 1975, pp. 31–32). Rape, unfortunately, also accompanied the war in the former Yugoslavia. As McGeough remarks (Vickers, 1993, p. 60), military sources rarely provide reliable information on what they euphemistically call a "collateral damage." Thus we do not have reliable statistics at our disposal on rape and other forms of sexual abuse in this war or in other wars. Moreover, the unreliability of statistics on rape in war is related to the usual and understandable unwillingness of women to speak about their experiences. Statistics are also rendered unreliable when used for political manipulation and the instigation of war. During war, as Brownmiller remarks, the emphasis on rape as a form of brutality specific to only one side of a conflict, to the army of one nation, was used to produce hatred and an emotional stimulus for the other side to continue fighting. Usually, neither side admits that its soldiers rape but they all readily point to the rapes performed by the enemy. And, "when the war was over, a wholly predictable reaction set in...The crime that is by reputation 'the easiest to charge and the hardest to prove' has traditionally been the easiest to disprove as well. The rational experts found it laughably easy to debunk accounts of rape, and laughably was the way they did it" (Brownmiller, 1975 p. 47).

An almost identical situation could also be found in the war in Bosnia-Herzegovina. The real sufferings of raped women were overshadowed by the state-controlled media campaigns. All sides involved in the war aimed to prove the culpability of the other side(s) and to promote the war by inciting their own people to vengeance (*Bosnia-Herzegovina—rape and sexual abuse by armed forces, Amnesty International Report*, January 1993, International Secretariat, London, p. 3). The consequences were new rapes and new female suffering. Unfortunately the international community and the media used this kind of propaganda all over the world as well. The Serb man was turned into the symbol of all rapists, and the Moslem woman into the symbol of all victims. As Žarkov pointed out, "in both cases the same process of ethnicization of the perpetrator and the victim was in play, obscuring many significant elements involved in these cases" (Žarkov, 1995, p. 115).

To illustrate this, we will present two examples from the foreign press and one from the domestic media. *Newsweek*, in its issue of January 11, 1993 (p. 21), for example, reproduced a photograph of a group of women with the following legend: "Bitter solidarity: Muslim women at a refugee center in Tuzla, Bosnia, relive the horrors of being raped by Serbian soldiers last June." *The Guardian* of January 20, 1993 (p. 2), also printed the same photograph, accompanied by the following text: "The Serbian soldiers who raped these women were 'normal' men, according to their victims. So what does that tell us about normal men?" On the other hand, the matter of identity protection for the victims who talked about their tragic experiences on Belgrade television is well illustrated by a case reported to us by one of the women that we interviewed. While talking about a woman who shared the same collective shelter with her, Anka said, "We learned true details of her case in a TV program, because somebody recognized her as she was talking, although she was shown from behind. Some reckless people invited her to watch the program and she had a nervous breakdown. I don't know what happened to her later."

Stigmatization, which may be a result of this kind of presentation of raped women, had obvious traumatic effects on these women. Similar effects may have been produced by foreign journalists' way of approaching women in refugee camps, usually followed by the question "Anyone here raped who speaks English?" (Zajović, 1994, p. 231). Also, the media's appetite for raped women sobbing out their tales of sexual violation resulted in a new kind of violence against them and new suffering for these women. One of the most drastic examples of media aggression towards rape victims was provided in the interview that Stiglmayer conducted with a 12-year-old Moslem girl from the town of Foča. Realizing how painful it was for the girl to answer the questions, Stiglmayer said, "I felt like a criminal while I pressed the little girl, who did not speak very much, with questions about her rape, and I was glad the interview was over" (Stiglmayer, 1994, p. 112). Stiglmayer's stubbornness in the conduct of the interview is indeed astonishing, especially as the girl's mother could have given her all the information she needed.

Given all we have already said, we can only agree with the opinion of McGeough (Vickers, 1993, p. 60) who claims that details about civilian suffering should be sought with refugees. What refugees lived, saw and heard about seems to be the best source of knowledge about the sexual violence against women in war.

As Seifert noted correctly, the international community had long ignored the rapes in Bosnia although the New York daily *Newsday,* as early as August 1992, published a report on rapes in Bosnian camps. "For only when sexual violence is perceived as a political event, when it is made public and analyzed, can its causes and contexts be probed and strategies to overcome it be considered" (Seifert, 1994, p. 68). The "numbers game" began at the end of 1992 and lasted through 1993. The Bosnian government spoke with about 50,000–60,000 raped Moslem women and claimed to possess information on 13,000 cases. On the other side, the commission for war crimes created in the Federal Republic of Yugoslavia brandished the statistic of 800 Serbian women raped in Moslem detention sites. Later on, a special report of the European Community (January 8, 1993) produced the number of 20,000 raped Moslem women, while drawing attention to "possible exaggerations." According to Jeri Laber, executive chief of Helsinki Watch, the report did not demonstrate the ways in which the data had been gathered. A team of UN experts, headed by the special UN envoy for human rights, Tadeusz Mazowiecki, spent eleven days (January 12–23, 1993) in Zagreb, Sarajevo, Zenica and Belgrade looking for data on rape and gathering evidence for 119 cases. In the conclusion of his report, Mazowiecki stressed that no reliable estimate of the total number of victimized women could be reached. Neither could Amnesty International, in its report of January 20, 1993, estimate the total number of rapes, although it claimed that the phenomenon was widespread.[1]

In March 1994, the special UN Commission of Experts sent teams of female lawyers and male and female mental health specialists to conduct interviews with victims and witnesses in Croatia, Slovenia and Austria. A total of 223 people were interviewed. However, as is stated in the Final Report, due to time constraints the teams were unable to meet with all those willing to come forward.[2] The Commission also sent a team of military personnel to conduct a pilot rape survey in Sarajevo in June and July of 1993, but the study was "relatively generalized" and not aimed at the exploration of specific cases. Unfortunately, the Commission had insufficient time to evaluate the data, as its Final Report was submitted only one month after the completion of interviews. The obvious hurry of the Commission to produce data that would confirm that rapes were a part of a typically Serbian strategy reveals the political manipulation of the statistics of raped women, especially raped Moslem women. However, it is interesting that despite all these circumstances which were supposed to contribute to unreliable conclusions, the Final Report stated that the results of the interviews were consistent with earlier conclusions. Yet it was recognized at the same time that it was difficult to discover the real number of raped women.[3]

The media and politicians from all parts of the world accepted data given by the Bosnian government as unquestionable. At the same time, the fact that Serbian women were raped as well was completely ignored. This kind of presentation of wartime rape promoted the hatred and hostility of Moslems and Croats and encouraged them to rape Serbian women in revenge. When political and military aims had been achieved, experts finally admitted that it was very difficult to find out the real number of victims. From the end of 1993 on, war rape reports have no longer made top news in the former Yugoslav and foreign media. Still, as *The Guardian*'s journalist Linda Grant wrote, "arguing how many women have been raped and why it was done has overshadowed another issue: What has happened to the women since the ordeal ended?"

The careless use of unverified numbers about rape in war is "efficient" from the standpoint of temporary propaganda effects. It is, however, usually counterproductive when the relation of the public toward the actual problem is taken into account. Exaggeration and the use of unverified numbers soon produce disbelief and doubt even about many truthful accounts. There is an obviously illogical contradiction between the extremely low rates of reported rape in pre-war Yugoslavia and the extremely high rate of reported rape during this war (as supported by numerous reports). The significant difference between the rates of report is not a consequence of a change in the attitude of women towards the reporting of rape in war, but a product of immediate military and political goals which are deemed priceless and which allow the manipulation of female suffering as a part of temporary war strategy. It is sad that some feminists, including some famous names such as MacKinnon and Chinkin, succumbed to media propaganda. Although curious about the sudden contrast with the usually low rate of report, they still easily asserted that rapes in the Bosnian war were frequently reported (Chinkin, 1993, p. 205); on the other hand, Serbian victims of rape were completely ignored (MacKinnon, 1993; 1994).

The media-fashioned black and white picture of the war in the former Yugoslavia has produced a biased approach in the study of the sexual abuse of women in the former Yugoslavia, as is well illustrated by Stiglmayer (italics ours).

> Because of the suffering of Muslim and Croatian rape victims, we frequently forget that Serbian women in Bosnia-Herzegovina are also being raped. Of course, they are not affected by rape as frequently as the Moslems. For one thing, the Serbian army is the victorious army and can better protect its civilians; for another, Moslems and Croats only rarely carried out "ethnic cleansing actions" in the territories under their control (where Serbs are still living)—although hostility towards Serbs is constantly growing and there are recurrent instances of misconduct toward Serbs...But the real reason that Serbian women seldom appear in the reports of rapes in Bosnia might be a different one: *they are the wives, sisters and daughters of the aggressors.* There is hardly a journalist who feels motivated to seek them out, to check up on what has happened to them and thus offer propaganda material to the Serbian side—that is, the bad side, the side "responsible for the war." (Stiglmayer, 1994, p. 138)

Thus, Stiglmayer has brilliantly defined the role of journalists in the creation of the image about war rape in the former Yugoslavia—an image which was uncritically accepted by the majority of experts (including feminists) worldwide. This image has inevitably included the male discourse, which treats women as objects, as a part of male property and not as individuals. By focusing their attention on Moslem rape victims (and to some extent on the Croatian ones), the majority of feminist authors have, willingly or unwillingly, contributed to the male political and military game in which women are divided according to whether they belong to the "good guys" or "bad guys."[4]

Unwillingness to talk with Serbian rape victims and to use data collected by Serbian anti-nationalist feminists and researchers, coupled with an exclusive reliance on Croatian nationalistic

sources and contacts (including nationalistic feminist groups such
as Kareta, which represents the main source for MacKinnon's and
Stiglmayer's analyses), meant the failure to understand rape in war
as an act directed primarily against women. The correction of a
similar position took considerable efforts when the Hague Tribunal was established and trials of war criminals were put on the
agenda.

In the period when rape statistics were being most brutally manipulated (the end of 1992 and the beginning of 1993) it was very
risky to approach the problem in terms of realistic and verified
data, regardless of the ethnic affiliation of victims. To talk about
the smaller—that is, realistic—number of raped Moslem women was
understood as a denial of the culpability of the Serbian side. Also,
talking about the realistic (again, smaller) number of victimized
Serbian women was often received on the other side with ironic
remarks, such as "Oh really, so few?" or "That's nothing in compari-
son with thousands of raped Moslem females." One could cynically
conclude that some people were sad because there was not a bigger number of raped women, as that would better suit their ideas
and actions. Or, as Chinkin notes, "there is the important question
of how women are portrayed by the government and the media at
a time of national crisis such as war. Images of women are typically
used both to justify the use of armed forces and to motivate men to
join the armed forces. The protection of women is an emotive
means of arousing domestic popular opinion in favor of the action" (Chinkin, 1993, p. 208). Or as Brownmiller correctly ob-
serves, when commenting on the propaganda surrounding rape in
World War I, "as propaganda, rape was remarkably effective, more
effective than the original German terror. It helped to lay the emotional groundwork that led us to war" (Brownmiller, 1975, p. 44).

The stories of the women we talked with demonstrated that
rape represents only one of a large number of the various forms of
sexual abuse of women in war, although the public attention
drawn to rape represents a certain development of public aware-
ness about violence against women (El Bushra, Lopez, 1993, p. 50).
Outside of rape, the sexual abuse of women in war also includes
the threat of rape, all kinds of sexual harassment and blackmail,
sexual slavery within the context of forced concubinage, and
forced prostitution (prostitution in brothels for soldiers and prostitution as a survival strategy). Women were abused in areas affected by the war (during war operations and occupations) as well
as in areas not directly affected by war, but where different ethnic
groups lived side by side. Women were also sexually victimized

when searched, arrested, interrogated, in prison, while demanding social assistance and as refugees. Of course, in war as well as in peace, women continue to be raped by the members of their own ethnic group, regardless of war and disturbed ethnic relations (Nikolić-Ristanović, 1996b).

General remarks about rape in war

Rape has always been considered "an unfortunate but inevitable by-product of the necessary game called war. Women, by this reasoning, are simply regrettable victims—incidental, unavoidable casualties...Rape is more than a symptom of war or evidence of its violent excess. Rape in war is a familiar excess with a familiar excuse" (Brownmiller, 1975, p. 32). In war, as well as in peace, rape results more from the imbalance of power between sexes than from a genuine sexual impulse. The purely sexual content of rape has only marginal meaning—rape is used as a means for goals that have nothing to do with sexuality. This meaning of rape is understood as such by all three participating parties: the man-rapist, the woman-victim and the man-rapist's war enemy. It is the relationship of force in the given moment in the given territory that determines to which side the rapist and the victim will belong.

As usual in a patriarchal society, in wartime women are seen as male property, as pure appendages to the territory and other male belongings. "The historic price of woman's protection by man against man was the imposition of chastity and monogamy. A crime committed against her body became a crime against the male estate" (Brownmiller, 1975, p. 40).

Within male-female relationships, rape corresponds to the behavior of conquering troops on the occupied territories (Chinkin, 1993, p. 206). Sexual conquest became an accepted evaluation of manhood, a manner of demonstrating dominance and superiority over women. "If sexuality was not bound up with power and aggression, rape would not be possible. When these attributes of masculinity are accentuated, as in war, rape reaches epidemic proportions" (Jackson, 1978, p. 31). Within the predominantly male character of war, the gap between the man who has power and the woman devoid of power becomes greater than usual. Rape in war is not only an accident produced by the fact that a woman found herself in the wrong place at the wrong time (Chinkin, 1993,

p. 205). Weapons increase the power of man, so that an ordinary man becomes un-ordinary by "entry into the most exclusive male-only club in the world" (Brownmiller, 1975, p. 32). On the other hand, women deprived of arms and the protection of "their" men, with their class and ethnic affiliation, educational and professional status, are exposed to the sexual violence of men.

The brutality of rape in war is especially amplified by the fact that in the eyes of the rapist the victim symbolizes the enemy. According to patriarchal principles, women are seen as the property of the enemy men, and the enemy has to be defeated by all means, including also the destruction of his property. Rape in war could be seen as a highly symbolic expression of the humiliation of the male enemy. The myth of the man-protector, which is usually activated in war, turns out to be, as Seifert notes, only a myth.

> Rape of women entails also another story: from man to man, so to speak, goes a rumor that the men whose women were attacked are not able to protect "their" women. That is a way to insult them and devaluate their manhood. This communication between men became clear during the war in the former Yugoslavia, when buses with women in sixth, seventh or even higher months of pregnancy were sent over the enemy lines—frequently with cynical inscriptions on the vehicles, about the children who will be born...The key point was the consequence for men, not the sufferings of women." (Seifert, 1994, p. 59)

Or, as Brownmiller wrote,

> A simple rule of thumb in war is that the winning side is the side that does the raping...a victorious army marches through the defeated people's territory, and thus it is obvious that if there is any raping to be done, it will be done on the bodies of the defeated enemy's women...Men of a conquered nation traditionally view the rape of "their" women as the ultimate humiliation, a sexual coup de grace...Apart from a genuine, human concern for wives and daughters near and dear to them, rape by a conqueror is a compelling evidence of the conquered's status of masculine impotence. Defense of women has long been a hallmark of masculine pride, as possession of women has been a hallmark of masculine success. Rape by a conquering soldier destroys all remaining illusions of power and property for men of the defeated side. The body of a raped woman becomes a ceremonial battlefield, a parade ground for the victor's trooping of the colors. The act that is played out upon her is a message passed between men—vivid proof of victory for one and loss and defeat for the other. (Brownmiller, 1975, pp. 35–38)

Of course, the men belonging to the losing side also rape, but in order to avenge themselves. When roles are changed, and the ex-losers become winners, they too tend to demonstrate their power to finally defeat the enemy. One of the most illustrative examples is the case of Russian soldiers who raped German women towards the end of World War II. A similar situation also occurred in the war in Bosnia-Herzegovina where the balance of forces in particular regions determined which nationality the rapist and his victim would be.

It is now possible to outline several "patterns" of war rapes in Bosnia-Herzegovina, regardless of the ethnic affiliation of the rapists and their victims. These patterns were determined on the basis of evidence discovered in our interviews, and taking into account the final report of the expert group contained in the letter addressed to the president of the UN Security Council by the secretary-general of the UN, in 1994.

- Before the general outbreak of hostilities in specific areas, the tension mounts and the ethnic group in control of power begins to terrorize its neighbors. Individuals and small groups of rapists, who simultaneously rob and threaten members of the other ethnic group(s), break into houses, search inhabitants, beat them, steal property and rape women.
- In the areas directly affected by war, during combat and while conquering territories, the winning army breaks into houses and rapes women there, or takes them away into camps or other places where they are publicly raped.
- In occupied territories or areas under siege, women are raped by individuals or small groups of men during the search of apartments, sudden inspections on fictional grounds, or during arrest. Also, women are abducted and then raped or taken to camps or brothels.
- In the regions not directly affected by war and that still have a mixed ethnic composition, individuals abduct, threaten and rape the women who belong to other group(s).
- Individuals or groups of men apply sexual violence.
- Women are raped who are confined in camps, prisons, hotels and other houses transformed into brothels, for the "amusement" of soldiers (often combined with cruel treatment and the infliction of suffering on women).
- Women are often sexually abused with the help of various objects, such as broken bottles, guns, clubs. There is also some evidence that animals were used.

The rape of women during military conquest and in the occupied territories

During a military conquest of enemy territories, men break into houses, kill men and rape and kill women, pillage and destroy property and burn houses. Sometimes men are forced to helplessly watch the rape, torture and murder of their women. Sometimes, men are the first to be killed, tortured or arrested. Afterwards, devoid of their possible protectors, women are raped, tortured and killed.

Marina, a Serb woman, told us about her neighbor, also a Serbian woman, who was tortured and raped in the town of Bratunac by four Moslem soldiers. The soldiers first broke into her apartment and shot her husband. He was wounded but did not lose consciousness, and pretended he was dead. Believing that her husband was dead, the soldiers raped the woman. Having raped her, they began torturing her in an extremely cruel fashion. They extinguished cigarettes on her body, cut off her breast and, at the end, dragged her into the bathroom and dumped her in the bathtub. When the torturers had left, the husband called for help and they were both transferred to the hospital. After four days, the woman died. Jana's cousin was raped in similar conditions. During the massacre of Serbs in the village of Sijekovac (by Croatian soldiers), the husband of Jana's cousin was killed, and afterwards she was raped. However, sometimes both husband and wife, found alone in their apartment, are killed, so that there is no way of telling what happened, and in what order. Still, as Sanija's report about a Moslem couple found killed in their apartment demonstrates, the state of the woman's body often suggests that the victim has been previously raped.

Rada reported the case of a 34-year-old Serbian woman from Zenica who was raped by Moslem soldiers while her husband was in prison. She was raped in her own house, in front of her father-in-law and her juvenile daughter. In general, it frequently happened that husbands, brothers, fathers and male cousins were forced to watch rape. Senada, a young woman interviewed by Helsinki Watch said, "A man broke into our house and raped me. He wore a green uniform and had a machine-gun and a knife. I did not know him. My husband had to watch the soldier raping me. There was no way of preventing him for he would have killed us both. He said, 'Your husband must watch this.'" Sometimes fathers were forced to rape their daughters. Brownmiller is obviously right when saying that, for the rapist, rape is an act that could be directed against the husband, brother or father, as well as against the female body (Brownmiller, 1975, p. 40).

Sometimes men prove their power by raping old women who live alone, and whose helplessness is only augmented by their bad mobility and the absence of a protector. As Sanija, a 76-year-old Moslem woman, recounted, in the town of Foča a 90-year-old Moslem woman who lived alone was raped and killed by Serbs. Nedžada reported a similar case happening in Brčko. A Moslem woman, aged 78, who lived alone in her house, was tortured, and, judging from the evidence, probably raped by Serbs.

> My aunt was left alone in the house, because she did not want to leave Brčko. Her children are refugees. Her sister lived next to her (they had a common backyard). The aunt is old, ill and illiterate. After the conquest of the town and expulsion of Moslems they remained in their houses. One day, three Serbian soldiers came into their backyard, where they spotted two old women. As the heavy fighting started in that moment, the soldiers said to the older one of the women, "Mother, why don't you enter your house?" The other aunt advised her to comply, thinking that the soldiers were benevolent. [The older woman] did not verify what was going on, because she hurried to enter her house instead. Later on the same evening she came to see her sister and she found her spread on the table, lying on her stomach; her clothes and lingerie were torn away and her back was covered with bruises. She was in such a state that she could not get back on her feet by herself.

During the conquest, soldiers not only broke into houses and raped the women they found there, they also broke into the houses which, due to their nature, sheltered larger numbers of women and were spatially and socially isolated. There, they raped the women as they saw fit. Dobrila recounted a similar case.

> I talked with the girls from the correctional facility in Ljubuško. I evacuated them and they recounted their experiences to me. The Croat army took the house. They found there sixteen girls, aged 16–18, who were mainly Serbian. There were also a few Hungarian and Slovak girls. They were raped and tortured. They could not take a bath. They had no regular food and attended no classes. Even correctional officers mistreated them and called them "Serbian whores." The whole thing lasted several months. We made great efforts to evacuate them through the Red Cross.

In the occupied territories and regions under siege, women were frequently raped, tortured and killed during or after the search of houses and apartments. Soldiers often searched houses under the pretext that they were looking for weapons. Sometimes they also raped and tortured women in their houses. However, cases of the abduction of women and their transfer to camps, prisons, brothels or other places were more frequent. That was the case of Bojana, a girl from Sarajevo. Since the beginning of the war, when the quarter of Dobrinja came under Moslem military control, soldiers broke into apartments under the pretext that they were looking for weapons almost daily. That was the usual system in her neighborhood. The soldiers used to open and search everything. One evening, three members of *Zelene beretke*[5] came and started knocking on her door, and she had to let them in. Having searched the flat, they took her to a cellar—a depot for food and ammunition. "The cellar," Bojana remembered, "was cold, dark, filthy, stinky, dusty and dizzy." She was raped there. They let her go around midnight, and she returned home alone. The next day they came back and everything started again. The ordeal lasted seven days. Olga talked with us about a similar case of abduction and rape in the occupied territory.

> A 54-year-old woman from Mostar was captured by the members of HOS.[6] They came into her apartment and took her away. She talked to me about that but was not able to give me all the details. Thirty to forty members of HOS, young men, raped her. They kept her locked up for several days. They also shaved her head. She was completely mortified. She was raped somewhere near the Neretva river. As she was tortured previously, she was unconscious when they raped her. However, she managed to run away; she swam the river and went into a monastery where Franciscan monks hid her and helped her to come to Serbia. When she was finally saved, she was completely psychically ruined.

While speaking about the rape of women in the region of Konjic, Stojanka stated, "There was a lot of that in my town. They used to take away women and rape them in apartments, cellars, and cars. It happened frequently. I came to know about that through reports of my neighbors who were returning from the front."

Soldiers usually break into apartments on some fictional grounds, such as the previous behavior of the victim, or the activities of some friends or cousins. Thus Milena reported Moslem soldiers breaking into her apartment and asking her and her friend about visits to her Moslem friends, and about the activities of her brother and brother-in-law. Then they began insulting them, calling them "chetnik whores," etc., eventually raping her friend. At the end, they locked them up and went away, threatening that the next day Milena too would be raped.

Sometimes, rape is preceded by the abduction of women from shelters, in the forest, or in the street. Anda mentions such a case. "Me and two other girls, also Serbian, were captured by a group of ten Moslems in the forest, not far from my home. I knew none of them because they were not from my town. They put us in a truck and drove us away. I did not recognize the road, as they were driving through the forest. They brought us to some kind of building and locked us in filthy, moist cells. We slept there one night. The next day, they transferred us to a prison. There, for the first time, we were beaten and raped by three soldiers."

Anka mentions abduction happening in the street.

> I came to know about the event, because I was with [the victim] in the same collective shelter. At the beginning of 1993, a very pregnant young woman came to the shelter. She was given special psychological treatment because of what she had had to go through. She had been abducted by Moslems, members of *Zelene beretke*, in front of a supermarket, in the street while she was waiting for a friend. They took her into a private apartment and gang-raped her. After a day or two, she was transferred to a brothel, where she spent three months.

Sometimes citizens, men and women alike, were ordered to resume their jobs, in spite of the war. They were kept there until they were transferred to camps.

> Radio-Čapljina summoned all physicians to the local hospital. My cousin was always conscientious and she left Tasovčići in order to go to the Čapljina hospital. Many did not come and thus they saved themselves. She worked fifteen to twenty days and could not return to Tasovčići because all bridges were blocked. The security personnel in the hospital did not allow anyone to leave, because they needed doctors. All doctors slept in the hospital. Later on, doctors of Serbian nationality were transferred to the camp of Dretelj. My cousin spent five months there. She was raped the whole time in the most brutal fashion.

Women were also taken away under the pretext that they were required to witness the search of apartments belonging to their neighbors or other people. Sometimes they were arrested because of their alleged membership in some political party or by virtue of some other political activity. Sometimes they were taken simply because they publicly expressed their attitudes about the enemy. Lepa reported a case of extreme brutality against a 30-year-old Serb woman from Sarajevo who publicly criticized the Moslem authorities. "My friend told me that a group of Moslem soldiers, five to six members of a private army, broke into the apartment of a girl who worked in the Revenue service. They tortured her and beat her; they all raped her and, at the end, they put a bottle into her vagina. She was wounded so badly that she died soon afterwards. The girl was very attractive and was known in Sarajevo for publicly criticizing Moslem authorities."

Besides political activity and political ideas, even apolitical or accidental behavior directed against the authorities could result in anger and terrible brutality. Gordana talked about a 38-year-old woman, who was characterized as attractive and slightly demented. She threw a stone at a car driven by Croats, members of HOS, and broke the windshield. Nobody knew if she had done it on purpose. "There was an accident and one Croat was wounded. After the incident, she was taken to prison in Ljubuško. There she was gang-raped. I heard that they were also using dogs. Finally, they killed her. I came to know about that through my cousin, who was in the prison and saw her tortured."

Very frequently the reason for an arrest was the political or military activity of husbands, sons and fathers. However, the simple fact that a woman belonged to the enemy nation was sometimes quite sufficient.

A telling example is the experience of Olga, a 34-year-old Serbian woman from Mostar. When arrested by members of HVO[7], she was told that the reason for her arrest was the fact that she had danced the "Čačak" (a Serbian folk dance) at her wedding ceremony. Jasminka too reported about Moslem girls who were abducted, kept in a camp and raped.

> In October of 1992 I was in the gynecological hospital in Sarajevo, where I was about to give birth. The hospital was evacuated because of shelling, and I spent ten days in the Clinical center. There, I saw two girls, aged 14, who had been raped by Serbs in Grbavica. They were very pregnant (in the fifth or sixth month). As they were not mature enough to have babies, doctors decided to take the risk and terminate the pregnancy. At that time, even the Clinical center was sometimes shelled. We all slept on the first floor (babies, mothers, pregnant women, women waiting for abortions) so that I was in a room next to the girls. They were in a special state of mind: not talking at all, crying all the time, waking up with screams. Their

parents were constantly by their side; they were desperate. The director of the clinic decided to help them. Their pregnancies were terminated, fortunately, with no consequences. We all were very uneasy about them. The people in the hospital were of mixed ethnic origin. As the girls' mothers recounted, one night they were taken out of their houses, brought into the common garage space and then transferred to a camp.

Sometimes men succeeded in protecting female members of their families, sometimes they failed. Nada explained that in the following way. "The fact that a woman or a child enjoys protection can influence the behavior of bullies in urban, more civilized environments. In more primitive, rural surroundings, they are more ruthless and pay no attention to anybody."

She described the case of her niece, whose grandfather succeeded in protecting his granddaughter.

It happened in 1992, in the town of Visoko, where Moslems held power. One day, Moslems came and ordered my parents and cousins, who are of Serbian nationality, to temporarily leave the apartment because they had to search the premises. My 14-year-old niece, who is well built and looks older than she is, was also there. They looked at her and said, "You little one, you will come with us to witness when we search an apartment." Then my father, her grandfather, energetically protested and said, "She can't go with you, she is a child, she's only 14 but looks older." And they did not take her away. Had he not acted thus she would have been taken away and nobody could tell what they would have done to her.

However, it seems that whether a woman is raped or not depends on more than the mentality of the people in the particular region. It also depends on how important she or some of her male relatives are to the enemy side. Ivana spoke about this.

During the first summer of war in Sarajevo (Dobrinja), two prisons were created: in one, girls were raped. In the other, they tortured men. A friend of mine spent a year and a half in one of these prisons. The behavior towards captured women varied from case to case. My friend wasn't harassed because her father, who is a physician, worked in the hospital where they treated Moslems. In general, soldiers sometimes broke into apartments to search people, in the middle of the night, and some women were taken while others were not. They usually did not harass the women who had somebody who was important for the Moslem side.

However, sometimes the husband could not protect the wife from rape. This could be either because he had no chance against more numerous armed enemies or because he could not persuade his wife to stay home from work or other activities. Given the fact that he is traditionally expected to protect the woman, if the husband fails in that obligation he himself is blamed, especially by his wife's male relatives. On the other hand, sometimes the husband cannot accept the fact that he has to continue to live with a woman who has been raped. This can happen regardless of whether he considers himself responsible and even if he has openly told her about his uneasiness. Gordana's report about the reaction of male relatives in connection with the female doctor who was raped in the camp of Dretelj is very telling. "While she was imprisoned, a conflict broke out between her brothers and her husband, because the brothers blamed the husband for letting her go to work when he knew what was happening. During a certain period, they forbade him to see his children...Her husband, who was educated in the patriarchal spirit, said to my brother that it was very hard for him to accept the fact that his wife had been raped, although he knew that she was not to blame."

In occupied territories, women are sometimes arrested and taken away into camps together with men. Several women told us about mass deportations to camps, including cases where whole villages were evacuated. Usually men were separated from women and sent to special prisons, although there were instances of mixed confinement. Imprisoned men were physically tortured, while women were physically and sexually abused both in prisons and brothels. Although there is some evidence of the sexual abuse of men (as quoted in the final report of the expert group), it happened less frequently than the abuse of women.

According to Olivera's testimony, women in Sarajevo were raped even when performing duties assigned to them by military authorities. While men were obliged to participate in combat, women aged 18–55 (except those with children younger than 8) were assigned various jobs. Some of them, especially young women, were ordered to clean apartments, and frequently they were raped on such occasions.

The sexual abuse of women in camps, prisons and brothels

In camps, prisons and brothels women were systematically raped. Although it is difficult and thankless to measure human suffering, it can be concluded that these rapes contained more brutality and humiliation than average rapes in peacetime. According to the results of many studies on rape, the brutality of rape increases with the increase of the number of rapists (Nikolić-Ristanović, 1989). While peacetime rapes usually involve one rapist and one victim, wartime rapes are characterized by a greater number of perpetrators, who rape each particular victim several times, consecutively or after short pauses. The sufferings thus inflicted were terrible, and other forms of physical and psychological mistreatment only increased them. Women were severely beaten, threatened with knives to their throats, and so on. Also, they were frequently forced to watch the torture and murder of other prisoners.

Anđa, a Serbian girl, who was abducted with two friends and taken into a Moslem prison, recounted her experience.

> They insulted us and called us names. I can't describe that to you; one has to live it in order to understand it. Three men raped us. They put knives to our throats, they wanted to slaughter us. It happened for days and days. When they beat prisoners and cut off parts of their bodies, we were brought to witness...Every day, the same thing happened to each one of us; we were tied and raped by several men. They did everything to us. It was unnatural, humiliating sexual violence...when I returned to my village, it took me a month to recover physically. Apart from being raped and tortured, we had only two meals per day: a piece of bread or boiled macaroni. There was some water in a corridor, and we could wash ourselves a bit, but not thoroughly, because there were always men circulating around. The only "shower" we had was when we fainted under torture. Then they used to pour water on us.

Desa retold experiences related to her by her daughter-in-law. "My neighbor was in the camp in Dobrinja (Sarajevo). The women were raped there. She was not touched but the younger ones were. They were tortured psychically. They were intentionally starved. From time to time they were given a piece of bread and some water. They were insulted, they were called names and asked to tell their husbands' whereabouts."

As Nedeljka recounted, women were taken away during the night, under the pretext of interrogation, at which time they were, in fact, raped.

> Bradina was attacked by Alija's[8] army, composed of Croats and Moslems. It was attacked in the morning. All the inhabitants were taken out of their houses (men, children and women). Men were tortured more than women and children. I watched men being beaten, insulted and menaced. They took us away to a sports hall in Konjic. There I slept one night. During the night, several times I saw pairs of soldiers coming and choosing pretty girls. They took them away, raped them and brought them back. One girl was taken away three times and raped. She said she had recognized her neighbor the third time and he managed to release her. In fact, they took away women under the pretext of interrogation. During the night around twenty.women were raped. The next morning, almost all women and children were released.

Svetlana reported about a men's and women's prison in Sarajevo watched over by Moslems. "There was a special way of torturing Serbs—they would tie all the prisoners with barbed wire and take them out into the part of Sarajevo under Serb shelling. Once, they untied a 76-year-old woman and raped her in front of all the prisoners. The woman died soon afterwards, as a consequence of the rape."

Some women managed to escape rape in camp thanks to their own or their mothers' cunning. Nedeljka, for example, saw a girl who was being personally sought by prison guards successfully hidden by her mother's body. Nedeljka succeeded in avoiding rape by disguising herself as an old woman—she put on old clothes, thick socks and her mother's kerchief. These are examples of what Smith-Haredah called "the cunning of the powerless," quoting a series of similar examples of cunning that German women during World War II used in order to escape being raped by Russians.

> Mothers—she says—dressed their juvenile daughters as young boys, cut off their hair and made them wear pants...The women who had to leave their homes in order to find food used to blacken their faces, mess up their hair, put on glasses, cover their heads with kerchiefs, put on band-aids or dress in old, gray and black rags...Sometimes courage and presence of spirit at the first moment were of the primary importance. A woman, for example, saved herself when six Russians broke into her apartment by taking out from her cupboard an electric model train and starting to play with them. (Sandher, Johr, 1992, p. 43)

Lepa, a Serb woman from Sarajevo, told us about the torture of Serb women in brothels.

> Starting with July 1992, the members of Alija's army started opening brothels in cafés in Sarajevo. Young Serbian women and girls from neighboring villages staffed the brothels. When entering a village Alija's boys took away men and women; men were put in prisons and girls were taken to brothels. A friend of mine told me about a similar brothel in the center of Sarajevo, staffed exclusively with minors. The brothel was "held" by a Moslem, a criminal and former convict who, at the time, was also the head of a prison. One evening, when I passed by the café-brothel I heard women yelling.

Svetlana provided a similar report. "Moslems used to bring juvenile Serbian girls into the prison-brothel in Toplana and rape them there. There had always been premises, annexed to their headquarters, where they tortured and raped Serbs."

Svetlana also described the suffering of women in another brothel in Sarajevo. "A 17-year-old daughter of a woman was taken into a brothel where she died under torture. She was bitten and raped; she was covered in wounds. Her mother was even forbidden to wear black. She was on the verge of madness. Brothels were staffed exclusively with young girls, while in prisons there were the old and the young ones alike."

Psychologically disturbed women could be the targets of particularly cruel sexual tortures and mistreatment, as illustrated by Marina's words.

> A 20-year-old Serb girl from Tuzla, who was known as mentally disturbed, was daily taken away by Moslem soldiers and brought back in front of a hospital. Her neighbors said the soldiers raped her the whole night in a brothel. Once I saw them throwing her out of a car and leaving her in front of the hospital. Somebody called the police then. The police came and several Moslems from the police began beating her on the street; she was covered in wounds. They dragged her along the street, forced her to walk. I heard that they had taken her afterwards to somewhere near the Jala river and continued to beat her so that maybe she succumbed.

Inter-ethnic rapes in the regions not directly affected by war

In ethnically mixed regions where one group predominated, women were raped simply because they were of the ethnic minority; they became victims of inter-ethnic retribution and the settling of scores. Rape was usually preceded by abduction, either by neighbors or by men known to the victim for years.

Milica, a 21-year-old Serb from a predominantly Serbian village, told us about her abduction and rape by a Croat neighbor.

> My house was at the beginning of the street and the youths usually gathered at the end of the street. On our way to the meeting point we usually called each other, waited for our friends to come out and then continued together. I have known him for years. He was 22, he was a Croat and he had gone several times to the front, but I didn't pay much attention to that fact. That night, I found him at his house. I called him and he came out. We continued together, talking. But, as we walked through the dark part of the street he suddenly put his hands on my mouth. He then called two men, who grabbed me and dragged me into a car. They covered my eyes with a band, stuffed my mouth with a piece of cloth and began beating me on the head, so that I don't remember what happened afterwards. When I woke up, I realized that I was in a field near my village. I looked terrible, every bit of my body ached. I was sick. It is a terrible, indescribable feeling: something insipid, sleazy. I realized what had happened to me. I came back home; I was shocked when I saw myself in the mirror. My mother called me while I was in the bathroom, but I did not want to come out immediately. I heard her asking behind the door, "How was your evening?" "Fine," I replied.

Rape: revenge against women or revenge against men

Apart from a woman's ethnic affiliation, her vulnerability to rape in civil war can also be related to her previous relations with some known man. The woman is the òne who has to pay for her previous behavior towards a particular man; or, as Ljiljana described it, "in wartime, the woman often has to pay if somebody was offended by her behavior in peacetime. And, with women, it almost always boils down to sex." In that respect, attractive young girls who in times of peace declined certain proposals are particularly vulnerable. The man seizes the opportunity provided by war and retaliates by rape.

However, revenge can also have another goal; it is meant to correct a perceived imbalance of power between women and men that existed in peacetime. A previous imbalance of power, in which a particular woman enjoyed a superior social status, has to be reversed and turned into the traditional relationship that favors the man. According to Gordana's report, in the Croat camp Dretelj (for Serbs and Moslems), every second woman was raped. The majority of the women were young girls, but there was also a physician and a teacher.

> The physician and the teacher were especially tortured, because rapists were provoked by their status and education...The physician, a 38-year-old Serb woman, was raped several times every day; they told her they wouldn't release her until she gave birth to an *ustaša*.[9] Fortunately, she did not become pregnant. They raped her, said they would kill her and sometimes left her to roam in the city, all maddened. As she herself said, she was on the verge of death several times and she thought she would die. They also used to take her away to tidy apartments and they raped her there too. She was raped by the people she had helped hundreds of times as a physician.

As Brownmiller writes, "the gun in the hand is power. The sickness of war feeds on itself. A certain number of soldiers must prove their newly won superiority—prove it to a woman, to themselves, to other men" (Brownmiller, 1975, p. 33).

However, more frequently, women had to "pay" for real or alleged, previous or actual ideas and acts of their husbands, sons, brothers, fathers. Or, more precisely, rape was used as a means to punish a woman's male relatives. This is a way to explain the abduction, rape, torture and murder of the women whose men were absent and presumed to be fighting on the opposite side.

Bosiljka, a Serb woman from Konjic, spoke about the case of her friend, also a Serb woman.

> She was 45. She was married and had two sons and a daughter. She was taken away to a camp, since the son and the husband did not surrender. In the camp, she was raped whenever rapists wanted it. There were several of them and she knew them all quite well. There were also some of her neighbors and customers, for she worked in a shop before the war. Since her husband was a policeman, she also recognized several individuals who had had troubles with the law.

> While she was detained, they broadcast over the radio the details of the mistreatment she was subjected to. During the war, her husband had been killed and his corpse (already in a state of advanced decay) was brought to her; she could recognize him solely by his sport shoes. Her son had been beaten so badly that he lost his eyesight. Her house was burnt in front of her eyes.

The price this woman had to pay, as the enemy's revenge against her husband and son, was terrible. By punishing the woman, the enemy obviously wanted to indirectly punish her husband and son for their previous or actual acts. This is demonstrated by the fact that the details of her torture were fully reported over radio. We think that the intention of such a procedure was twofold: a) to deter other men, whose women were left at home, from fighting against the enemy, and b) to wear away the morale of the other side. However, the circle of horror was closed by definite and direct punishment, the death of her husband and the heavy incapacitation of her son. By this her mistreatment in camp was rendered absurd; nevertheless, it was the woman who was directly punished, probably without the torturers being aware that they were punishing her. That is the chain of violence that follows the fate of a woman in war, whose destiny is closely interwoven with the destiny of men close to her. This chain usually remains invisible and hidden behind "heroic" combat and the wounding or death of men. Moreover, this case brings up the possibility that rape in the war was used for pornographic purposes. MacKinnon believes that the video recording of the rapes of Moslem women and their use for pornographic purposes was exclusively done by Serbs (MacKinnon, 1994, p. 75). Since our research did not produce sufficient evidence to enable us to speak about the scope of the phenomenon, we can only draw attention to two things. First of all, the example mentioned above suggests the possibility that other belligerent parties may also have used rape for similar purposes. However, it is important to point out that MacKinnon's conclusion, and her explanation of pornography as "the motivator and instructional manual for sexual atrocities in this genocide" (used exclusively by Serbs, as she believes), is based on a rather impressive ignorance of historical and social characteristics of the former Yugoslavia. Most of all, her initial thesis that pre-war Yugoslavia was flooded by pornography which paved the way for the sexually obsessed genocide enacted by the Serbian side seems very problematic. As an illustration of the pornography flood, MacKinnon mentions a rather old Croatian weekly, *Start*, which, as she said, published photographs of naked women in its middle pages. Yet another example, according to MacKinnon, is the pile of pornographic reviews found in the bedroom of Borislav Herak, a Serb soldier who had confessed to numerous rapes and killings in Bosnia. However, it is hard to understand how the alleged "pornography flood" which submerged the whole of the former Yugoslavia and which, moreover, was channeled through a Croatian review, could lead only one ethnic group (Serbs) to commit atrocities. We think that this over-simplified explanation, based on a poor knowledge of relevant facts, has unfortunately displaced attention from the essential explanation of crimes against women in this war. These violations represent an expression of misogyny which, in the communist era, was carefully concealed by ideological slogans about gender equality. The nationalistic hysteria and the ensuing war have only denuded and reinforced misogyny among males from all warring camps. Thus, MacKinnon's explanation appears contradictory in itself. She places rape within male/female dynamics, without discussing ethnicized groups and how they were constituted (Rejali, 1996, p. 366). Furthermore, neglecting the process of the ethnicization of the female body makes her unable to grasp the essential character of rape. She reduces it exclusively to the dynamics between Serb males and Croat and Moslem females. As Žarkov correctly points out "it is a 'natural' element of male power to define the boundaries of its own 'ethnic group' by defining the women of the 'Other' through rape, and thus defining the female body as the ethnic female body" (Žarkov, 1995, p. 113). Women's bodies become a battlefield where men communicate their rage to other men, because women's bodies have been the implicit political battlefield all along. Rape in the context of war is the means by which differentials of power and identity are defined (Rejali, 1996, p. 366). Therefore, power differences that exist within male/female and male/male relationships (i.e., differences among various ethnic groups) determine the scope of rape among members of different ethnic groups. That is a way to explain the fact that Serb males probably committed the largest number of rapes of Moslem women, and also the fact that the number of raped Serbian women continued to grow as the war unfolded and military success shifted towards Croats and Moslems.

The female body as a means of male inter-ethnic "communication"

Women married to men of another nationality were potential victims of rape by men of their own nationality, their husband's nationality or men of some other (third) nationality.

In the first case, members of the woman's own ethnic group want to offend and humiliate her husband. In a letter to her sister, Nataša described such a case. "A Croat woman, married to a Moslem man, was raped by Croats, in the presence of her daughter." From the standpoint of the rapists, the rape was obviously meant as a message sent to her husband.

In the second case, the husband's compatriots want to punish the victim's husband through her rape because he did not get rid of a woman who belonged to the enemy nation and who, as such, is not worthy of being the "property" of his nation. Nataša, daughter of a Serbian father and Moslem mother, is married to a Croat. She describes her fear of Croats in the following way. "My husband is no longer able to protect me and my mother. There were instances where they said 'If it is a mixed marriage, you either go away or make your woman go away.' I'm so afraid."

Finally, in the third case, a member of a third nationality, to which neither the husband nor the wife belongs, intrudes into the conflict. He mistreats the woman, aiming thus to punish her husband simply for his connection to the enemy nation. The vulnerability of women in mixed marriages is especially accentuated when the husband is directly involved in military actions against the rapist's nation, or when he is accused of participating in such actions.

Emina, a 28-year-old Moslem woman, told us about the fate of her sister, who remained in Mostar.

> My mother-in-law, who is a Croat, told me about that when she came to Belgrade to visit us. Croats mistreated my sister because her husband, a Serb, had decided to stay in the Croatian part of Mostar. They used to live there together. When the war broke out, she thought she would be more secure in the Moslem part (where my mother lived), so she moved there, together with her children. One day, our Croat neighbors came and took her and our mother away. They took them to the left bank, in the park called Buna. There, they began sharpening their knives in the car and threatening them with murder. They threatened my sister with rape and viciously in-

sulted her. Because her husband was absent, the neighbors thought that he was on the front line, fighting against Croats. Fortunately, another Croat neighbor came who knew my father well and he managed to release them. My sister was very shaken by the whole event, especially because she was separated from her husband, who was so near yet so far (fifty meters), since she couldn't cross over and knew nothing of him. For eight months my sister had no news of her husband. Finally, he sent her a letter, in which he stated he would kill himself because he couldn't stand to live that way anymore. Besides, since her mental health seriously deteriorated after the Croat mistreatment, I fear that my sister was not only threatened with rape but also indeed raped. However, neither she nor my mother wants to talk about that.

This case demonstrates again to what extent the psychological suffering of mistreated women becomes accentuated in the context of war, on top of the usual general insecurity and severed family ties.

The cases described in this chapter draw attention to the fact that women who lived in so-called mixed marriages were particularly exposed to the possibility of rape—a fact that is almost completely ignored in all analyses. Rapes of women who lived in mixed marriages have undoubtedly confirmed Brownmiller's thesis that rape in war represents a way for men to settle accounts with other men. Rape is directed against "all women who belong to other men" (Brownmiller, 1994, p. 181). This introduces the third, and it seems the essential, element of the explanation of rape, the fact that the woman belongs to a man of another nationality. In war a woman is raped because she represents the "female and ethnic Other," and her ethnic difference is defined by the man whose "property" she is, without taking into account her own ethnic origin.

Rape as a part of war strategy

Rape as an instrument of expulsion. Rape was obviously used as part of a more general war strategy; it became an instrument of war and a method of "ethnic cleansing." The threat of rape was used as "an instrument of forced exile, to make you leave your home and never want to come back" (MacKinnon, 1993, p. 88). Or, as the final report of the UN expert group demonstrated, rape was intentionally used in order to expel a particular ethnic group from a particular area. This was demonstrated by the humiliation and dishonoring of the victim through rape in front of her relatives, in front of other prisoners, in public places or by forcing family members to rape each other. Moreover, young women and virgins were frequent targets of rape, together with educated girls and women from respectable families.

Although existing information is not sufficient to point to a conclusion about the existence of an overall policy of rape for the sake of expulsion, it is obvious that there was such an aim and that it was frequently achieved. However, one must distinguish two types of case. In the first type, rape is used as an instrument of threat, direct pressure on the victim to make her leave. In the second, women leave the territory where they live because they become disturbed by what they see or hear happening to other women. This second type of case includes examples where parents, especially mothers concerned for their female offspring, decide to send them to a safe place, away from the region affected by war.

While talking about the physician who was raped in the camp of Dretelj, Gordana said she had left, with her husband and children, to live somewhere else. When mentioning Čapljina, she said she would never again set foot there.

An example of emigration provoked by the fear of rape is well illustrated by Olivera. She explained how she and her husband decided to send their two daughters into refuge.

When the war started, I was ready to leave Sarajevo immediately. My husband did not agree because he had heard that there was mobilization in Serbia and he thought that there were ways of avoiding mobilization in Sarajevo. Indifferent, as men mainly are, he did not even understand that we had to put our children in a safe place. It was a bloody mess: there was shelling, people were taken away and killed, girls were raped. Once, my younger daughter, aged 15, came home all desperate, saying "I'd rather be killed than raped." Then I lost patience and said to my husband, "We have to move the children out immediately. Our daughters are young and pretty. I could be beaten, raped or even killed, but I could put up with everything and continue to live because I have them. But they can't deal with that; just think what they would become if somebody raped them. Their lives would be destroyed." Thus, we decided that they should leave.

Lepa was guided by similar reasons when she decided to send her daughters to refuge. "We decided that our daughter should leave Sarajevo because we had heard that there were brothels; we had heard about assassinations, abductions, mistreatment."

The fear of rape was present in women with young daughters as well as in very old women, due to the cruel and humiliating rapes to which not only young women but even little girls and old women were exposed. While writing about the reality of the fear of rape in Berlin at the end of World War II, Smith-Harchah concludes that "rape of women was an order of the day. It did not matter if they were children or old women. A 14-year-old girl had to lay her head on a stone and she was the object of several men who transmitted a venereal disease to her" (Sandher, Johr, 1992, p. 85). Similar things also happened in the war in Bangladesh (Brown-miller, 1975, p. 40).

While talking about the fear that she had to face while she was in Sarajevo, Desa said that she especially feared for her 8-year-old daughter.

Jasminka had similar thoughts when she was in a maternity hospital, together with two raped and pregnant girls. Vera told us about the events of World War II, similar to the present war in Bosnia. "They came into our house and drove us all away. There were thirty to one. My grandmother begged us to take her with us. 'Don't leave me, please, they can rape me,' she said, 'there are some animals who rape even grandmothers.'"

Rape and the abuse of women's reproductive rights: a deconstruction of the idea of rape as a method of ethnic cleansing. In the Bosnian war rape was also used for the "production" of children of the rapist's nationality. According to the patriarchal pattern, a woman symbolizes family, and family is seen as the basis of society. Within that context, the rape of women with the aim of producing children of the enemy's nationality represents a means for the destruction of the foundations of the enemy's life. In other words, rape is used as a tool to destroy the enemy.

The idea of rape as a method of ethnic cleansing contains a very deep patriarchal construction; women are seen as objects, "recipients" that passively accept male seed without adding anything original, anything personal. Within that context, the identity of the child, a human being, depends only on the man. Thus, the children of the women impregnated through enemy rape will be of the rapist's nationality. "Milena, we have to make Moslem children," replied a Moslem soldier to Milena, when she begged him to stop his "brother in arms" raping her friend in the next room. I. J., a woman raped in the camp of Slavonski Brod, allowed her testimony to be published in the refugee paper *Odgovor*, in 1993. "When they knew that many of us, including me, had become pregnant, they left us alone for a while. They said they did it for the benefit of future Croat children. They were not bothered by the fact that these are Serb women who will give birth, because, as they said, their fathers are Croats and therefore the children will be Croats too."

It is high time to deconstruct the notion of rape as a method of ethnic cleansing (through forcing women to give birth to children conceived through inter-ethnic rape). The essence of such rape, first of all, is constituted by another crime, that of forced pregnancy, which is still not defined as a crime either by the international community or by the International Court for War Crimes in the former Yugoslavia. We agree with Chinkin that rape as a method of ethnic cleansing has to be investigated and prosecuted separately. This would highlight the seriousness of rape and violent sexual abuse in war outside their relations to other war tactics such as ethnic cleansing (Chinkin, 1993). We think that the phenomenon of children conceived through rape authorizes us to talk about ethnic mixing rather than ethnic cleansing, although men of all warring sides are not ready to accept that. Writing about rape in World War II, Sandher and Johr observe a great historic irony—the war which was made in the name of racial purity, among other things, laid the ground for a gigantic mixing, so that contemporary Europe really does look different from the Europe of the 1940s (Sandher, Johr, 1992, p. 34).

The refusal to accept that rape between members of different nationalities in fact constitutes ethnic mixing produces terrible suffering of women. The rapists want to ensure that raped women will give birth to children of the rapist's nationality, and to remind women forever of the horrors of rape. Unfortunately, they succeed; to feel the rapist's child in their wombs and to be sure that everybody knows these are the children of the enemy, yet knowing, at the same time, that they are also their own children, represents one of the cruelest forms of torture of women in war. At the same time, rapists want to deliver a message to the husbands of the raped women (as well as to other men belonging to the enemy) that their women have become worthless. Instead of giving birth to children of their husband's nationality, the victims give birth to the children of their enemies. This is how the husbands of raped women, as well as other men, understand the message. They despise and reject women who have been raped and have given birth. A Bosnian Serb, the husband of a raped woman, handed a gun to his wife, advising her to commit suicide.[10] Sandher and Johr quote a similar example from World War II. "A father sent his raped daughter to death, with the following words 'If honor is lost—everything is lost.' He even defined for her the way of dying: he handed her a rope to hang herself" (Sandher, Johr, 1992, p. 100). Husbands' incapacity to accept shame sometimes produces the destruction of the whole family, because "the hallowed rights of property have been abused, and the property itself is held culpable" (Brownmiller, 1975, p. 40).

The male abuse of female sexuality and reproductive rights is unlimited, and it is bound up with immediate political and military goals. For example, unlike Serbs and men from other ethnic groups involved in the conflicts in the former Yugoslavia, in World War II the Germans had other priorities. They were prohibited from raping Jewish women (which, however, does not preclude disobedience), as these acts were defined as "race pollution." This, in fact, was very similar to the "race mixing" prohibited in the American South during and after the age of slavery (Brownmiller, 1975, p. 51). According to MacKinnon, race rape was treated in the American context as "pollution." Children were seen as "filthy" and "contaminated" and they were defined by the race of the mother (assuming white rapist and black victim, as was usual), that is, they were seen as black children. This is in contrast to inter-ethnic rape where the children are seen as miraculously purified. Their ethnic affiliation is defined exclusively by the ethnicity of the father, as "pure" as if there was no drop of mother's blood in them at all (MacKinnon, 1993, p. 89).

The irony goes even further. The Catholic Church gave its blessing to the children of forced pregnancies resulting from inter-ethnic rapes. Promoting an image of woman as a passive recipient of every injustice done to her, the pope publicly invited forcibly impregnated women to "accept the enemy" by giving birth, instead of interrupting pregnancy (El Bushra, Lopez, 1993, p. 57).

Forced impregnation aimed at giving birth to children of another nationality is almost always seen as a product of rape. However, as we will see later, the problem appeared also as a consequence of other forms of sexual abuse, such as sexual blackmail. Moreover, we have formed the impression that the discussion of rape as a method of ethnic cleansing largely overshadowed complex and negative consequences of rape in war. Thus, the problem of women who had been impregnated through rape and who could not abort or give birth in wartime conditions—because of serious health risks—was completely ignored. The termination of pregnancy was sometimes rendered impossible due to religious prohibitions, blackmail or by detention until a moment when abortion was no longer possible. Some women were rendered sterile by abortions while others who could not accept their pregnancy committed suicide. In war, when food, medication and accommodation are lacking, and when medical care is principally oriented toward the army, childbirth can be an incredibly heavy material and psychic burden for a woman. The psychic state of the woman is furthermore complicated by the fact that the child is frequently seen by her family and/or other compatriots as a "proof" of the woman's collaboration with the enemy, or as evidence of her immoral behavior. Moreover, rape, as well as abortion and childbirth in inadequate conditions, brings an increased risk of venereal diseases, including AIDS (Chinkin, 1993, p. 206).

Anka and Emira talked about the problems of women who were sexually abused in war and who wanted to abort. For some time Anka shared the same collective shelter with a woman who was raped by Moslems. "She was already pregnant and wanted to abort. However, in the hospital she was told that they would perform an abortion only if she declared that Serbs had raped her. She refused. She took the first convoy out from Sarajevo, in 1993, and arrived here. However, as her pregnancy was already advanced, an abortion could not have been performed. She had to give birth."

Emina talked about her cousin from Mostar. "As she was in the Croat part of Mostar where abortion was not allowed [every gynecological examination was also witnessed by a nun who insisted that the child had to be born], she could not abort in time."

In this war, as well as in the previous ones, even women impregnated through rape who were not forced to give birth had a very hard time. Milica's account illustrates this point well.

> I did not know I was pregnant, because I had my regular periods even until the fifth month after the rape. I did not have a medical examination immediately after the rape because I feared that it might become known. Sometime in the fifth month I went to see the doctor, because I realized there was something happening with me. In my town abortion is performed only until the third month, and after that, you can do it provided you have money and connections. I was poor. I did not succeed. I was ashamed to give birth in my town, so I decided to go to Belgrade. I gave my baby up for adoption. The ambience in my town is such that if you are not a whore, if you don't break marriages, if you are not scum, you can't survive. You don't realize where you live until something happens

to you. Only then you can see who's your real friend. I could not accept my baby because it would have always reminded me of the
thing that happened to me. I think it would have killed me.

Milica gave birth to a boy which was given up for adoption. After
childbirth she was accommodated in a home for unprotected children. She was in a room with her baby, and the personnel constantly reminded her that she had to take care of the child, although she had declared before giving birth that she did not want
to see it. However, because of the closeness of the child and the
care she provided, she ended up bonding with the baby. She even
gave him a name, although she kept refusing the very thought of
keeping the child for herself. The conflict between reason and
emotions eventually produced a horribly painful trauma, as happened with many women who gave birth to children conceived
through rape in war. And not only in war. This is perhaps best illustrated by a letter that Milica sent us, after she had returned to
her town. "There is nothing new here. There is war. People are
killed. Nothing new, indeed. We can barely make two ends meet.
I'm not feeling well. I feel so bad, depressed, irritated. I became
withdrawn. My nerves went down the drain. I have nightmares.
I don't know what to do. I only smoke and worry. I can't eat, I've
lost my appetite. I lost ten to twelve kilos. The other day, I was
given an infusion. I don't know what to do."

Mixed, conflicting emotions, constant clashes between love and
hatred, between acceptance and rejection, are even more dramati-
cally expressed in the lives of women who decided to keep and
rear children conceived through rape. There is not much evidence
about the dramas that are experienced by the mothers of children
who became living monuments of their suffering, but even those
few accounts that we have point out a painful fact; these children
very often bear a physical resemblance to their father-rapists.
A very telling example is provided by a Jewish girl raped in a concentration camp in World War II. Her confession is reproduced in
Simon Wiesenthal's book *Max and Helen*.

But, you would probably like to ask: "Why did you give birth to a
child of that evildoer?" That is the question I have often posed to
myself too. The whole of my being strongly resisted the idea of
abortion. In fact, what was the culpability of that little being in my
womb? It did not beg anyone to come to this world. Of course,
I could have left him in an orphanage or given him for adoption.
But it was my baby, and I was his mother...The child grew. It resembled Schultze more and more. I thought I could not bear it. Will he

also inherit his impulsiveness, his brutality? Will fear ever stop? (Wiesenthal, 1991, p. 117)

The drama of the mother inevitably influences the life of the child. Sandher and Johr interviewed children conceived through rape who lived with their mothers. They found that their relationships were very traumatic, because children constantly reminded mothers of the horrors of rape, and that inevitably influenced mutual relations (Sandher, Johr, 1992, p. 94).[11]

Milena, another woman we talked with, was traumatized at the very beginning of her attempt to live with the child that was conceived during a seven-day rape performed by three Moslem soldiers. Milena arrived in Belgrade in the seventh month of her pregnancy without realizing that she was pregnant. She was accommodated in a home for unprotected children. She wanted first to have a cesarean in her seventh month, just to get rid of the fetus. She thought it was feasible. She was, however, advised by the doctors that it was better to give birth. While the baby was being delivered, the nurse covered her eyes so that she could not see it. After recovering from childbirth, she returned to her town, but could not find peace of mind because she was torn between her desire for the baby and the emotions produced by her memories of rape. She decided to give up the baby for adoption, then changed her mind and tried to live with the child. She could not bear that test. Due to a serious psychological state, which demanded hospitalization, she could not take care of the baby.

Forced concubinage or sexual slavery

Sometimes, apart from being raped, women are taken away and forced to live in concubinage with men who are members of the enemy side. Thus they become slaves, completely subjugated by their forced husbands. Sexual slavery, which sometimes lasts several years, is usually accompanied by domestic chores, and a general satisfaction of all of the master's needs, including acting as a receptacle for physical abuse. Examples of such treatment of women in war can be found in literature and movies which demonstrate the Nazi abuse of Jewish women in World War II (Wiesenthal, 1991; Steven Spielberg's film *Schindler's list*, etc.). Similar cases also existed in the former Yugoslavia in World War II, as well as in the present war.

In some regions of Croatia, for example, some very young girls, no older than 14, were systematically raped and abducted. Some of them never reappeared. Borka, speaking about similar crimes in the region of Western Lika, said that all the raped girls were Serbs abducted by Croatian soldiers. She could not tell what had happened with them, but there were some indications that they were taken to brothels or made sexual slaves through forced concubinage with Croatian soldiers. The latter seems probable, since it resembles the events that, according to Vera, happened in Croatia during World War II. "In the Second World War, *ustaše* used to kidnap girls aged 12–13. They took them into a barn and raped them. Afterwards, they killed some of them and took the rest (seven to eight girls) to their houses where they were forced to live with them. These forcibly married women lived with the bullies until the end of the war. It is interesting that only one of these girls conceived with her violent husband. At the end of the war, all of these women, except one, had quit their ravishers and married Serbs."

It is interesting that Vera's daughter Gordana, commenting on her mother's story, recognized that the essence of forced concubinage is hidden rape, which provokes a different social reaction from open rape. "It is interesting for a patriarchal surrounding, that all of these women married afterwards, while raped women usually had problems with their husbands, and had difficulty in marrying."

There are several possible explanations for such attitudes of husbands. Perhaps the situation was different due to the fact that the women were not their women prior to rape. The women were not seen as their property at the time of the rape, and thus it was easier to accept the fact that the women "temporarily" belonged to the enemy. Or perhaps it was the matter of reconquering territories, including the women who were "conquered" by the enemy. However, it is most probable that future husbands did not understand life in concubinage of these women as rape. It seems that marriage, formal or informal and regardless of its content, represents a mask that men can accept more easily (and more readily forget) than the barren and total sexual violence that women were exposed to.

Prostitution as a survival strategy

It seems apparent that some sort of exterior form similar to a marriage or relationship (even with the enemy) guarantees a woman moral purity and a sufficient excuse; she is not stigmatized as a raped woman or prostitute. It seems that women are conscious of this male opinion. Many women in Bosnia, as well as in other wars (Sandher, Johr, 1992, p. 62), chose to become mistresses of men of their own or another nationality in order to protect themselves or to survive. In that way, they attempted to protect themselves without losing their dignity. Women were forced into a situation where they had to choose some discreet form of prostitution which more closely corresponded with the male definition of female dignity and chastity. In that respect, Stanislava's story is very illustrative. During the war in Bosnia she met a shadowy character, a trucker, who delivered some services to Serbian paramilitary units. She met him at the beginning of the war, in May of 1992. As she herself said, she was happy with him, because she thought that a woman in war conditions has to have some protection. She believes that he was good and kind to her and her relationship with him helped her save her dignity. "At least nobody could say that I was a whore during the war," said Stanislava. She continued, "I know a whole bunch of Moslem women who escorted their husbands and children from Grbavica to the Moslem part of the city, and who remained to guard their apartments. Every one of them has found herself a 'protector' and strolls with him around Grbavica, hand in hand."

However, a similar mode of protection can end tragically, as several of our interviewees confirmed. Ana, for example, told us about a 30-year-old Serb woman from Mostar. "She was not originally from Mostar. She was a translator, single, attractive. She lived alone in her apartment. A Croat first raped her, and after that she started dating a Moslem, in order to get some protection. However, he started acting like a pimp for his friends. She was killed afterwards."

Sandra talked about her friend, a 32-year-old Serb woman from Sarajevo, mistreated by a Moslem friend who offered her "protection." "On the insistence of a Moslem friend, who was an older man, my friend accepted living in his apartment. She knew him well, because he was the father of her best friend, a Moslem woman married to a Serb. Given the war situation in Sarajevo, she thought she would be more secure in his apartment. However, as soon as she moved in, he changed his behavior. He became cruel. He mistreated her, beat her, and sexually abused her."

The hard economic situation produced by war sometimes forces women to engage in more open forms of prostitution in order to survive (Chinkin, 1993, p. 207). Stanislava, for example, said that "the morality of the women who sold themselves for food and clothes fell incredibly." Or as Gorica said, talking about the hard times of women refugees, women are sometimes forced to sell themselves for ten eggs or for a can of food, in order to feed their children.

Ivana told us about very young girls who engaged in prostitution in order to save their families from hunger in the besieged Sarajevo.

> The mother of my friend told me that many girls prostituted themselves in order to get some food for their parents. She said, "Thank God that you are here, girls! There were some girls of your age who had to do it only to get food for their parents." The majority were Serbs whose entire families lived there and who did not have anyone to send them a package. They prostituted themselves with the men from the Army of Bosnia-Herzegovina, which, besides Moslems, contains also forcibly mobilized Serbs and Croats.

Sexual blackmail and humiliation

Women were sometimes forced to accept sexual blackmail and humiliation in order to obtain some rights: leaving a besieged city or joining their children in refuge, for example. In similar situations, women's love for their children often overpowers all fears. Women sometimes sacrifice themselves consciously in order to join their children as soon as possible. However, sometimes the sacrifice turns out to be greater than supposed.

Emina talks about the terrible price that her relative had to pay in order to leave Mostar and join her children in refuge.

> My husband's sister, a Serb woman, lived alone in her apartment in Mostar. Her ex-husband went off to fight, and her elderly parents lived in Mostar but could not protect her. All the time, Croats used to break into her apartment, search her, and mistreat her. During two and a half years she tried to obtain permission to leave the city and join her three children who lived with her sister in refuge. A Croat, who could decide about permissions, blackmailed her and pressed her to sleep with him. She accepted. She claims that she

was not raped; she accepted it only in order to get the permission. After the act, he told her he would not let her go until she gave birth to an *ustaša*.[12] He knew that she already had three children, and he said that besides these three Serb children she had to give birth to an *ustaša*. It was impossible to obtain any contraception in Mostar and she indeed got pregnant. He let her go when she was already in the fourth month of pregnancy. She came to Belgrade, all desperate. She did not dare to talk about that even to her parents (although her mother had some doubts) or to her brother, and especially not to her children who had already adapted to the new environment and made friends. She did not want the child at all, and since an abortion in an advanced pregnancy demands the opinion of a commission, she did not know whether she would succeed in obtaining abortion. She feared that her husband would say that she had come here to give birth to an *ustaša* bastard. She thought that childbirth would provoke rejection from her children, brother and other relatives. Knowing them, I think it is not far from the truth.

Again, it is obvious that rape was not the only method of forced impregnation. The hard condition in which women lived, their emotional dependence on their children as well as the suffering produced by separation were used as grounds for blackmail. Women were forced to have sexual intercourse, forced to conceive a child who, by general consensus, would belong to the enemy nation.

Olivera told us about the humiliating treatment she was exposed to when she was leaving Sarajevo. However, the desire to join her children, whom she had not seen for two years, overcame her fear of possible rape. "When I had to leave Sarajevo I was searched in a tobacco shop/improvised customs-office. I had to take my clothes off in front of three men, Moslems. There was also a woman who performed a gynecological examination on me. As I stood there naked, a thought came to me, 'It's done, they will rape me, but I will survive. That will be my last suffering and then I will go to my children.' No suffering on that road would be difficult for me, because I had my goal: to finally be with my children."

Notes

1 The data can be found in *Amnesty International i UN za silovanje kao ratni zločin* (Amnesty International and the UN report on rape as a war crime). *Ark*, Zagreb, 1993, No. 1, p. 6.

2 United Nations Security Council, *Final Report of the Commission of Experts Pursuant to Security Council Resolution 780 (1992)*, Annex 241, n. 65, UN Doc. S/1994/674 (1994).

3 Ibid.

4 This approach to rapes during the war in the former Yugoslavia strongly resembles the American approach to the race element of rape. The American context emphasizes the stereotype of the black rapist or the idea that black women are less worthy rape victims (Rejali, 1996, p. 365).

5 *Zelene beretke* (Green Berets), a Moslem paramilitary organization.

6 HOS stands for *Hrvatske oružane snage* (Croatian armed forces), a highly brutal paramilitary organization, whose members were mainly recruited from the extremely right-wing/fascist party *Hrvatska stranka prava* (Croatian Party of the Right).

7 *Hrvatsko vijeće odbrane* (Croatian Council of Defense), a military organization of Bosnian Croats, created at the beginning of the Bosnian war in 1992.

8 Alija Izetbegović, president of Bosnia–Herzegovina.

9 *Ustaše*, Croatian fascists, were members of the Croatian army during the Nazi-protected Independent Croatian State (1941–45). As Gordana's report reveals, the name is also used as a self-designation of radical Croatian nationalists. On the Serbian side, the name is used as an insult.

10 "Zločin nad zločinima", *Politika*, January 17, 1993, p. 23.

11 Jann Queffelec, in his book *Les noces barbares*, gave a particularly interesting analysis of ambivalent attitudes of the mother towards the child conceived through rape.

12 See 9.

CHAPTER 5

The Hague Tribunal and rape in the former Yugoslavia

VESNA NIKOLIĆ-RISTANOVIĆ

Concerning rape, as Niarchos pointed out, "from a feminist perspective, international human rights law has mischaracterized the crime and has ignored its gender aspects. Rape is regarded not as a violent attack on women but as a challenge to honor (whose honor is not entirely clear), and it has yet to be recognized as an assault motivated by gender, not simply by membership in the enemy camp. In these respects, international human rights law must be seen as a gender-biased body of law" (Niarchos, 1995, p. 674). The "immunity" of human rights law from dealing with women's human rights is evident both in the abundance and the framework of human rights law, and can be analyzed in the areas of implementation and the language of human rights law itself. The invisibility of women within human rights law is evident in human rights conventions and customary law, and, in particular, that which underlies humanitarian law (Smiljanić, 1997, p. 55). Although the point has frequently been made that the Statute of the Hague Tribunal represents progress in the field of female rights, a more detailed analysis reveals that rape is explicitly treated as a crime against humanity (Article 5) only when it is systematic and widespread, or, in other words, when it occurs as a part of ethnic cleansing. This makes it clear that women's interests are not what count in the first place. Again, rape is understood as a crime against a particular ethnic community, against women as a form of male property, and not as a crime against the female body, against the woman as an individual. As Smiljanić brilliantly points out,

> There are still difficulties with adopting the idea that, due to this development, human rights law has acknowledged the woman's presence as possession of her own body. The female body. The female

body as an embodiment of a particular site for sexual violence, entwined within a particular political/nationalistic environment is reflected in how human rights discourse has constructed the female body and incorporated it in the Statute. Women living in the countries of the former Yugoslavia are subject to specific discourses and representations emanating from the social order, defining their bodies in particular ways, and law is complicit in stabilizing and maintaining these ways of being. (Smiljanić, 1997, pp. 55–56)

Rape and sexual violations have also been acknowledged as grave breaches of the Geneva Conventions (Article 2), violations of the Laws or Customs of War (Article 3), and as genocide (Article 4). Although rape is not explicitly a grave breach, it has been recognized by feminist lawyers as falling within the definition of one in particular ("inhuman treatment") and would seem to qualify under two others ("torture" and "willfully causing great suffering or serious injury to body or health") (Copelon and Meron, in Niarchos, 1995, p. 207). Moreover, the International Committee of the Red Cross and the US State Department have declared that rape is a grave breach, and it has been subsequently prosecuted as such in the Čelebići case and Tadić indictment. However, this proposition should not rest on interpretation. As Niarchos suggested, an amendment is needed (Niarchos, 1995).

In the Čelebići case, the defendants were charged with a grave breach of the Geneva Convention under Article 2b of the Statute (inhuman treatment) and two violations of the Laws or Customs of War, punishable under Article 3 of the Statute of the Tribunal as Article 3/1a (torture) and 3/1a (cruel treatment) of the Geneva Conventions. Here, rape and sexual assault do not warrant their own names as war crimes. Instead, "torture" and "cruel and inhuman treatment" are deemed to cover rape and sexual violence, although the Tribunal has not yet determined what actually constitutes rape and sexual assault as torture and cruel and inhuman treatment. Within these classifications, particular requirements have been established for prosecution—rape and sexual violence as crimes of gender are not included (Smiljanić, 1997). However, independently of this, and independently of the confusion of terminology thus created, this mode of interpretation of the Statute has worked to ameliorate the former—completely unacceptable—legal situation. The new interpretation is significant because it makes it more probable that a larger number of victims will decide to act as witnesses at the Tribunal and thus help decide a larger number of instances of rape cases. However, rape as a part of ethnic cleansing is far more difficult to prove than rape outside the strategy of ethnic cleansing, so we can expect many ethnically motivated rapes to remain unproved. Or, in other words, we expect that it will only be possible to prove a number of individual rapes, without the possibility of demonstrating that those cases were systematic and widespread, committed as a part of a preconceived plan. We can conclude that it is in the clear interest of rape victims that rape should be principally regarded as a crime against women and as such proved and punished. All other considerations have little to do with the interests of the raped women.

The narrow definition of rape as a crime against humanity, or in its exclusive incarnation as a form of mass and genocidal rape, has provoked concern among some commentators and some victims, especially Serbians. As Smiljanić says, "commentators are concerned that acknowledging rape on the basis of a particular program and on mass numbers will obscure rapes which have occurred outside of these definitions" (Smiljanić, 1997, p. 59). Raped Serbian women are concerned with the possibility that their cases will not be considered as rape if the rape was not part of the strategy of ethnic cleansing, or that such a strategy will be more difficult to prove than in the case of raped Moslem women (Jovanović, 1997, p. 68).

If we bear in mind the way rapes in the former Yugoslavia were presented by the politicians and the media, and how some feminist authors spoke about them, we should not be much surprised. A one-sided perspective on rape in the Yugoslav war has inspired one-sided proof-gathering in order to prove the existence of rape as a part of ethnic cleansing, which basically means rape as a crime against man's honor, property and territory. Moreover, some (reputed) feminists have not opted for the female interest as such, but for the interest of the women belonging to the side that was, according to the dominant political (male) assessment, the good side in this war. By their very procedures, feminist authors have subjugated gender to ethnicity, and female interests to male interests. The Statutes of the Hague Tribunal have largely actualized the ideas that animated discussions about rape in the war. Therefore, it is not surprising that forced impregnation, which according to the results of our survey represents the most traumatic female experience in war, is neither explicitly nor implicitly defined as a crime unless part of ethnic cleansing and genocide. Thus Copelan seems quite right in saying that "the crime of forced impregnation—central as it is to genocidal rape—also elucidates the gender component...When examined through a feminist lens, forced impregnation appears as an assault on the reproductive self-determination of women; it expresses the desire to mark the rape and rapist upon the woman's body and upon the woman's life" (Copelan, 1994, p. 207).

However, Copelan herself casts a shadow of doubt on the above-mentioned thesis that forced impregnation is the key element of genocidal rape, when remarking that "the taunt that Muslim women will bear Serbian babies is not simply an ethnic harm, particularly in light of the prevalence of ethnically mixed families" (Copelan, 1994, p. 206). Copelan's attitude remains contradictory, since she advocates the recognition of forced impregnation as a crime against women while only taking into account crimes against Moslem women. However, as the results of our survey, Amnesty International reports and some rare studies of rape against Serbian women (Stiglmayer, 1994) have demonstrated, Serbian women as well were victims of forced impregnation, although the scope of the phenomenon remains unknown.

If feminist authors expect the Hague Tribunal to recognize the gender dimension of rape and sexual persecution (Copelan, 1994), first of all they have to rid themselves of the prejudices that political agendas and propaganda wars (which ran parallel with the military actions in the former Yugoslavia) have imposed on them. As it stands today, the Statute of the Hague Tribunal does not guarantee a fair punishment for the perpetrators of gender crimes, regardless of their nationality and the nationality of their victims. However, its critics, especially feminist ones, must understand that only the Tribunal is competent to determine crimes and the responsibility of perpetrators. Moreover, all data gathered so far must be taken with a grain of salt, because of the inaccessibility of many victims and the partiality of those who have gathered evidence.

The protection granted to rape victims by the Tribunal was related to the way the problem of raped women was dealt with during the war. It is quite clear now that the huge media coverage and the ways in which journalists and other data "collectors" approached raped women was very counterproductive for the victims. The alleged "concern for women's rights" was only a pretext for the abuse and instrumentalization of female suffering (on the national as well as on the international level), with no organized assistance to those women. Now they are expected to give evidence to the Hague Tribunal. Almost nobody asks if those women can overcome their mental, existential and status problems. The Tribunal cannot guarantee their protection either before or after the trial (Nikolić-Ristanović, 1998, p. 18). This means that, for the time being at least, it would not be realistic to expect a significant number of women to risk the little that is left of their lives in order to fight for justice. Moreover, if we take into account the lack of appropriate support and protection during the trial itself, as well as the risk of secondary victimization due to the inconsistent application of the rules of evidence, we can conclude that the overall situation is more likely to discourage possible witnesses from reporting the rapes they have survived or appearing before the Tribunal.

If the international community indeed wishes to reach the truth about war crimes and adequately punish the perpetrators, it is first of all necessary that the witnesses be granted a stable immigrant status[1] and assured that they will not be deported to their country of origin. Moreover, before the establishment of a Permanent International Criminal Tribunal, it is necessary to ensure adequate funds for the normal functioning of all services of the Tribunal, as well as for the consequent application of the rules of evidence relating to the protection of rape victims. An important element would be the establishment of a department for victims and witnesses that would offer psychological assistance and give victims feelings of security and confidence. Moreover, one of the possible lines of action in the future could be cooperation with state agencies and non-governmental organizations in all the regions where possible witnesses might come from. Also needed is financial support for the non-governmental organizations that are ready to support and assist victims and possible witnesses. Special attention should be paid to cooperation with those non-governmental organizations in the Federal Republic of Yugoslavia that are willing to work with the Tribunal, especially in regards to the invisibility of raped Serbian women, a consequence of the black-and-white image of the war in the former Yugoslavia. In that way, the consequences of the inadequate treatment of rape victims in general, and raped Serbian women in particular, would be partially compensated for. Needless to say, the current state of affairs has resulted in the neglect of their interests and their further victimization.

Note

1 The recent Canadian offer to grant citizenship to Tribunal witnesses represents a significant step forward.

CHAPTER 6

Physical abuse and homicide

VESNA NIKOLIĆ-RISTANOVIĆ

Women and children represent the most frequent civilian victims
of war-related physical abuse, bodily injury and homicide. Physical
abuse, as it can be seen from the preceding chapters, often accompanied sexual abuse. Yet quite often women were physically
abused, injured or killed without being sexually abused. This does
not mean, however, that their gender was of no consequence in
those cases, or that they were victimized under the same conditions as men. Although cases were found of mass retaliations
against civilians where men and women were victimized together,
the victimization of women was largely determined by the fact that
they, together with children and the old, formed the majority of
the civilian population. This important characteristic of the suffering of women in war can be perceived regardless of whether attacks were focused on a larger group of people or on a single female. Another reason women are exposed to suffering in war is
because they are, most often, unarmed, and do not know how to
handle weapons. Moreover, women are attached to their homes,
less mobile than men, and therefore less able to flee and save
themselves, either because they are old, pregnant, or have small
children. Perhaps only in the case of elderly people does the exposure of women to physical abuse approximate the exposure of
men, since the reduced mobility imposed by old age, as we will
discuss, often produces a situation in which old couples are tortured or killed together. On the other hand, women are exposed to
numerous risks when they have to go out of their homes, during
war. When men leave to fight, women are left alone to take care of
children and old and sick members of the family. This, in a war
situation, contains numerous risks (El Bushra, Lopez, 1993, p. 56).
In order to secure food, water or fuel they have to go out, and thus

run the risk of being wounded or killed. Conversely, fear of violence sometimes restrains women's mobility, reducing their possibilities of dealing adequately with the situation. This is a woman's burden in wartime; due to the absence of men, caring for the biological survival of the family becomes uniquely the woman's responsibility (El Bushra, Lopez, 1993, p. 56).

Generally, we can state that women are victimized:

— During military actions directed against civilian objects and civilian populations;
— Because of explosions in places where large crowds gather;
— During the "cleansing" of a territory;
— During isolated attacks, which are performed more selectively.

In isolated attacks on a particular woman, physical violence most often represents:

— Retaliation for the military participation of her men (a punishment and message directed to a man close to her);
— Retaliation against the woman herself;
— A measure intended to terrorize whole groups of people and thus achieve a particular military goal.

The victimization of women during massacres, retaliatory measures or terrorist actions against civilians

Mass torture and the murder of civilians are committed during territorial conquest, in occupied territories and in detention camps and prisons. Vida, Slobodanka, Zorica and Jana told us about cases of the victimization of women during a massacre that accompanied territorial conquest.

According to Vida, in the summer of 1992, when Moslem forces were taking the town of Trnovo, they committed mass murder, looting and arson. Many people were killed at the time, including a Serbian friend of hers who was burned alive.

Slobodanka talked about the special vulnerability of old women. They were not able to flee the enemy, which, while conquering the territory, burned the houses and killed the civilians that happened to be there. "We were forced to flee the Moslem army twice, but they did not remain long in the village. The third time they came, they burned all the houses. Twenty-three died in the fire. Afterwards, we all left the village, except one old man who could not flee. He was saved by a Moslem soldier who knew him. The soldier said he would kill him and then let him off when the other soldiers had left. The old women who had remained because they could not flee were all killed."

Stojanka related the case of an old woman who had to leave her home to find some food. "My mother-in-law, aged 80, who lived in the town of Konjic, was killed and then burnt by Moslem irregulars. Besides her, there were nine other old women who could not flee. The soldiers also killed and scalped my sister-in-law. She was killed while she was going to the village to find some food. I don't know what happened with my other sister-in-law."

Zorica witnessed the suffering of whole families and the terrible psychological suffering of the women who, although wounded, somehow survived the pogroms where their dearest ones were killed.

One day in October 1992, in the village of Čemerno (where I fled from Sarajevo together with my father, mother and brother) I saw a group of some thirty Moslem irregulars who burned down the house of our cousins, some fifty meters away from the house where we had found shelter. They first called the residents (there were ten of them) to come out, promising they would not do them any harm. Our cousins began to come out, one by one, since they recognized the voice of one man from the group who was the godfather of their child. When they all came out, the irregulars began shooting them, one by one. (In fact, I saw them firing at my cousins and later on I checked it out and they were all dead, except a female cousin of mine who, by a miracle, survived.) Afterwards, they set the house on fire. This cousin of mine fell by her parents but she was only wounded and rendered unconscious. Her brother, a boy, also wounded, lay by her side as well. The irregulars were carefully examining if someone had remained alive, so they turned her on her back. But as she was unconscious they thought she was dead. When they finally left, although wounded (she had five wounds on her leg), she succeeded in leaving the scene and reaching the nearby forest where we met. I gave her first aid by tying her leg with a piece of cloth. Later on, I heard that she had completely gone out of her mind. You know, she lost her mother, father and one brother in the event. The other brother, who by chance had not been in the house at the time, was later killed at the front.

Jana recounts the suffering of men and women during mass killings, and how women tried to escape when enemy attacks were anticipated.

> On March 26, 1992, Croats committed a massacre of Serbs in the village of Sijekovac. A couple of days before, on March 21, I had brought my three children to the village of Lešće, because there were rumors that something terrible would happen. During the massacre, my husband was taken hostage and many people were killed. My mother and sister used to run away every night and hide in their pigsty in order to survive. My brother and my aunt's daughter were slain and thrown to pigs. The majority of people were killed by their neighbors, near the fishpond. Many people were burned in bathtubs. There were corpses floating in the Sava river.

During the sudden enemy raids, women who remained in their homes, either because they did not anticipate anything or because they could not or did not want to leave, were the first to be killed. Their chances of escaping massacres were slim because they were forced to hide in the immediate vicinity of their houses, so that they could survive only by pure chance. Many, however, found a terrible death, alone or together with male relatives who happened to be at home. Vera, for example, recounted the case of an old woman who lived alone, completely isolated from external events. Since she was not aware that Croats had come to her village and begun searching houses, she protested their intrusion, which would be a normal reaction in peacetime. Irritated by her reaction, the soldiers brought her to her cellar and set her on fire.

During the massacres of women and children, the perpetrators sometimes leave some grisly symbolic message to the men of the opposite side, which is meant to signify their utter defeat and destruction. Thus Vera, while recounting the suffering of her grandmother during a Croat massacre of Serbs in World War II, said that the perpetrators had first slain her aunt's child, put it into its mother's arms and then killed her as well.

During systematic raids in the occupied territories, the thugs sometimes "settled for" physical abuse of those they found in their houses. Sometimes they took them away to detention camps, where they were starved, tortured and often killed.

Marina, for example, came to know through her neighbors about the torture of a Serbian couple from the city of Tuzla. Two masked Moslems, probably irregulars, had forcefully entered the house where the couple lived. They were both badly beaten, and the woman sustained serious injuries; all her limbs were broken and she barely survived. Branka, Slobodanka and Rada recounted the torture their female friends had to suffer in detention camps.

Branka commented on the case of a female friend taken forcibly to the Koševo football stadium, in Sarajevo. "Almost nobody got out of there alive. They were kept without food and water. It's terrible to say, but I think that shooting them would have been much more humane. I don't know if she's still alive."

Slobodanka said, "A woman from the village of Ljuta told me how her daughter had been taken away to a detention camp and how [the woman] was taken away herself. She was beaten and tortured, just like the other prisoners."

Quite often, women were taken hostage and held in captivity, waiting for the other side to agree to an exchange of prisoners. Rada, for example, reported the case of her grandmother, a Serbian from the town of Duvno, who had been taken hostage. She was held captive, together with other older men and women, and mentally and physically abused by Croats, who kept her without food and medication.

Jasminka described her feeling of the risk people ran when having to stand in a line for food.

> I lived in Vasa Miskin Street. I also had to wait in line from time to time, although I didn't like it because it was very dangerous. That day I did the same, while my husband and a friend of mine remained at home. By chance, I came back a little bit earlier because I was too bored to continue waiting. Then we heard a terrible detonation. One of my neighbors lost a leg, while her son-in-law was killed. It was terrible to think that I might have remained there and experienced the same...I got out of the city with the Jewish convoy. We entered the territory of Republika Srpska and from noon to 8 p.m. waited for other buses to come. Some soldiers came in. We asked them why we were waiting and they replied that a shell had fallen on the Markale market. They said that quite coldly. More than sixty people were killed, and I began thinking about what had happened to my mother, my husband and my neighbors.

Branka's memories of suffering in the Serb-controlled part of Sarajevo were rather similar.

> After the Vasa Miskin Street tragedy, the same happened in Titova Street. My mother and me, we were walking at ten meter's distance from each other, so that one could be safe if something happened to the other. We were in Titova Street. There were injured people all over the place. Shells were falling and people were screaming.

> I will never forget those screams. There were puddles of blood all over the place. Then we found a shop where we spent some thirty minutes, in order to recover from the shock. I remember a woman asking me there if she had shell splinters in her hair.

Women are often victims of strategies that are calculated to terrorize the civilian population, instigate ethnic conflicts and produce the expulsion of members of particular ethnic groups.

The women from Sarajevo we talked with, Serb and Moslem, were particularly bitter about the case of an innocent Serbian girl who was killed on the Brotherhood and Unity bridge, immediately before the outbreak of the war. We think that the symbolism of that murder needs no comment. Juliana, a Serb, while saying that there had been rumors in the city that the girl had been killed by Serbs, added, "The girl began crossing the bridge when somebody fired at her without any reason. She was unarmed and innocent. I don't know what her nationality was."

Women who lived alone were sometimes threatened with murder, in order to terrorize and isolate them. Members of her ethnic group would be threatened so that they would eventually leave. Sanija, a Moslem, related a similar case.

> I used to get along with my Serbian neighbors quite well and they helped me a number of times. For example, they fixed my door so that I could be better protected. At the beginning of the war, my Serbian neighbors continued coming to my place and I did the same. One day, my first neighbor, a Serb, when I invited her to come, replied that she was afraid because she had been told that she would be killed if she continued to socialize with Moslems. The other neighbors continued coming to my place. I believe she was really afraid because she lived alone and had no protection.

The threats she was frequently exposed to, as well as the knowledge of what happened to other girls, made Branka leave Sarajevo. Here is her story.

> Having listened to the radio news, while we were in a shelter, one friend of mine and a neighbor, a Moslem, all angry said to me, "That's what they do to Moslems and you are the only Serb here and we don't do anything to you. We should kill all Serbs, and we should begin with you." I didn't know what to do because I just felt terrible. Finally, in order to reduce the tension I made a kind of joke and said, "Well, why kill first? Let's begin with rape." Others also felt a little bit relieved after I had said that, because it helped us change the topic.

As part of the strategy of ethnic cleansing, sometimes women are evicted from their apartments by open threats of physical abuse, as Merima mentioned. A woman told Merima how she had been evicted from her apartment with a gun against her throat. She was evicted and transported to Serb-controlled territory.

Individual assault, torture and the killing of women

Aside from being victimized during massacres and mass campaigns of intimidation against civilians of a particular ethnic group, some women were exposed to individual assaults motivated by reasons other than ethnic hatred. The most frequent grounds for such events included retaliation for the military engagement of the male members of their families, and punishment for their own political ideas and actions. Very frequently women were abused because of their profession or property. Women who were married to the members of another ethnic group were particularly exposed to the risks of physical violence. It is important to point out that the women were frequently abused by their own husbands who were from another ethnic group, or by some other individuals belonging to their own, their husband's or some other ethnic group.

Very frequently, mothers who had sent their daughters away to save them from rape became victims themselves. The revenge for the daughter's absence could go from threats and intimidation (as described by Olivera in Chapter 4) to rape and murder.

Brownmiller described the tragic epilogue of the rape of one Miss MacIsaacs, who hid her daughters in a cellar when she realized that enemy troops were coming. Realizing that she herself was in danger, she ran away and hid in a marsh. As they were drunk and it was dark, the soldiers could not spot her. However, Miss MacIsaacs was pregnant and she died of a miscarriage before dawn (Brownmiller, 1975, p. 39). This event occurred in 1746 after the battle of Culloden Moor, when the British conquerors decimated the Scottish army. It is very similar to the fate of mothers in modern wars, including the one waged in Bosnia-Herzegovina. Jasminka's story is a very telling one.

My neighbor's sister, a Moslem, was killed in the municipality of Grbavica, Sarajevo. She was a professor of English and had two daughters. Since there were rumors in the neighborhood that Serbs were taking away young girls, and fearing they would come to pick up their daughters as well, the parents hid them away. When the Serb soldiers came and could not find the girls, they brought the mother to a detention camp, where she was killed afterwards.

However, sometimes daughters were taken together with mothers and forced to experience the same things. "One of my class-mates, a lawyer who had been in a detention camp," said Jasminka, "told me that there were many mothers and daughters who had been taken and tortured together."

Women of certain professions (especially those that implied the possession of considerable sums of money or other valuable items that are highly appreciated in wartime) were especially exposed to robbery committed either by the criminals belonging to their own or to the enemy ethnic group(s). Thus, Marina recalled how a Serb woman from the city of Tuzla, owner of a goldsmith's shop, had been attacked by a group of Moslem criminals. "In September 1993, three young armed Moslems came to her shop. She was there with a friend and she opened the door because she recognized one of them, since he was living in her neighborhood. When they came in, they shot her in the head. They also fired at the other woman and then robbed the shop. The owner of the shop survived but she lost an eye."

Women whose professions are especially important in wartime, like doctors, are not only threatened by rape but also by death. Women from ethnically mixed marriages were especially endangered. Natalija told us a story that strongly resembled the one told by Gordana, but with a different end and within a different ethnic context.

It is about my best neighbor's daughter. The neighbor remained in the municipality of Grbavica, Sarajevo, only to pull [her daughter] out from the Moslem-controlled part of the city where [the daughter] had remained with her husband. She was a doctor, married to a Moslem. Long before the war, they had lived in Višegrad and then they moved to Sarajevo. She never paid attention to what ethnic group people belong to. I knew her well, since she was of the same age as my sons. She was a real good child, one of the best students of the Sarajevo Medical School. When the war began, they did not let her go to Grbavica, so she remained in the Moslem-controlled part of the city. She continued working, but as she was Serbian, they transferred her to another hospital, in order to better control her and prevent escape. I do not know what she had to go through during that period, but there were rumors that she, together with other Serb doctors, was put on a liquidation list. One night, she and her husband tried to escape to the Serbian side. However, they were discovered and she was killed, while her husband was badly wounded and captured. I don't even dare to think how they will torture him.

Stressing the complexity of decision making in similar situations, Natalija added, "The most terrible thing is that in June I read in the newspapers that Moslems had liberated a group of Serb doctors and transferred them to the Serbian side. Had she not tried to escape, she would perhaps have survived."

Due to their vulnerability to the enemy, women are victimized because of the military engagement of their husbands, sons, fathers and other male relatives. During the war in Bosnia-Herzegovina, women and girls who lived without male relatives to protect them were intimidated and brutally abused both inside and outside their homes. Moreover, as we have already said, the husband's military engagement was an excuse for the arrest of women and their transfer to detention camps. Very frequently, when a son was engaged in fighting and the parents remained at home, the parents were victimized, especially if they were older.

A unique feature of victimization in the war in the former Yugoslavia concerns women whose husbands were officers in the Yugoslav People's Army (YPA). These women were especially exposed to physical abuse, regardless of their husbands' nationality or actual participation in the conflict. This was a result of a general hatred against the YPA, as a communist supra-national army involved in the conflict. Sometimes, only women were victims of this specific hatred—wives, daughters or female relatives of YPA officers—especially if they happened to be alone at home. However, during the widespread manhunt against YPA officers, which occurred immediately after the outbreak of the war, many males and couples were victimized as well. Revenge against YPA officers and their families had a broader context, since it did not occur only during the Bosnian war, but also during the war in Slovenia (in the summer of 1991) and even in territories not directly affected by war.

Marina recounted a case of physical abuse and intimidation of a girl whose father was at the front.

A girl from my neighborhood told me that Moslem soldiers constantly mistreated her and beat her on the street, and that some people constantly harassed them over the phone. In the autumn of

1993, I witnessed such an event. I saw a group of Moslem soldiers mistreating the girl on the street. They pushed her around, called her names, beat her...The girl lived alone with her mother, since the father had gone to fight, so they were unprotected. The girl complained to me that the harassment took place several times and that she could not stand it anymore. She was especially frightened by the anonymous phone calls and threats.

Snežana related the case of a couple who were tortured because their son was in combat. "A month or two ago, a woman from the town of Visoko was here. Her mother-in-law, a Serb, was badly beaten by Moslems. Eventually, she had a stroke and died. Before that, over several months, she and her husband had been mistreated in their own house. Moslems used to force them to put their hands on the table. Then they threatened to cut off their fingers. Their son was taken prisoner. Although both were mistreated, only her husband survived."

Blaženka, a Croat from Zagreb, recounted how women who were married to YPA officers were brutally abused, even by members of their own ethnic group, and in territories not directly affected by the war. "Some zengas[1] broke into the apartment of a Croat woman whose husband, a Serb, was an ex-YPA officer. She was forced to leave her flat together with her children and brought to the entrance of the building where she lived. The zengas cut off both her arms: one for her husband, and one for her father-in-law. The children ended up in a psychiatric clinic."

Natalija described the manhunt against ex-YPA officers in Sarajevo when, among others, an elderly Moslem couple were brutally killed because of the alleged participation of their sons in the Army of Bosnia-Herzegovina.

I remained in Grbavica until mid-September, because I was waiting for my older son and sister-in-law to leave the Moslem-controlled part of the city. I saw there everything you can imagine, because, immediately after the outbreak of the war, chetniks[2] descended on Grbavica. Those were all unknown people who lived in surrounding villages and who began terrorizing people in the municipality. Grbavica had a relatively big number of ex-YPA officers of all ethnic affiliations. However, everybody was exposed to violence—Croats and Moslems especially, but also Serbs from ex-YPA officer families, because they were "commies." Anybody at anytime could enter their homes and nobody would dare to protest. I will tell you about the Aslanagićs, an old Moslem couple aged 80 or so. They remained in Grbavica because they did not have any other place to go and they had lived in Sarajevo for decades, anyway. One of their sons is a refugee now, while the other one is in the Moslem-controlled part of the city, together with his family. I know those children and am sure that none of them had joined the Army of Bosnia-Herzegovina. The old couple had a beautiful flat and some paintings of great value. One night they were both slain and their flat was sacked. Their corpses were buried in a nearby park.

Natalija, while reflecting on the brutality of this murder which was obviously calculated to intimidate the remaining Moslems and make them leave the city, said, "They were very old and completely powerless people. The father had a serious cardiac condition. The perpetrators did not have to cut their throats—it would have been enough to push them from the Vrbanja bridge. They lived near the bridge, anyway."

Natalija remembers the overall inhumane ambience of the war, where there was not even an elementary respect for dead bodies. Thus, female corpses were (perhaps not accidentally) used to send some horrible messages, as the following example illustrates. "When their son, who lived in the Moslem-controlled part of the city, came to know about their death, he demanded that their bodies be sent over to him. The Serbs accepted to exchange them for the bodies of some Serbs who had remained in the city. However, since the Moslems did not deliver all the bodies demanded, the Serbs exhumed only the mother's body and sent it to the son, while the father's corpse remained buried."

The fate of Slovenes, wives of ex-YPA officers, was especially dramatic and difficult after the war in Slovenia (July 1991), particularly if they were married to Serbs. They were victimized not only by their compatriots but also by persons of other ethnic origins, and their vulnerability increased if they remained alone after their husbands had left.

After the insults I had to put up with and after an attempt by a group of Moslems to forcibly enter my flat and abuse me physically, I began feeling completely unsafe in my place, because I remained alone and they could enter whenever they wanted. I don't believe that anyone would have protected me. That's why I decided, after some two hours of reflection, to go to my sister's place and demand police protection. I sneaked out of my building and began walking towards my bus station. However, all the time I had a feeling that something bad would happen to me. I was walking by a wall, about two meters high, on one side of the road. Led by a strange premonition, I looked up and saw two masked heads. They immediately withdrew when they realized I had seen them. At that very moment

I froze and saw a huge stone falling in front of me. In a second, I turned around and began to run. I heard curses and two gunshots behind me. After some time, I found a supermarket, entered it, mingled with the crowd for some time and then exited the back door, from where I took a taxi that drove me to my sister's place. I still can't explain what made me look up in that moment and why I decided to turn back. Had I continued to walk towards the bus station I'm sure they would have killed me, because it was obvious that they had been waiting for me. Afterwards, my cousins found me a big dog, and there was always someone staying at home with me.

The etiology of physical abuse against women living in ethnically mixed marriages is very similar to the etiology of sexual abuse against those same women. However, based on our data about the ethnic affiliation of the woman, her husband and the perpetrator(s), we cannot say whether physical abuse was more frequent than sexual abuse or whether there was any regularity in the application of these forms of violence. It seems that abuse is highly contingent and varies greatly from case to case. However, there was one constant; women from mixed marriages were in wartime physically abused, raped and murdered by the members of their own, their husband's or some other ethnic group. It seems that in times of ethnic conflict women in mixed marriages could be abused by anybody, regardless of the perpetrator's ethnic affiliation.

As we have already said, physical abuse of a woman by a perpetrator of the same ethnicity as her husband is meant as a way of sending a message to the husband to get rid of a wife who belongs to the enemy ethnic group. Should he fail do to so, the wife will be brutally abused, in spite of all her efforts to demonstrate loyalty, as Jovana's story demonstrated. It seems that *physical* abuse not followed by sexual violence represents a way of "punishing" the woman for her ethnic affiliation, while the "punishment" of the husband is of secondary importance. This is suggested by the cases of brutal murders of mothers in front of their children. In cases of *sexual* violence the order seems to be reversed. It seems that rape was principally used as a way of settling accounts between men of different ethnic origins, not a surprising fact given the predominant male discourse. Within male-male communication, it is obvious that rape, far more than physical violence, represents an attack on the honor of the man to whom the raped woman "belongs." In that context, rape demonstrates his impotency in contrast to the rapist's potency, extrapolated as the potency of the rapist's ethnic group. Thus, Jovana said,

That woman, a Serb, was married to a Croat and lived in a Croatian village controlled by the *zengas*.[3] Her husband was at the front, in Benkovac, and she was very loyal to the new authorities. In order to demonstrate her loyalty, she decided to continue to live in the village. She worked in a kitchen and regularly prepared meals for the soldiers. One day, a group of soldiers attacked her. They cut open her stomach, tied her to a tree with her own bowels and left her to die there in the worst imaginable way. But that wasn't enough: in front of her, they killed her 2-year-old child and burned it on a stake.

This case unambiguously demonstrates the difference between rape as a war tactic and individual cases of the physical abuse and murder of women whose husbands belonged to the same ethnic group as the perpetrator(s). On one hand, there is rape as a way to produce children belonging to the rapist's ethnic group. On the other hand, there is a pure infliction of pain on women belonging to an enemy ethnic group, even when they and their children, according to the widely accepted definition, belong to the perpetrator's ethnic group. Quite simply, when we peel off all the layers of nationalistic and warlike discourse, there remains only a barren misogyny and the terrible suffering women and children have to undergo for the sake of various ill-minded plans.

In conditions of ethnic conflict, women married to members of the enemy ethnic groups are often physically abused by their own husbands. Unfortunately, ethnic conflict permeates all relationships, even the most intimate ones. As Smith (1989, p. 15) put it, "everything that happens in global society is reflected in the family. The abstract ethnic hatred very easily transforms itself into animosity towards the closest persons, such as a wife, children or cousins. They come to be seen as very concrete symbols of the enemy. Furthermore, women are considered as a part of male property that has become bad or worthless on account of its ethnic origin" (Nikolić-Ristanović, 1996, p. 76). Therefore, the wife becomes the source of the husband's shame and the root of the problems he encounters when relating to others. This is illustrated by a case of marital violence described by Milica.

They loved each other enormously, he especially was strongly in love with her and everybody knew it. He was Serb and she was Moslem. When the war began, his Serb friends began criticizing him for having married a Moslem woman. They said, "Man, there were plenty of Serbian girls around, and you've decided to marry a Moslem." It was the terrible time when Serbs and Moslems fought each other. Serbs began to blame his wife, as if she was responsible for the irregulars who began to sporadically terrorize the village. He became very nervous and began beating her. Once he told me how his neighbors had been talking against Moslems from the very beginning of the war. Every time he visited them, he would begin beating her as soon as he got home. Afterwards he would be sorry, and so on and on. He beat her every other day once the hostilities between Serbs and Moslems began. She defended herself, saying it wasn't her fault that she was Moslem. Rumors began circulating, saying he was drinking and seeing other women, so that there was a huge dispute between him and her. On that occasion, he beat her so badly that she couldn't get out of bed for ten days.

This is how Milica explains the way ethnic conflict affects marital violence in ethnically mixed marriages. "The war made people who had loved each other now hate each other. I think one shouldn't listen to what others say. I think that they themselves now wonder what happened to them. If they had not listened to what other people were saying, they would have loved each other still."

Notes

1 A popular term for the members of *Zbor Narodne Garde* (Council of the National Guard), a hastily formed Croatian armed organization which was created immediately at the time of the Croatian declaration of independence from Yugoslavia (June 25, 1991). Although commanded by professional soldiers, ex-officers of the YPA, the force included numerous rogue elements and was dissolved later on to form the regular Croatian Army.
2 Extreme Serbian nationalists organized in various paramilitary units.
3 See 1.

CHAPTER 7

Psychological violence and fear in war, and their consequences for the psychological health of women

SLOBODANKA KONSTANTINOVIĆ-VILIĆ

Some general remarks about psychological violence and fear in war:

> War, which produces large-scale destruction of visible objects, does so even more with humans. Only some individuals, and only gradually, become aware of this type of destruction. It takes off from our faces the last mask of humanity, turns us inside out and brings to the surface some unexpected qualities, radically different from what others believed us to be and what we believed we were. Moreover, it transforms the family system and produces changes of the sanctified social rules and relations, including those deemed eternal and immutable, such as gender relations. (Ivo Andrić, *Destruction*)

War and war-related events endanger not only the physical integrity of human beings but also produce various forms of psychological violence. These, in the long run, change the victim's personality, his/her self-image and his/her world-view. War also produces a serious crisis of identity and moral values. "The exclusive right to the truth claimed by both parties in conflict produces the synchronicity of the main emotional current to the extent where participants become fanatical in their thoughts and emotions...they let out all the dark they bear in their souls and morality disappears as if it has never existed" (Bojanin, Išpanović-Radojković, 1994, p. 79).

Ethnically or religiously motivated hatred eventually produces a serious identity crisis. Ethnic or religious affiliation becomes the most important element of individual self-definition, since it is this which decides whether someone has the right to live. "The feeling of being snatched away from the cradle of existence produces anxiety and provokes the eternal question: 'Who am I in this world?'"(Bojanin, Išpanović-Radojković, 1994, p. 78).

War, first of all, implies the existence of various forms of violence, used either against those immediately participating in military actions or against civilians, especially women and children. All methods are deemed good which destroy security and produce national or religious hatred, insecurity, contradictory emotions, helplessness and fear.

Psychological warfare includes compulsion, blackmail, insults, humiliation, hate-mongering, intimidation and the like. Experts in military psychology frequently state that psychological violence often represents the best way of crushing the enemy's resistance (Arnautović et al., 1988, pp. 222–223). Propaganda through radio and TV programs, videos and public announcements represents the most efficient method of psychological warfare, since it forcefully changes emotional states and the actions of individuals and groups.

One of the main goals of psychological warfare is to reinforce the stressful character of war. War is a major stressor in itself, since it involves a considerable number of severely stressful situations and events (killing, bodily injury, scenes of torture, participation in combat, separation from the family, forced change of habitation and more). Intentional psychological violence only reinforces negative emotional reactions. The bulk of stress research suggests that to understand stress reactions and determine stress severity one must take into account the way subjects experience a given event or situation. A lack of control—a lack of perception about control, a lack of choice in a given situation—is a major element of stress. Stress and emotions are mutually dependent, so that emotions are defined as the emotional dimension of stress. The stronger the emotion is, the more intense stress reaction becomes. In war, there is an objective existing situation of external danger, and personal resistance to anxiety is seriously reduced. One of the most frequent manifestations of emotional reaction in war, especially when psychological warfare is applied, is the syndrome of anxious reaction, characterized by emotional tension, restlessness, fear and a sentiment of threat. All these emotional states are accompanied by numerous physical symptoms. Resilience towards stressors, intensity of stress reaction and its outcome all depend on age, gender and bio-psychological characteristics of personality, social adaptation and social status. There are significant individual differences, even when stressors are the same or of the same intensity. That is why experts believe that stress reaction is a highly personalized process which depends on personality characteristics. Or more precisely, cognitive and conative personality traits, defense mechanisms and the psychic organization of the personality represent significant factors in understanding stress reaction. The individual energy of adaptation is different for different stressful situations, so that experts speak about a specific resilience. This depends on an individual's current psychological status, as well as on the specific psychological history, that is, previous individual experiences. As for the age variable, children and the young are more sensitive to stress and more likely to develop stress-related disorders than are adults. The old are more resistant to psychosocial stressors, but "the weakening of their economic power, physical fitness and adaptability to changes makes the old have the impression that they are less and less able to control their destiny" (Kaličanin, Lečić-Toševski, 1994, p. 30). Resistance to stressors also depends on gender. Men and women react differently to stressors, which can be explained by various biological and social factors. Men and women differ in their status, roles and the cultural and social expectations they are faced with.

Past research on psychological reactions to mass disasters, including war, has demonstrated that we can distinguish among the immediate and intermediate reactions to stress events, and that stress reactions develop through a series of phases (Kaličanin, Lečić-Toševski, 1994, p. 60; El Bushra, Lopez, 1993).

The first phase (also called the phase of shock) is characterized by intense emotional uneasiness and fear due to exposure to life-threatening danger. Consciousness is narrowed and there are disorders in the perception of external stimuli. Even partial amnesia of events from the initial phase is possible. The second phase (the phase of organization and overcoming shock) is characterized by a more realistic evaluation of the new situation. In this phase organized activity and planning are possible. As well, psychologically vulnerable individuals may experience anxiety, which, in its turn, can lead to panic, irritability and aggression. The phase of unjustified optimism (euphoria and uncritical behavior) is characterized by the pleasure produced by surviving a life-threatening situation. In the phase of "sobering" and disillusionment, the subject gains realistic insight into his/her situation and forms more realistic expectations, but depressive moods, anxiety, disenchantment about the assistance offered and oversensitivity to the actions of others remain quite frequent, while some individuals even develop apathy and feelings of helplessness. The phase of definitive reorganization is the last phase of stress reaction. During this phase, subjects begin to genuinely organize a new life and develop plans for the future. Failure to achieve the goals set up in this phase may produce bitterness, depressive moods, loss of self-esteem and a tendency to blame others who could become the target of hostile emotions.

Stress reactions and their consequences can be especially severe in the victims of psychological torture—individuals who were exposed to various forms of psychological abuse accompanied by constant and intentional life threats. Individual and group reactions to psychological torture depend on a series of factors, such as motivation for war and beliefs about the righteousness of one's goals and values. Analyses of psychological reactions of individuals detained in concentration camps during the Second World War have demonstrated that a certain percentage of the detainees reacted by withdrawing from the immediate reality and by idealizing the world outside the camps. Their emotional picture was characterized by numbness and disengagement ("the problem of surviving"). On the other hand, other subjects, especially those exhausted by the camp regime, had reacted by developing feelings of helplessness, passivity and extreme apathy ("conditioned helplessness"). Yet another group of detainees had developed absolute submission to the torturers. They had even tried to identify with them, and strong feelings of guilt and a loss of self-esteem accompanied the whole process. In contrast to the "utterly submissive" group were those who had reacted to torture by developing an intense hatred of the torturers. This was regularly accompanied by strong desire for revenge, even if it meant sacrificing life (Kaličanin, Lečić-Toševski, 1994, pp. 46–47).

Various forms of psychological violence in war produce a constant state of fear, characterized by intense trepidation and anxiety. Fear, as a reaction to danger, is determined by an individual's specific genetic constitution and previous personal experience. The perception of external or internal danger always produces fear. As an emotional response to danger, fear is most frequently associated with stress. Anxiety is followed by the activation of the autonomous nervous system and is expressed in feelings of general restlessness, insecurity, loneliness, helplessness and constant worrying (Vukov, Baba-Milkić, 1992, p. 60). Psychology distinguishes between fear (which implies that danger is obvious and objective) and anxiety (which appears when danger is hidden and subjective). The intensity of anxiety is determined by the degree of importance that a particular person attributes to some specific situation or event, while the true reasons for anxiety usually remain hidden for the person in question (Hornaj, 1987, p. 54). The overall context of war produces fear and anxiety. The general ambience of violence and the knowledge that some people have been killed, taken to camps or expelled may produce anxiety and fear of some abstract danger. Precise events (such as forcible entry and search of houses by enemy forces, the abuse and abduction of family members) produce intense fear. Fear accompanies all forms of violence, and its intensity is determined by the particular form of violence and by the way a person reacts to it. Because of the woman's bio-psychological constitution and her role as mother and wife, the fear of possible attacks against her closest relatives becomes so intense that it can weaken her willpower, seriously disturb rational decision making, obscure moral values and produce an overall psychological breakdown. It has been observed that stress in women, in association with an intense fear of war, affects their children as well. A survey that Margaret McCallin and Shirley Fozard, from the International Catholic Bureau, carried out on a sample of women and children from Zambia and Mozambique demonstrated that higher levels of stress in mothers (compared to everyday events and traumatic experiences) produced a higher occurrence of stress-related behavioral disorders in their children (*Izbeglice i lica koja traže azil*, 1993, pp. 96–97). Moreover, there was a cyclical connection between stress in the mothers and stress in their children.

The emotion of fear cannot be exclusively reduced to survival instincts. It has been observed that women experience not only fear for their own survival but also some other types of fear: fear for the destiny of close ones (if the family is dispersed), fear of responsibility and decision making in a situation of war danger ("to go to refuge or to remain and save the house?"), or fear of the responsibility for family care.

Psychological violence against the women we have talked with

"War is not...something outside of the female experience of life; it is a part of life, interwoven with all the rest" (Hayton-Keeva, 1987, p. VII).

Women in war are exposed to various forms of victimization, including psychological abuse. As Gordana said, "women experience the whole scale of violence, from pre-war violence to war violence." In the matter of emotional response to psychological vio-

lence, females react more intensely than males, because the violence disturbs female psychological stability and security more
deeply than it does with males. Past research has demonstrated
that women's emotional vulnerability is increased by their biology,
but also by the social construction of gender roles and a series of
socioeconomic factors. All together, these factors make women
less resistant to strong stress and less capable of assuming their
numerous responsibilities. It was also quite possible for women to
be personally exposed to strong war-related traumatic events and
situations, such as rape, physical torture or participation in combat. Most often, these kinds of physical and sexual violence were
accompanied by psychological violence. On the other hand, many
women were only exposed to various forms of psychological violence, on top of the burden of additional worries and stressful
situations imposed by everyday family care. Generally speaking,
women suffered because their husbands left to participate in combat, because their closest relatives had been killed, tortured or arrested, or because they came to know about, or had to witness, the
killing, torture and rape of others.

The women we talked with defined psychological violence as
"suffering, sorrow, violation, starvation, intimidation and fear"
(Bosiljka), "being forced to witness abuse" (Nada), "killing our children, fighting for survival, psychological trauma, dread, harassment
and blackmail" (Smiljka). Women are "the mothers, the widows, the
exiles. Women give birth to sons and daughters whom, after all their
care and love, they must lose to war. They must bury loved ones and
leave the graves behind. They must hide children and feed children
and carry them when they are too weak from hunger to walk. They
must endure rape and abuse of both body and spirit and manage to
go on" (Hayton-Keeva, 1987, p. VIII).

In war, gender roles change, and may lead to a woman's unpre-
paredness to accept the newly created situation in which she is left
alone to provide for the family. These conditions reinforce stress,
which may lead to the development of stress-related mental disorders. In war, the woman is made "the pillar of the home" and "the
head of the family" because her husband has left to fight. In such a
situation, women's responsibility is huge, whether they stay in the
war zone or seek refuge together with their children. They are
made responsible for the economic and emotional survival of the
family, and they have to satisfy the everyday needs of their families
and maintain emotional bonds with dispersed family members.

The absence of control over their own lives makes both men
and women feel helpless. This is how Natalija described it: "The

most terrible thing is psychic violence—when you feel completely powerless to change anything and yet you dread every moment that a sniper or a shell might kill you."

Socialization through the learning of traditional female roles, which leaves women with little or no influence and control over their lives and the lives of their family members in peacetime, only reinforces the feeling of helplessness in wartime. The impossibility of changing the existing conditions or failing to do so makes some women passive and "psychologically paralyzed." "Reactions are absent because of the emotional state, characterized by depression and fear that the positive outcome will not occur, as it was proved a number of times before" (Nikolić-Ristanović, 1993, p. 30). The psychological state of helplessness, the lack of fortitude in both body and mind ("I am completely devoid of physical and mental strength," said Sofija), in some women can lead to a reduced feeling of control over their lives, depressive moods and crises of motivation.

The final consequences of this helplessness are manifested in fear, restlessness, illness and even death (El Bushra, Lopez, 1993). The state of helplessness, loneliness and anxiety imposed by war and separation from family can inspire suicidal ideas. Thus, Nataša wrote from Mostar to her sister, "I think I would just like to swallow a handful of pills. Anyway, that's what I think about sometimes, because this is not life...This is too much for me" (letter of June 25, 1993). Nataša's contemplation of suicide was inspired by a family conflict, produced by the general ambience of ethnic intolerance which had penetrated in her family as well. "I just wanted to jump beneath a car" (letter of September 1, 1993). Nataša's depression and desire for self-destruction were accompanied by desire for total annihilation, which she later explained as a moment of weakness. "An alarm siren is my only music; it sounded today as well, and I just began crying, not out of fear, but anger. I thought 'I would like an A-bomb to fall, to wipe us all out and thus terminate our suffering.' But it was just a moment of weakness." Even women who survived the horrors of war and became refugees met new problems, and also contemplated suicide.

The psychological state of helplessness can make women who have children react unusually. Women who have children and who have lost close relatives often develop depression. They cannot bear the regression or over-dependence of their children and often react by frustration, anger or rejection. The disappearance of her husband or the father of her children frequently makes the woman anxious, depressed and lacking the energy that child-care and adaptation to a new environment demand.

In some women, still, helplessness and desperation give place to a strong survival wish and efforts, well described by the survivor theory. After the initial reaction to stress and psychological warfare, after the phase of strong emotional uneasiness, there comes the phase of resistance. In this phase the woman strives to overcome stress and takes appropriate measures to obtain assistance and social support. Thus, Nada said, "I understood that I had to find strength and continue to live...I found a reserve of energy in myself and I think that every woman can do the same."

How a situation of psychological conflict will be resolved depends on the biological foundation of the female personality, her experiences, her resistance to stress, her capacity to adapt and her social and economic status. Concerning the latter, our survey demonstrated that women who had enjoyed superior economic or social status, as well as those who had been independent before the war, suffered more in refuge than did women who had had inferior status. The formerly independent women did not have control over their lives anymore, could not provide for their existence and had to accept bigger, different responsibilities than they had had before. Olga commented on the situation in the following way: "Highly educated women refugees are in particularly bad shape. They are completely confused and cannot find themselves."

Psychiatric experts think that not all stress reactions should be regarded as pathological. Stress-related mental disorders (i.e., reactive disorders and especially reactive psychoses) can be triggered by "dominant and prolonged exposure to stress," accompanied by reduced capabilities of adjustment. Research into the psychological consequences of war for women has demonstrated that the most frequent disorders are anxiety and depression.

Psychological violence against the women we talked with took different forms in various periods (before, during and after the war, when going to refuge, in refuge, etc.). The general impression of all the women was that the overall ambience of war was a major source of the most intense mental suffering. They all deeply lived the civil war, which abounded in severely stressful situations and events. The loss of the closest family members, the military engagement of their husbands and sons, witnessing the torture of others, news about the terrible experiences of others, ethnic intolerance, harassment and humiliation because of their own or their family's ethnic affiliation, forced expropriation, expulsion from the home, exile and refuge—all these took their toll on women's psychological state. Stress was accompanied by the fear of shelling, forcible entry and search of apartments, rape and detention in concentration camps. Although the majority of the women left the war zone immediately or several months after the outbreak of the war, they became victims of psychological violence, stress and fear. Some of our interviewees explained their exposure to psychological violence by the fact that they had remained alone and without male relatives who could have protected them.

On the basis of their testimonies, it was possible to differentiate among several forms of psychological violence against women: threats and intimidation, humiliation and mistreatment, harassment in the workplace, witnessing the suffering of others, restriction of their freedom of movement, forced deprivation from the essential necessities for survival, eviction from their houses and flats and expulsion from their homeland.

Threats and intimidation. In all wars, threats and intimidation, as forms of psychological compulsion, are used to compel people to make wrong decisions or engage in particular forms of behavior that suit the propaganda mongers.

> When you realize that you are under surveillance or that you will be arrested, pressure begins to rise. At the beginning, all you feel is just a little stress, but, if the situation continues, you soon remark that when you turn the light on, for example, the sound of the bulb, feeble as it is, unbearably irritates you. That means that your nerves have become quite shaky. Everyone who knocks on your door is suspect, and you don't answer until you know who's at the door, and that's something that lasts for months and even years (*Izbeglice i lica koja traže azil*, 1993, p. 29).

The stories of the women we talked with demonstrated that threats and intimidation were most often related to ethnic hatred and intolerance. The insistence on ethnic affiliation and the encouragement of intolerance of other ethnic groups soon produced intense conflicts. The vaguely defined enemy could have been anybody: neighbors, friends, colleagues. The change of erstwhile normal relations among people produced a particular mixture of disdain, anger, hatred, aggression, helplessness, disillusionment and disorientation. It was impossible to predict from whom danger might come, how serious it might be and whom they should guard themselves against. Sanija's neighbor, a Serb, was threatened with murder if she continued to socialize with Moslem women. The woman took the threats seriously because "she lived alone and had no protection," and stopped seeing Sanija.

The most common victims of threats and intimidation, were the women who lived alone and without any defense. Most frequently they were threatened by irregulars and policemen, but also by neighbors, acquaintances and former friends of various ethnic affiliations. The point of such threats and intimidation varied: the production of tension and fear, revenge, or expulsion from houses and flats in order to sack and appropriate them when they became vacant.

Sanija's experience shows the dangers of solitude.

> I lived alone. One day some soldiers came. They wore uniforms of one of those paramilitary units, but I couldn't distinguish which one it was. They began intimidating me, saying they wanted to enter my house. They asked me if it was a Moslem house, and I immediately began shouting that they would by no means enter, that the house was mine and that I had protection. They asked again if it was a Moslem house and I replied again that the house was mine and that they better not enter or I would call the police...They backed down, but, still, when they went to the street they began throwing pebbles at my window, which they finally broke. Fortunately enough, I remained unharmed, but I could hear them cursing and threatening they would come back and set my house on fire. I was terribly afraid.

Merima told us about a Moslem woman from Mostar who lived alone in Ilidža (Sarajevo) and who was threatened by armed irregulars. They forcibly entered her flat and intimidated her "with a gun against her neck," demanding that she abandon the premises and leave the city. Similar was the case of a Serb woman who lived alone in her flat in Mostar. As Emina said, Croats used to enter her flat, search it and harass her. Sometimes the main reason for psychological abuse is revenge, as was the case with an elderly Serb couple from the town of Visoko (Bosnia). As Svetlana reported, during a period of several months Moslem irregulars sometimes forced the couple to put their hands on a table and then threatened to cut their fingers off. The reason for the abuse was that their son had left to fight for the Serbian side. Sometimes, as Marina's case shows, threats and intimidation were used to obtain information.

> When the war began, my husband did not want to join the Moslem army and he went into hiding at a friend's place...From March 1993 to September 1993 (when they finally found him), armed Moslem soldiers constantly entered our flat to search it. I remained there alone with two young children...I heard that people in my city had been abused and killed and I feared that the same might happen to my children. They did not abuse me physically, but they constantly asked me about my husband's whereabouts. Once I was ordered to

take the younger child with me and go with them to look for my husband. Three Moslem policemen took us to the city, where we strolled all over the place, from the morning until the evening. They probably thought that we would meet my husband and that the child would recognize him. In the evening they used to take us to their headquarters. The child cried and begged to go home, because he was tired and hungry. The policemen paid no heed at all; they kept asking information about me, my husband, and my parents and relatives. Then they told me I had two alternatives, either to find my husband myself and turn him in or to renounce him by a written document. I chose the second possibility, so they gave me a declaration to sign whereby "I renounce my husband and all his deeds." Afterwards, they frequently summoned me to their head-quarters, where they tried to provoke me by saying that somebody had called me over the phone, and the like.

Lies and misinformation dogged some women when their children had gone to refuge while they remained with their husbands in the war zone. Psychological violence against mothers with daughters is experienced in a particularly strong manner. Olivera's story reveals that she experienced considerable Moslem harassment when her children had left. Armed irregulars used to enter and search her house whenever they wanted. Once, four Moslem soldiers (former class-mates of her daughter) came, pointed rifles at her and said "So, where's your daughter?" She replied that her daughter had left at the beginning of the war and they asked ironically where she had gone and why. Then they said they knew that her older daugh-ter was an instructor in a camp for Moslems. The lie hurt her but she was more hurt by the idea of what would have happened to her children if they had been there.

Olivera thinks that her family was particularly abused, because it was "respectable, always distant from others," while she herself was always "well dressed," which suggests that during war hatred and intolerance are expressed towards those who enjoyed supe-rior social and economic status.

Aside from intimidation during forcible entry into houses and flats, armed irregulars have relied on other means; threatening phone calls were very frequent. Dobrila, a Serb who lived alone in the city of Osijek, was harassed by Croat irregulars. "I was harassed by intimidating phone calls and constant intrusions. Once, four men came and said that I was a sniper and that I had just fired at a military convoy that had passed nearby."

Especially frightening and disturbing were threats by neighbors and acquaintances before and during the war. Branka, Emina and

Tatjana all spoke about that. Branka, who had remained alone in her flat with her mother, could hardly endure the threats of their neighbors. They were the only Serb women in their building, and their fear was only reinforced by the fact that her brother was at the front at that time. The neighbors next door, whom they did not especially socialize with but whom they saw every day, began following them and reproaching them for not publicly taking a stand against Radovan Karadžić.[1] Branka and her mother were treated as if they were guilty for everything that was happening. According to Branka, the heaviest threats and humiliations came when people of different ethnic origins had to share shelter—usually a cellar—before and during military actions.

> Once, while we were in a cellar, a Moslem acquaintance, a man of roughly the same age as me, invited me to sing some anti-Serbian songs in English, from some local radio program. I did not dare to refuse directly, and, on the other hand, I felt terrible when I imagined that I had to sing a songs like "The Thompsons and Kalashnikovs[2] are blasting, let's drive all Serbs across the Drina river and into Serbia." I replied that I did not know English...That was psychological pressure to make me act against my ethnic group.

Branka used to socialize with a Moslem girl whose friends cursed chetniks and demanded Branka do the same. They kept insisting, although she said she never swore. She experienced major stress when the brother of one of her Moslem friends began threatening he would kill her and her mother.

> Two Moslem boys, aged 18–19, with whom me and my sister used to socialize, were recruited and sent to the frontline. It was September 1992, a period when Moslems had serious casualties. As the boys did not return for twenty days, everybody was afraid that something terrible had happened to them. Then, one day, the brother of one of the boys came to our place (together with his commander) to meet the girls the boys socialized with, and there was a lot of provocation. For example, the guy looked at my mother and me and said "If I come to know that my brother has been killed, I will kill the first innocent I encounter, including a little baby." My mother and me, we were shaking. When the boys returned from the front, they said, "You are lucky because God only knows what could have happened to you if something had happened to us." Others were silent, but I could see on their faces that they would be glad if the brother had a reason to pour his anger on us. They just enjoyed our fear.

Hostile attitudes towards Branka and her mother, provoked by the fact that they are Serbs, also manifested through declarations that all Serbs must be killed. When Moslems burned a part of Branka's city, neighbors invited Branka to watch it and said, "Come to see how your brother Serbs are burning!" Alone and unprotected, afraid that the threats addressed to them might finally happen, Branka and her mother decided to use Moslem names in their everyday communication.

Branka and her mother also had to endure threats when they were leaving Sarajevo. Simply waiting for a bus was filled with tension and insecurity. They also had to worry whether they were on the evacuation list and whether the convoy would be stopped and harassed along the way. And last but not least, there was a lot of misinformation about the convoy itinerary and the possible attacks they were exposing themselves to. "We began to panic when we heard over the radio that the convoy for Split had been stopped and that Moslem and Croats had been mistreated. However, the information turned out to be false, because an hour later Aida, my Moslem friend who had been in the convoy, called and said that everything was alright."

The tension and insecurity of evacuation were only reinforced by threats addressed to the people intending to go to refuge. "Moslems used to come and say, 'Go away, we will arrest you all and take you to concentration camps,' and, the next day, they would say, 'Don't leave, stay to live together with us,' and then again 'Go away, we will expel you anyway,' and so on. They spat at us and said 'We will not only expel you but also kill you.'"

Milka also experienced expressions of hostility when she and her daughter were abandoning their home in Tuzla. There were people around, shouting at them, calling them chetniks, cursing and throwing stones at them.

Emina, a Moslem woman, told us how cruel neighbors of another nationality could be during war. Emina came to know through her mother-in-law that her mother and sister had been severely mistreated by their Croat neighbors. They took the women away from their flat, brought them to the right bank of the Neretva river, sharpened knives in front of them, threatened them with rape and murder and insulted them.

Tatjana's mother-in-law, an elderly Serb woman, also experienced intimidation when her Moslem neighbors forcibly entered her home to search for weapons. They also searched her husband and hit him on this occasion. As she said, although her mother-in-law was not physically abused, it was terrible to watch how they tortured her father-in-law and how the people they had lived with so well before the war smashed things and ruined her apartment.

However, not all ethnically different neighbors reacted in the same way. There were people who, in spite of the overall ambience of ethnic intolerance, tried to help their ethnically different neighbors. Thus, Branka, a Serb, was secretly assisted by her Moslem neighbor, who used to give her bread and yeast. Natalija, a Serb, was ready to offer a Croat neighbor the opportunity to spend a night at her place, but she had to warn her in advance. "Come, if it means something to you, but I have to tell you that if something happens to us it will happen to you as well, because we won't be able to protect you."

Especially frightening were the repeated mock executions and psychological violence against hostages in prisons and detention camps. Jasminka, for example, talked about a female Croat neighbor who was brought three times to face a firing squad. Desa came to know that her neighbor was in a Moslem-held camp where women were sexually, physically and psychically abused in order to make them tell their husbands' whereabouts. Aside from that, they were also insulted, threatened and starved. Rada recounted how her grandmother, a 90-year-old Serbian woman from the city of Duvno, was taken hostage, arrested, starved, denied medication and psychologically abused by Croatian soldiers. Olga, a Serbian from Mostar, was arrested several times by members of the local Croat armed forces. During the first arrest, they blinded her with flashlights, tapping on a table with a huge metal club. The second time, they broke into her flat and smashed everything; then they took her to a police station, where they again blinded her with flashlights, saying that her husband was a chetnik who had left to fight against Croats.

Propaganda is largely why threats and terror campaigns are taken seriously. It helps create an overall ambience of insecurity that eventually makes many women feel completely unprotected. Television propaganda was much more effective than newspaper articles or orally transmitted news. One-sided and heavily biased reporting about intentional large-scale property destruction, the torture of prisoners, mass killings, terror and violence against civilians, as well as reports from individuals who had been taken hostage or tortured, produced various negative reactions. Propaganda significantly influenced many women's decision to leave the war zone.

Mirjana, for example, had many sleepless nights because there were rumors in her city that Croats would round up all Serbs and that "they would first throw hand grenades into our houses then take away the survivors to form a living shield in front of the military barracks which, at the time, were under siege. I did not know what to do," said Mirjana, "because my child was little and I did not know whom I could entrust her to." Milka too decided to leave Tuzla because she could no longer stand the ongoing propaganda. "[It said that] Serbs kill and torture Moslems. I couldn't stand those stories anymore, nor could I watch the TV reports about Serbian crimes against Moslems. There was heavy propaganda in that sense and I just wondered if there was any truth in that and whether some of my neighbors would have attacked me on that account."

Vera was also scared by the public threats. "The voice from the TV said that the three villages, especially Tasovčići, would be taken by all means, while those who wouldn't go would be killed." Natalija described the dread and psychological pressure created by propaganda. "But psychological pressure is worst of all. For example, you hear Moslems in the market bragging that the next day they will take Grbavica by storm, and then you cannot sleep all night, thinking what will happen to you and where could you go."

Insults and humiliations. A certain number of the women we talked with were victims of verbal violence, which took the form of ethnic insults and humiliations. Women whose ethnic affiliation differed from that of their husbands were especially vulnerable on this count. They had to put up with insults and humiliations coming from members of their own and other ethnic groups, as well as sometimes from their own husbands. Wives of ex-YPA officers were also exposed to harassment. Verbal violence frequently accompanied physical and sexual violence against women.

Svetlana had difficulty enduring ethnically inspired insults and humiliation. "I was astonished by that hatred...the way people look at you, humiliate you. They blame you as if you were guilty for all. As soon as you try to protest, they label you 'chetnik.' I constantly had to listen to insults, calumnies on my account, like 'You Serbs are all genocidal and chetniks, Juka's right when he throws you out of the window.'"

Insults were often accompanied by a kind of surveillance: stalking and spying by neighbors. In some buildings the concierge would keep records about the people coming in, whom they wanted to see, how long they wanted to stay, and so on. This meant, practically speaking, that one left one's home and contacted friends only when it was really necessary. Our interviewees frequently reported that their neighbors, on top of insulting them, also followed them and controlled their movements and visits. It was also neighbors who constantly reproached them for preparing to leave or for having sent children out of the war zone.

Lepa, who remained alone in the Moslem-controlled part of Sarajevo where Moslems predominated, was constantly reproached for being Serb. She was the only one left without electricity and running water and she was the only one who was omitted from the food lists. She was also constantly monitored. She was mainly followed and spied on by a Moslem neighbor who kept telling her that she should remain in Sarajevo and call her children to return, but on condition that she renounce her Serbian nationality. "All Serbs should be killed and Belgrade should be bombed," she used to say. Lepa's example demonstrates that an invitation to remain was sometimes on condition of losing one's ethnic identity.

Ethnically inspired insults were addressed to women whose ethnic origin was different from that of their husbands. Emina, a Moslem, had worked for the YPA prior to the war and "swore her Serb husband, on their child, not to go to fight" because they had members of three different ethnic groups in their extended family. Emina hardly endured the threatening insults of her Croatian neighbor, who once, while making an allusion to the ethnic origin of Emina's husband, told her, "You chetnik whore, you too will pay in the end!"

Blaženka, a Croat married to a Serb, also had to put up with insults and humiliation. She said that the attitude towards the YPA and the way her children were treated—they called them chetniks—in school and in their apartment building were the most difficult things for her while she was in Croatia.

Natalija recounted how a Moslem friend, whose elderly husband had been killed by chetniks, did not dare to speak to her anymore. "She did not know whom she could count on, and, on the other hand, our neighbors had begun to call Moslem women 'balinkuše'[3] and to treat them as second-class citizens."

At the beginning of the war, Ana, who was born of a Serb father and Moslem mother, and who was married to a Serb, left Mostar together with her husband and children. Her mother, sister and brother-in-law remained in the city. Afterwards, she was deeply affected when she came to know that during a search of her flat in Mostar, a group of Croat and Moslem soldiers had written "četnikuša" over a photograph of her daughter.

The ethnic divide most deeply affected the so-called mixed marriages, because it was impossible to take sides, so that what frequently happened was that women were abused by their ethnically different husbands. Milica talked to us about a couple that lived in her neighborhood. The husband, a Serb, took the reproaches of his fellow Serbs seriously when they criticized him for having married a Moslem woman. He began beating his wife, while telling her, "You Moslem one, you can return to your village but you can't take the child with you because she's Serb."

The verbal violence that accompanied rape was meant to further aggravate suffering and humiliation. Thus, Anđa had to endure rape and psychological torture in a Moslem-held detention camp. "They swore and called us names; they put knives against our necks, threatening they would kill us." Dobrila, who met several Serb women who had been raped by Croatian soldiers, said that they had been insulted and called "Serbian whores." As Nedeljka said, at the initial interrogations upon arrival in detention camps, psychological abuse and insults such as "you chetnik mothers!" regularly accompanied rape.

During the war in the former Yugoslavia, women were also psychologically abused if they happened to be married to YPA officers or because their husbands, sons and other male relatives had been recruited for the regular Serbian armed forces. Hatred towards the YPA took the most brutal forms, regardless of the ethnic affiliation of the women married to YPA officers.

Before the actual outbreak of the civil war in Slovenia (June–July 1991), there was a period of special war against YPA officers and members of their families. The civilians, home-guard members and police officers exposed them to considerable psychological pressure through verbal aggression, intimidation, mockery and widespread harassment. The fate of the Slovene women married to YPA officers, especially when those were Serbs, was particularly dramatic. They were exposed to threats and insults, especially after the war in Slovenia, when their husbands had left and they remained alone. Thus, Katja, a Slovene, reported the ambience of alienation, fear and violence.

> My husband is a YPA officer, a Serb, who had lived in Slovenia all his life. After the war in Slovenia, he was among the last ones to leave the country. I am a born Slovenian, undoubtedly of "Aryan" origin, so to say. I was shocked by the whole preparation of the war and hate-mongering against Serbs and the YPA officers. I experienced a lot of harassment, because I'm married to a YPA officer. Most bizarre of all is that, when the YPA retreated and Slovenia began making new registers of citizens, the wives of the YPA officers were most often harassed by individuals whose family names ended in "*ić*"[4] and who were in the same situation as we were. I suf-

fered terribly when, some time in October 1991, I saw a picture of my husband on TV with his full name and inscription "Serbian chetnik."

Katja's story reveals that she felt threatened by non-Slovenes as well. The general anti-Serbian attitude of Slovenian public opinion even encouraged some Moslem refugees to stalk and threaten her. After her husband had left, she remained alone in her flat. One day, in the spring of 1992, somebody rang at her door. She partly opened it and saw a girl of about 20 and a man. They told her that they were refugees collecting donations. She replied that she had already given some donation at her workplace and began to close the door. The girl suddenly approached, cursing and trying to stop her from closing the door. She also tried to hit her. Fortunately, Katja somehow managed to close the door. She heard the couple behind threatening that they would come back. She believes that the couple were Moslems who had been encouraged by the fact that every Serb who had not been granted Slovenian citizenship had to leave Slovenia.

Other forms of psychological violence. Other than threats, insults and humiliation, there were other forms of suffering that women experienced as psychological violence, and to which they were exposed before and during the war. These included harassment in the workplace, eviction from houses and flats, forced expulsion from their regions, restrictions on their freedom of movement and being present at scenes of suffering and the humiliation of others. As Branka said, women who experience these forms of violence feel like "second-class citizens, utterly unprotected and unable to do or change anything."

Harassment in the workplace

The main reason for harassment as a form of psychological violence was the victim's ethnic affiliation. Especially vulnerable were women in higher managerial positions or those in the upper echelons of state agencies. The widespread ambience of ethnic intolerance offered a handy opportunity to humiliate and mistreat those women who had enjoyed superior economic and social positions in peacetime.

Women who had been employed before the war told us how the attitude of their colleagues changed when ethnic intolerance set in. The sheer fact of ethnic affiliation was a sufficient reason to lose a job or to be sent on compulsory leave. Mirjana and Gordana's examples demonstrate that ethnic intolerance was expressed first towards the highly educated women who held higher managerial positions and who enjoyed a superior social status.

Mirjana, a Serb, worked as the chief legal consultant of her firm in Croatia. As the situation deteriorated her Croat colleagues began harassing her because of her ethnic affiliation.

> One day...an ex-worker dropped by in the uniform of the Croatian Guard. We had initiated a lawsuit against him, which was not finished. He ordered me to come to his office and told me that the suit must be finished the next day. I said that it was up to the court to decide when the suit would finish, to which he told me "not to kid around with him." I told him not to threaten me or else I would go to see the manager, which I did, but the manager was also wearing the same uniform. He said he would see to it that I was no longer harassed. I asked not to be sent to the court this time. I participated in administrative board meetings where everybody, except Serbs, wore a uniform and had a gun. I felt terrible. I said I did not want to go to the court because I was afraid, and then others began criticizing my behavior.

Another reason Mirjana's colleagues changed their attitude towards her was because her mother lived in a Serb-controlled area. Thus Mirjana was seen as a disloyal citizen and as such was exposed to threats. Before a Croatian attack on the area where Mirjana's mother lived, Mirjana's boss and other colleagues told her that the area would be attacked and "cleaned," and when Mirjana replied that her mother would then be killed as well, they said that nobody would touch her if she went into hiding. When Mirjana came back from accompanying her child to Serbia, her colleagues asked her how many chetniks she had brought with her. At that time Mirjana lived in the town of Požega, where Croats were in the majority, and she was afraid of the overall ambience that reigned in the town. Her boss pressed her several times to tell him why she had sent her child to Serbia. He also told her that she would be suspicious if she went there too frequently. He said that he had constant problems with Serbs and that they could not be allowed to hold managerial positions. Others told Mirjana not to bring food to her mother because that would be a way of assisting chetniks.

Gordana as well was afraid of the changed attitudes of her Croatian colleagues. She was employed as a sales manager, and was constantly exposed to psychological abuse because of her ethnic affiliation. "Without any reason, some people suddenly stopped saying hello...When the war began I was stigmatized in a way. Once, a colleague of mine turned his head away from me 'because Vukovar fell.' I felt completely insecure. Anybody could come and arrest me in my workplace."

Lepa found that her Moslem colleagues changed their attitude toward her before the beginning of the war. Lepa held a high-ranking position in a state agency and was frequently told to remain in Sarajevo and to publicly renounce her ethnic affiliation.

Danica described the ethnic cleavage in her firm. "My bosses made a selection according to the ethnic affiliation of the employees. A couple of my Serbian colleagues and me were given orders to take a year of compulsory leave, while Moslems were favored at the expense of the employed Serbs...I heard many times that Serbs should go to Serbia, Croats to Croatia, while Moslems should remain in Bosnia."

Some women were fired on account of their ethnicity, regardless of whether they had been loyal to the newly established authorities or not. Jovana told us that her Serbian cousin, who worked as a nurse in the city of Bjelovar (Croatia) and who had always maintained good relations with Croats, had been fired just because she was a Serb. The woman was expecting to retire normally and could not find any job in the public sector after the dismissal. Jelena, who worked as a shop assistant in a Serbia-based firm, was fired as well.

In November 1994, Stanislava returned to the firm where she had worked for more than thirty years. She wanted to assume her job again but was seriously insulted by her erstwhile colleagues, with whom she had had excellent relations before the war. One of them asked her "What do you Serbs want?" Stanislava replied that she wanted to work and live normally, as before the war, to which the colleague replied that she was a "chetnik bitch." Svetlana's ex-boss made his contribution as well, saying that she must be denied access to the firm.

Ranka worked as an economist in her firm and her colleagues constantly provoked and insulted her, before and during the war. "It was terribly hard to endure those provocations, especially by my colleagues," said Ranka.

Eviction from houses and flats and forced expulsion from home regions

Women had serious difficulties in coping with eviction and loss of property. The most serious stress was related to loss of property that had sometimes taken years to accumulate. The severity of this reaction is deeply related to their social roles as carers of the family and home. For them, the war meant being forced to leave what they had been strongly attached to, as well as being forced to watch other people settle in their homes. Women refugees often came to know, painfully, that the homes they had left behind had subsequently been sacked or destroyed, so that they had no place to return.

SNEŽANA: "My building was destroyed and my apartment was completely sacked. My husband only succeeded in saving two photo albums...Now I have no place to go."

OLGA: "They gave me the key back but they took away my flat. There was a plate with my name on my door. That is how they knew what flats belonged to Serbs and whom they should evict or take away."

Nataša remained in Mostar during the heaviest fighting. In a letter to her sister she wrote about the people who came to other people's flats. "The authorities have invited everyone to return to Mostar before the end of July and those who do not return will have their flats confiscated." Nataša watched over her mother's apartment, which had remained vacant. Merima also spoke about ethnic cleansing and forced expulsion from the home area.

> My distant relatives with whom I lived told me about a Croat girl who was dating one of my distant relatives. In August that year she became quite depressed because she came to know that her parents had been expelled. The army "cleansed" the area and one day her mother phoned her and said that it might be the last time she heard from her. There were trucks, she said, transporting people and she was waiting for her turn as well...The very knowledge that people are being transferred from one region to another, that they go into the unknown, is something horrifying.

Senka told us about Serb soldiers who evicted an elderly couple from their house in order to set up a brothel to be staffed by Moslem girls. People from some cities and villages were given open orders to leave their homes. Thus, Sanija had to leave the city of Foča because "there were loudspeakers saying that all Moslems must leave the city."

Eviction and forced expulsion was not only carried out as part of "ethnic cleansing," but also in order to loot the abandoned property. Here is Natalija's story.

> War profiteers used to carry away truckloads of things that belonged to the inhabitants of Grbavica [Sarajevo]...They stole everything they could. All abandoned flats were sacked, with no exception. As for the non-vacant flats, the method was the following. They would come saying they had to mount a machine-gun on the window to respond to Moslem fire. Then they would begin carrying away everything they could. One group would take rags and carpets, the other one would load electric appliances, while the third one would pick up the smaller items they found interesting... My flat was sacked after we had left for Serbia. They asked for the keys from one of my neighbors (they knew exactly whom to press). They regularly took him away to their headquarters. Eventually, he broke and gave them the keys.

Nataša wrote to her sister that everything had been utterly destroyed. Soldiers would enter shops or flats, sack them and eventually set them on fire. Dobrila, who had been frequently harassed by Croatian irregulars, eventually concluded that they wanted her to leave her flat so that they could sack it with ease.

Vida and her husband spent twelve years building their house, then lived there only six months before it was destroyed. "My house was completely sacked and burned when Moslems took Trnovo. So, I packed all my life in just one bag and left the city."

Restricting freedom of movement

Some women who remained in the war zone had to live under permanent surveillance and control, with restrained freedom of movement and without the possibility of leaving. This form of psychological violence was also related to disturbed ethnic relations, the social status and profession of women and the military engagement of their male relatives. It never depended at all on their actual behavior or will. Women exposed to this form of violence felt helpless and dependent on the decisions made by somebody else, most frequently a male from the regular or irregular armed forces or some other male who took the role of "protector," thus displaying his power. Lepa, Dragica and Sandra talked about that.

Before the war, Lepa lived in an "élite neighborhood" in Sarajevo, which, when the war began, came under Moslem control. Her husband had left Sarajevo, her son had been recruited into the Serb forces and she herself was Serb. The police constantly monitored her movements and social contacts. The letters she sent or received were opened and read. She could leave her flat only in order to go to work and whenever she wanted to see a friend she had to inform a Moslem neighbor or the guard who stood in front of her building. There was no legal way for her to leave Sarajevo because, as she came to know, she had a file in the state security service. For two years and a half she was, as she said, "a political and war prisoner" because she "was deprived of freedom just because she was Serb." This life "under surveillance," with limited freedom of movement, was particularly hard for her. She said that she was not physically abused but she was deeply marked by the constant fear and insecurity, and the possibility that anyone could break into her apartment. She began suffering from insomnia and was constantly thinking about getting out of the situation. In exchange for a free and legal exit from the besieged city Lepa voluntarily offered her flat, but the proposition was declined.

Dragica, a 60-year-old pensioner, remained alone in her flat in the besieged city of Zenica. Fearing that somebody might attack her and sack her flat, she had to reduce her movements about the city. As she said, "I used to leave my flat only when I had to sell something and buy some food."

Sandra also recounted the psychological suffering that accompanied a restrained freedom of movement. Her female friend, a Serb from Sarajevo, was physically and psychologically abused by the Moslem father of a friend, who had offered her "protection." He denied her food and ordered her not to talk to other people or leave the building. She lived like a prisoner. She tried to escape several times but it was too dangerous—there were snipers all over the place. The torturer's daughter, her friend, knew all about the situation. Although she did not approve of it at all, she was powerless against her father. The victim thought that the man changed his behavior towards her because of her ethnic affiliation, since all at once Moslems began treating Serbs as enemies and chetniks. She endured the suffering for a month and then succeeded in escaping and reaching the Serb-controlled village of Pale. To the Moslem soldiers that she met on her way she said that she was a Croat going to find some food.

Witnessing scenes of suffering and the humiliation of others

The witnessing of suffering, humiliation, torture or execution leaves profound marks on the souls of the survivors. The stories of our interviewees reveal that during this war civilians were exposed to the dangers of shelling, sniper shots, land mines and torture in detention camps. These are all highly stressful events that not only represent an immediate life-threatening danger but are also liable to produce severe fear and panic, thus deeply affecting even those who were not directly exposed to them.

Other people's torture and distress had terrifying effects on the witnesses and made many women suffer profoundly. That is what transpired from the stories told by Desa, Slobodanka, Jovana, Snežana, Nedeljka and Olga.

Desa recounted witnessing the aftermath of the massacre in the village of Čelebići, where Moslem soldiers left twelve decapitated corpses behind them. Desa also came to know through a female cousin that her neighbor, a Serb woman from Sarajevo, had been taken to the concentration camp of Dretelj, where she had been psychologically abused, insulted and deprived of food and water.

A Serb woman from the village of Ljuta, about whom Slobodanka talked, had been taken to a concentration camp, together with her daughter. Aside from being physically abused, the women watched Moslems taking buckets full of blood out from the next room, where prisoners were interrogated and tortured. The scene provoked intense suffering and fear in the woman.

Jovana used to work as a nurse in a hospital near the city of Pakrac (Croatia). She describes the psychic trauma she experienced when assisting the wounded. "My personal experience—I had to see crippled boys of about the same age as me or boys with napalm-made wounds that couldn't heal—affected me so profoundly that I could not recover for a long time."

The suffering of others deeply affected Snežana. She heard that her Moslem neighbors abducted fifteen males, Serbs, shot them in the legs and let them bleed to death. Snežana had a cousin who was murdered on that occasion and she told us that the whole event had terribly shocked her. Nedeljka came to know that her aunt was in a camp through a Serbian acquaintance who had been taken prisoner by Croatian and Moslem soldiers. This woman told Nedeljka how her aunt had once been taken to identify the bodies of her husband and sons. After she recognized the bodies, the soldiers began cursing and shooting at the corpses that lay in front of her.

Olga gave us a very moving example of ethnically based humiliation and torture of the weak and elderly.

> I was present when they took away two old couples of about 60 years of age: a Croat woman married to a Serb man and a Croat man married to a Serb woman. They lived in Mostar. The second couple offered shelter to the first as well as to my children and me, because we were afraid to sleep alone. One night, around 10 p.m., two HOS soldiers broke in. They were dead drunk and obviously wanted to have some "fun" during the curfew, when HVO did not allow any arrests. Nevertheless, the soldiers took away the old couple without any charges. Aunt Z. tried to jump from the balcony, but they did not let her. They shouted at the old people, hit them. They asked them "What do you become when you jump into a tree?" and they had to answer "Monkeys." Then they would ask "And what do you become when you descend the tree?" and the others would have to reply "chetniks." The soldiers took away those people and nobody ever saw them afterwards.

Olga continued, saying "That was the most terrible thing I ever experienced in my life." Olga reported the case to HVO and they said "All right, you have reported the case but try not to sleep alone anymore."

Witnessing scenes of humiliation and torture drove some women to openly protest and express their bitterness against members of their own ethnic group, sometimes endangering their lives.

Fear experienced by the women we talked with

Excluding exposure to psychological violence, our interviewees were also exposed to fears of varying intensity related to the overall situation of vulnerability in a state of war. The sudden and unexpected outbreak of immediate danger provoked various kinds of fear in women. Many of them were completely unprepared for such a possibility, having been born, and having spent years, in peace. Some women, especially the older ones, lived through the Second World War, and their fears of renewed ethnic violence were both strong and justified. The women who had never lived during a war took considerable time accepting reality, while continuing to believe that "the situation will settle down and normal life will continue."

At the beginning of the war, the majority of women experienced the fear of shelling, snipers, barricades, arbitrary and forcible entry by the police and soldiers, stalking, searches and arrests. Afterwards, women experienced intense fears relating to survival in war conditions. Those who attempted to leave the war zone—which almost always happened on the spur of the moment—experienced profound fear while trying to reach safe areas. Fear in women was related to the general insecurity and danger in which war abounds, but it was also produced by some specific conditions and risks that they were exposed to. Women become afraid because they are quite aware of the risks they run due to their gender, profession, social status, ethnic background, earlier lifestyle, or the military engagement of their male relatives. Particularly intense is the fear women feel for their children, husbands, parents and other close relatives.

Given the situation, fear could be classified in the following categories:

— Fear that appeared before the outbreak of the war and which took the form of anxiety, concern, tension and restlessness;
— Fear appearing during the war itself, experienced as a realistic fear of shelling, sniper shots, searches, arrests, killings, torture, bodily injury, restriction of movement and the impossibility of leaving the war zone;
— Fear experienced during transfers from the war zone to safe areas, related to the insecurity and danger inherent in the endeavor;
— Fear concerning the conditions in refuge, related to the concern for the lives of relatives who remained in the war zone.

Fear in the pre-war period

Women became restless and anxious when, during the pre-war period, they noticed that the ambience of confidence and security had disappeared. Even before the war, neighbors began to hate, spy on and insult each other. Security was ensured by the possession of weapons. Suddenly there were people wearing new and strange uniforms, and there was a possibility that males could be

drafted. Daunted by war preparations, powerless to change or influence anything, unable to protect themselves or their family
members, with experience (first- or second-hand) of the previous
war, some women decided to leave the war zone altogether. They
took their children, wishing, first of all, to protect them. The
women who chose this course were mainly women who had close
relatives in some place unaffected by war. Women made those decisions believing that the departure was only temporary and would
last a couple of months at most, until the situation became normal
again. Departure represented the last exit, and it was resorted to
when fear became truly unbearable.

Gordana told us about her anxiety and insecurity before the
outbreak of the war in Bosnia.

> It was the autumn of 1991. The war was already going on in Croatia
> and there was terrible tension in Bosnia. During the Catholic
> Christmas I was on duty in my factory. There were no buses and
> I had to walk alone, at 5 a.m., and there were drunken men in uni-
> forms all around me. On my way I saw a café exploding. When
> I reached the factory I saw that the guards were half-drunk, and
> I was on duty alone. I was terribly afraid, because I had a cousin
> who had been tortured in a detention camp (they stabbed him with
> a red-hot knife, for example). He told me "Don't be ever alone when
> they are around." And there I was, with three half-drunk, armed
> guards. In the morning, they called me to come to the guardroom.
> I realized they were acting quite unusually that night and began
> thinking of finding an iron bar (in case I had to defend myself) but
> then I realized the bar wouldn't be of any use.

The fear that precipitates the decision to leave the war zone can be
aggravated by some additional circumstances, such as children,
pregnancy, knowledge about what happened in the previous war
or what was happening in the current one. Tamara's story is very
telling in this respect.

Tamara came from a partisan family from the region of Lika
(Croatia). Her father's relatives, Serbs, had all been killed by Croatian fascists during the Second World War. After the political
changes in 1991, and after the first news about the massacres of
Serbs in Lika, Tamara, who was pregnant at the time, decided to
leave her city (Otočac) and go to the city of Knin. There as well she
felt insecure and eventually moved to Belgrade.

> We used to walk in long rows and hide in caves. It affected me so
> deeply that I decided to go to Belgrade for six months, together

with my child who was only six months at the time. At that time, a dozen *ustaše* were arrested in Knin and we were told that they had necklaces made of baby fingers (cut off from Serb babies). I was terribly afraid and anguished by the idea of what would happen if the Croats took Knin. Therefore, I decided to move on and go to Serbia. On our way to Serbia I was terribly afraid when traveling through Croatia and Bosnia. Every now and then the irregulars would stop our bus and, as we had to travel by night and through the war zone, the military controls were quite frequent. I was overwhelmed by fear and was feeling completely powerless because, unless you see the signs on the soldiers' caps, you don't know whom you have to deal with.

Merima, a Moslem, and Svetlana, a Serb, recounted how they lived through the sudden appearance of barricades and the division of their city. In Merima's words,

> When the partition of Sarajevo began and when the nationalistic parties appeared, we knew that some parts of the city belonged to Serbs and some others to Moslems, but neither I nor my friends took it seriously, because Sarajevo was unified and people of different ethnic origin lived side by side, everywhere in the city. I lived in a part of the city where Moslems were the majority. I was born there and I worked there as well. Before the war we joked about what part belonged to whom, but these were only jokes, indeed. We lived all together, side by side, and that's why we were shocked when the first barricades appeared. Everything stopped, including the public transportation system. That day I did not go to my job. Quite simply, I was shocked, I was out of my mind.

When the war was imminent, it announced itself by some sinister signs, such as lack of street lighting and the ever more frequent gunfire. "We went to bed peacefully. The next morning I went out to buy some bread and milk and I saw armed men all over the place. Those were the neighborhood boys I knew. I just froze. Some time later, on April 5, there were those barricades so we could not go to work and I was filled with some unspeakable fear."

After the tragic event in front of the Assembly of Bosnia-Herzegovina, Svetlana, whose two daughters had attended the demonstration, decided with her husband to send them out of Sarajevo.

In the period of the growing ethnic intolerance in Croatia, Mirjana traveled every second week to Belgrade, where she had sent her daughter. She believed that the safest way would be to travel in her own car, regardless of numerous checkpoints on the road.

"When you are on the road you have to pass a hundred check-points. My kid was sleeping in the car and yet I had to open everything because they were searching for weapons." Once, while returning from Belgrade, she experienced strong fear both as a woman and as a Serb when she was not able to refuse to give a ride to members of the Croatian army.

Immediately before the outbreak of the war, Mirjana worried a lot about the destiny of her child, which she cared for alone. "The Croatian Guard was accommodated in the school that my daughter had to attend...There were rumors that the YPA was shelling the school...My firm was turned into a bomb production facility and you can imagine how I felt knowing for whom the shells were destined...It was the time of terror. Whenever you went shopping, for example, you felt fear. You were afraid all the time. I was shivering when I went to the school to see when classes would begin."

Mirjana finally realized that she could not cope with the fear and worries anymore. "I was completely helpless and the authorities weren't protecting us at all." Eventually she decided to leave Croatia and join her daughter in Belgrade.

Fear during the war

Women who remained in the war zone when the war began were constantly exposed to life-threatening danger and therefore experienced very intense fear. Mothers who had to take care of their children were rendered particularly vulnerable. "The woman is overpowered by fear for her children," said Gordana.

Senka spent several months with her children in besieged Sarajevo, fearing most the fate of her children. "My children slept in our toilet. On May 28 there was a terrible shelling and my building was hit five times. We were in the cellar at the time and our house burned but we were lucky to survive."

In fact, flats and houses offered no safety at all, which only aggravated the fear and insecurity. That is what Vera, Emina, Natalija and Biserka told us.

VERA: "A shell fell in front of our house, causing damage to four spots."

EMINA: "In April 1992, a bullet passed through our flat, missing my child by just about thirty centimeters."

BISERKA: "I lived in Grbavica (Sarajevo). One evening in May 1992, a stream of bullets from an automatic weapon splintered my window and hit the armchair where my husband would normally sit at that time of the day."

Until December 1992, Natalija was in Sarajevo with her husband, with whom she shared her intense fear of shelling.

> Our house was constantly targeted by shells and snipers. In my flat all the windows and upper portions of the furniture were smashed and drilled with bullets. Every day we could hear the screams of somebody who had been shot by a sniper at the entrance of our building...But most terrible of all was psychological pressure...During shelling, we descended into the cellar, but my husband found it too hard to descend and then mount again so that once he refused to go. I left him alone two or three times but then I realized that I would have gone out of my mind if something had happened to him. Therefore, I decided to keep him company. When we had to go to bed, we would put mattresses on the floor, in the hall, since it was too dangerous to sleep in our bedroom because a bullet or a shell splinter might easily reach us there.

The fear of shelling was coupled with the anxiety that one could lose one's life in shelters as well, because, most often, they were not designed for that purpose. As Merima told us, these were, in fact, large cellars that offered no real protection.

> I was obsessed with protecting my children from shells...Children, as children are, just wanted to continue to play outside the house, as if nothing was happening. That drove me crazy, because the shells were not choosing their victims and they were falling every second. I was terribly afraid for my children. The cellar we were in, in fact, presented no shelter at all. It was an ordinary cellar in an ordinary apartment building. And we were all there: Serbs, Moslems and Croats, all together. Nobody understood what was going on and, because of the position we were in, you just could not know anything. All you knew was that you were trapped and that you could not go out when you wished.

Some women were completely paralyzed by fear and unable to act. Ivana, a 17-year-old girl from Sarajevo, did not remain long in the war-affected city yet she experienced intense fear. In fact, at the very beginning of hostilities she experienced a fear so strong that she could not leave her home for any reason whatsoever. Vesna had a similar experience and since she was not able to cope with the fear, she left Sarajevo together with her children at the beginning of the conflict. "I was so paralyzed by fear that I did not dare to go to the street. I used to wake up at night thinking that somebody was screaming in my ear."

As Olivera and Zorica let us know, intense fear experienced during stressful war-related events and situations continues to haunt the victims long after they have left the war zone.

Olivera spent two and a half years in the Moslem-controlled part of Sarajevo because she did not want to leave her husband alone and because she feared that their children would blame her if something happened to their father. Eventually, however, she decided to send the children to refuge alone. "All kinds of terrible things were happening, shells were falling, people were being taken away and killed, girls were raped." This long-lasting period of intense fear, coupled with concern for children who had gone to refuge, affected Olivera so deeply that long after she had left Sarajevo she continued to feel restless and anxious. Even after having made it to refuge, she still experienced the feeling that when she was walking on the street somebody was stalking her or that somebody would shoot her in the back or assault her otherwise.

Zorica recounted how for the first time in her life she had experienced the fear of death. It happened when Moslem irregulars attacked the village of Čemerno where she had found refuge together with her family.

> I thought it was our end. I shivered by my mother's side and my brother was crying silently. We heard them entering the house, shooting randomly and looking for something. I understood they were looking for a lighter or matches or something similar to set the house on fire. They cursed and protested because they couldn't find anything. I understood they were in a hurry but would return later. Finally, they got out of the house and we swiftly ran to the forest. We spent almost four hours in that terribly cold forest and I still shiver when I recall that.

The experience made Zorica depressed long after the event. Her fear for her life and the lives of her family members was justified, because before the soldiers entered her house she had seen them killing her cousins and setting their house on fire. She could not talk about her experience with anybody, because in that case the horrifying images would surface in her memory. After two and a half years she finally succeeded in overcoming the memory of this traumatic event.

During the war, women also frequently had to worry about sudden house searches, usually performed by unknown, armed and sometimes masked men. There were rumors that the search parties sometimes planted weapons, which served as a pretext for arrest, physical and psychological abuse and deportation to detention sites. The whole procedure was ridden with fear and insecurity.

Maja recounted her fear and anxiety provoked by the frequent inspection of her home.

> I felt very insecure in my flat, because every now and then the home guard would forcibly enter. My neighbors told me that some people had indicated us as chetniks. They interrogated my husband, who suffers from asthma, and asked him why he did not go to his job. I was terribly afraid of anonymous denunciations, because you could lose your head just because someone had denounced you for some personal reasons. What was worse, we were the only Serb family in the whole apartment building. There were also two mixed families. I knew that my best friend, a Moslem and a pacifist, could not have helped me in such a situation.

Natalija, as well, related the fear she felt when armed soldiers searched her house. "I remained alone and could hear them. I heard their boots echoing in the hall and just could not breathe out of panic. I heard them going to the upper floor and banging the rifle butts against a door. As there was nobody at home, they came out angry."

Svetlana described her fear in the following way. "Soldiers used to drop in our flats, mistreat us, arrest us...We had to throw away many books. If they found a *gusle*[5] in your home you would be instantly arrested...The first search of our flat happened at the beginning of May, 1992...Some men in uniforms came and rang at our door. As my husband was in the bathroom, it was me who opened. They said they were from the Bosnian police and that they were informed that a man had been shooting from the third floor of our building."

Women who had remained alone with their children experienced even more intense fear in similar situations. Marina spent almost the entire war in her flat with her two children, in the besieged city of Tuzla. Her husband was in hiding because he had refused to join the Moslem army. During a period of several months in 1993, Marina experienced almost constant apprehension, because "armed Moslem soldiers were constantly coming to our house to look for my husband. I was constantly fearing that they might come, because I heard that they were torturing and killing people, and I feared that the same might happen to me and my children." Later on, when her husband had been caught and taken away to a detention camp, her anxiety was only aggravated. "While he was in the camp I was afraid even more because I was completely unprotected. Every day I heard stories about people disappearing, being tortured, killed, called chetniks...My former Moslem friends all began turning a blind eye to me and I was completely ostracized."

All women who spent some time in the war zone experienced a strong fear of arrest and deportation to detention sites. Their alarm was well grounded, since they had ample opportunity to watch various armed groups entering the flats of their neighbors, who were then insulted and physically abused.

When women remain alone in a war zone and send their children or other relatives to safe areas, aside from worrying about their own lives, women are also concerned and in suspense about the lives and well-being of family members. In wartime, it is quite difficult to obtain timely and accurate information about those who have moved elsewhere. In similar situations, as Svetlana said, "separation from children becomes more difficult than war."

Olivera, who spent two and a half years torn between loyalty to her husband and love for her children, also said that the separation from her children was the most difficult thing for her in this war. Nataša also found it extremely painful to endure being apart from her child, mother and sister. In every letter that she wrote it was apparent how much she missed them and how strong was her concern about their fate. Yet, having remained in Mostar which was fully involved in war, she could have rightfully been more worried about her own life.

Fear experienced during evacuation from the war zone

Evacuation from the war zone, from a woman's home (i.e., "uprooting" and "separation from the hearth"), results in deep insecurity, confusion, vulnerability and anxiety. All these feelings are accompanied by the fear of what might happen on the road, for no road was safe at the time (1991–95).

Nedeljka, Nadežda, Jelena and Lepa talked about the fear that accompanied evacuation.

NEDELJKA: "I was constantly afraid and yet I had to move. I walked twenty-two kilometers until I reached the Serb-controlled territory and I did not feel sorry at all about the house I had left behind. All I was thinking of was how to get out with my children, because, during the three years since the beginning of the war, I didn't sleep at all."

Nadežda left Sarajevo together with her daughters. "We headed for the unknown, overwhelmed by fear. We passed through the parts of the city where all the houses were burned, destroyed and deserted. I left behind all the comfort I had, which I experience as major violence."

Jelena was in the third month of pregnancy when she left the city of Čapljina (Bosnia). She was afraid because she had to take a bus filled with Moslems. After two and a half years of life in the be-sieged Sarajevo, Lepa had to leave the city by illegal means. This is how she describes the fear that made her finally decide:

> The constant waiting, fear that soldiers might forcibly enter my apartment and evict me because I lived alone, affected me really badly. Then, secretly and intensely, I began to collect information about the illegal ways of leaving Sarajevo. I took a serious risk but I couldn't wait any longer. I succeeded in finding a connection and was very cautious in covering all traces. The day I finished my preparations, I told my neighbor and my guard that I was going to attend a birthday party and that I would remain there all night. That's how I succeeded in leaving Sarajevo. I will never forget how scared I was that night. A Moslem man led me through one part of the no-man's-land and I had to cross the other part alone, not know-ing if the field was mined, where the guards were, would they fire without asking, etc.

Fear in refuge, related to family care in refuge

Even in refuge, women remain anxious and in suspense about the situation of their relatives. They are frequently anxious about fam-ily members who remain in the war zone. The consequences of this particular kind of fear take the form of depression, anxious moods, restlessness and hopelessness.

Thus, Gordana talked about her concern about her parents, who had remained behind.

> The twenty days that preceded the fall of the village of Tasovčići were the worst time in my life. My parents lived in a house on the right bank of the Neretva and were therefore heavily exposed. I was

feeling completely hopeless; seventeen local residents were arrested and killed...Therefore, I was incredibly relieved when I came to know that they had gotten out of the city and thus avoided being massacred...Mother wore a torn dress; she had two teeth missing and her hair was long and twisted, while Daddy was completely exhausted. He had pneumonia and was sweating heavily. Mother dressed him in her clothes and I was completely shocked when I saw them.

Jelena left the town of Čapljina when the war began but was constantly concerned about her parents, who had remained in the village of Tasovčići. Emina's parents as well remained in Mostar when she left for refuge together with her children, and she was very concerned about the destiny of her mother and sister.

Notes

1 Former leader of the Bosnian branch of the Serbian Democratic Party and wartime leader of Bosnian Serbs, who presently stands accused of war crimes.
2 The Thompson submachine gun and the AK–47, an automatic gun of Soviet production.
3 A highly insulting term for Moslem women.
4 The vast majority of Serbian family names end in "*ić.*"
5 "A bowed stringed musical instrument found in the Balkans, usually having only a single string, and used chiefly to accompany and support the chanting of the epic poems of the southern Slavs," *The Oxford English Dictionary,* CD, Second Edition.

CHAPTER 8

Separation and dissolution of the family

NATAŠA MRVIĆ-PETROVIĆ

Generally speaking, apart from the immediate physical, sexual and psychic violence that women in wartime are exposed to, wartime violence also implies the murder of close relatives, separation from other members of the family, impoverishment, forcible emigration and the loss of home, property and regular income (El Bushra, Lopez, 1993). War and the accompanying conflict affects women in a multitude of ways; it immediately endangers their physical and psychic integrity while temporarily or irretrievably severing their marriage and family ties, disturbing their status as members of a broader social community. Although the female experience of war is a very complex one, we have limited ourselves in this chapter to explaining the influence of disturbed family integrity on the psychic state of women. In the following chapter we will study the ways through which in refuge the changed family structure affects the family role of women, and influences their relationships with the children and elderly who share refuge with them.

One of the characteristics of traditional, culturally transmitted, female values, determined by gender-specific socialization, is that women, differently from men, show a greater concern for the lives and welfare of their close relatives and friends. This difference between sexes is accentuated in wartime, as demonstrated by surveys of refugee camps in Mozambique, Zambia and Latin America. It was shown that women were more preoccupied with family care and their relations with children and husbands. Men were most concerned with some external factors, such as the lack of information about the development of the war (El Bushra, Lopez, 1993). In Yugoslav society, women were not exclusively reduced to the roles of wives and mothers. However, it did appear that separation from family members or the loss of such (especially the husband) in wartime produced not only suffering but also a change of women's social status or even a crisis or loss of identity. Deprived of male protection (especially the protection of a father or husband), women became a marginal social group which could only with great difficulty affirm itself in the new social environment (Lerner, 1986).

Suffering caused by separation from family members
"There's no life without joy of life"

Usually, the outbreak of hostilities separates male and female members of a family. Men (fathers, brothers, husbands and sons) are mobilized or assigned various work duties, while women with children leave the region affected by war. However, the sudden outbreak of civil war in Yugoslavia prevented citizens from preparing themselves appropriately for the approaching war; people were in a state of shock, which is always the first reaction to a situation of mass disaster (Kaličanin, Lečić-Toševski, 1994). The dominant opinion (especially in Bosnia-Herzegovina) was that the conflict would last only several days and that it would not spread into many regions (especially not to Sarajevo, a multiethnic city). Thus families temporarily evacuated some women and children to safer areas, while men, employed women and old people remained in order to preserve their apartments, houses and workplaces. However, as the war advanced, it turned out that civilians were by no means safe, even when they were completely loyal to the new authorities in the regions affected by war. Family members who remained in the war-affected regions in order to safeguard their property, or those who planned a later evacuation, became victims of the violence of war, including loss of life or property.

Very few families, like Anka's or Biserka's, could move to the Federal Republic of Yugoslavia[1] in an organized manner. In Anka's case, the comrades of her husband, who had lost his life in the war, helped Anka and her children to move out of Bosnia with all her furniture and movable property. In the second case, Biserka, who was a member of SDS[2], conceded her property to the government of Bosnian Serbs and thus made it possible to transfer her family into the Federal Republic of Yugoslavia, together with her movable property.

Far more frequent were the cases in which women with children (Sofija, Ana, Snežana, Vesna, Stana, Borjana and Nada) left their homes thinking that the war would last only several days. The solution, accepted as a temporary one, and efficient from the standpoint of protecting the children, turned out to be very rational. These women thus escaped the destiny of their husbands or other women who did not move out and who remained a national minority in the regions affected by war. However, the development of war meant that the length of separation was uncertain. This burdened women with fear for their loved ones, while giving them a feeling of culpability and guilt because they had not remained with them.

These emotions, in fact, reflect socialized values, according to which family care, and even caring for the husband, should take priority over a woman's care for herself. A typical example of similar thinking was provided by Olivera. "I can't forgive myself for leaving with the children. You know, I was taught to be always by my husband's side. I thought, 'What would happen if he has to go to fight and then gets killed? Would my children tell me that I had left and let him manage everything alone and get killed?'"

Women refugees experienced serious traumas provoked by separation from their loved ones. They were not only faced with their own individual problems but also burdened by the thought that everything and everybody dear to them had remained in the war-affected regions, thus they were unable to adapt quickly to poverty and refuge. Moreover, an initially warm welcome offered by relatives and friends frequently turned cold. In addition, women refugees were often incorrectly treated by Red Cross personnel and other government agents charged with refugee care. Especially less emancipated women, who had built their identities as "somebody's wife" and who had accepted that their fathers and husbands would decide for them, found it difficult to deal with the new situation. They frequently became withdrawn and experienced serious emotional troubles. This is confirmed by Nada, a widow with two children. "The majority of the women refugees that I know are depressed and keep telling themselves that they can't do anything without their husbands. My sister-in-law, for example, said the following when I told her that my husband had been killed. 'God forbid that anything similar should happen to me! What could I do alone, with these two children?'"

This kind of separation was particularly hard for women from so-called mixed marriages. Their own ethnic affiliation could be a source of trouble in the new environment, no matter how much loyalty they showed towards their husbands' nationality. They "betrayed" their nation without gaining a place among compatriots of their husbands. Cut off from support in the new surroundings, they oriented themselves exclusively towards the emotional exchange within their nuclear families. Separation or the loss of husbands and/or children represented for these women an additional source of anxiety, depressive or even psychotic disorders.

Emina, a Moslem woman in refuge from Mostar, explains.

I lost 17 kilos, in few weeks. My eyes are constantly filled with tears, and I can cry anytime. I loved my husband too much, he remained there, there were no letters from him. My sister was in Macedonia with two children and she returned to Mostar, where she was arrested in the Croatian part of the city. I cursed the day when I came here, but then I began thinking about the child and I realized it was better this way...I suffer a lot because of my sister and mother. I am so burdened with care for my sister—will somebody kill her? What could they do to the children?

The absence of news
"A letter means hope"

Fear for the fate of family members is amplified by the absence of reliable news about their lives and living conditions. Women in particular are distressed by their passive condition and their incapacity to help their dear ones. They are often torn between the need to remain with those who stayed in the region affected by war and the need to remain in refuge in order to secure the future of their children or to provide care for sick and weak members of the family.

MERIMA: "In fact, all the time I dreamed about returning. I was born in Sarajevo, my roots are there. That's why I had, and I still have, a sentiment of guilt. However, I have a hope that we will be back together again. On the other hand, I saved my children from shelling."

SNEŽANA: "I haven't seen my husband for two years. There's no way of seeing him. He can't come here, because they won't let him go, fearing that he might desert. I wanted to go there to see him, but as there was heavy fighting going on, he refused. On the other hand, how could I leave my children?"

Olivera and Svetlana, who had been separated from their children for more than two years, revealed the suffering and strong guilt felt by mothers who had decided to stay in the town.

OLIVERA: Separation from the children was the toughest thing for me in this war. I couldn't stand any longer to be without them. The last month I only vegetated...I went to see the doctor in order to get permission to leave Sarajevo. I told him I couldn't stand it anymore...I said I would commit suicide, because the sorrow for my children tore me apart. I think they blame me now, because they had to live so long without parents, alone. They don't blame the father, because it was me who always decided about everything in the family; they think that I should have persuaded him to leave Sarajevo immediately, all together. They don't say it, but I feel it, and I feel very bad about it.

SVETLANA: I always cried when I received a letter from my children. They suffered. I felt guilty for making them go, for not joining them. When you realize that you have committed a crime against your children, you also realize that you can't change anything. At the beginning you think that it will not last long, and that it's better to stay in order to preserve your apartment and property for your children. I knew that in the material sense they were well cared for but their suffering represented for me a special, additional suffering. ADRA[3] was really a light at the end of the tunnel—not only because of packages, but more because of letters. Separation from my children was for me worse than the war itself—that uneasiness, the fear that something might have happened to them. I interpreted every word in their letters.

Concern for children dominates; regardless of the age of the mother or child, the suffering of mothers is equal. Especially affected were those women whose sons remained in danger: as civilians doing their jobs, as members of a minority in enemy-controlled territory, or as forced recruits.

VUKOSAVA: My older son (an economist) remained with his wife (a Croat woman) in the Moslem part of Sarajevo. He is 43. I am very concerned about him. He's not very resourceful and he was surely assigned work-duty. Without his wife, he would have been lost, because he does not know how to lie and wriggle out, and besides, he is a Serb...I can't decide to go to Sarajevo, I think I'd rather die than see him sick or wounded. Sometimes, I hear from him through amateur radio operators, but then again, their messages are censored.

NATALIJA: I feared so much for my son who remained with his wife in the Moslem part of Sarajevo...We have not had any news from them since May. We did not even know if he had been taken into a camp...Thus, even when we were hungry and while we were waiting for the children to come out of the city, I saved a salami and a bottle of *šljivovica*,[4] to celebrate when they come out. I was so superstitious; I believed if I opened it something bad would happen to them, if I preserved it then everything would be alright.

Mothers who had female children were particularly anguished by rumors about young girls being raped in the city and abducted for brothels. As we have seen, that was a decisive factor for Olivera and Svetlana when choosing to send their daughters away from the besieged city.

The kind of suffering we have elaborated was especially accentuated when a woman felt insecure in her new environment because of her nationality. In such conditions she could not openly seek information but had to rely instead on radio and TV news, as well as on unreliable information obtained through friends and relatives. This is well illustrated by Jelena's[5] account.

> At that time, approximately, Tasovčići fell. My region was constantly portrayed on the Croatian TV as chetniks' country. Then I began having terrible fear for my kinfolk. My parents are old. I knew that my father and uncle would never leave their homes. My mother is ill and has been bed-ridden for seven years already. I thought that they should leave by all means. A cousin told me that they all had moved out. I couldn't believe...I thought that she did not want to tell me the truth, because I was pregnant. It was really a terrible feeling.

If a husband disappeared in war and nobody knew if he had been killed or not, the situation was further complicated for the woman, who was thus not legally widowed. She could not remarry or claim her welfare rights as a widow (Vickers, 1993). The situation was especially involved when the missing person (a husband or son) was of a different nationality. In that case a woman could not get any reliable information since communications were severed, and contacts with remaining relatives rendered more difficult.

> NEDŽADA: My husband remained in Brčko, to safeguard the house. I know that he was not in the Army of Bosnia-Herzegovina, because I contacted the Red Cross and UNPROFOR[6] and they told me that they had no information about him (they would know something if he had been taken prisoner). All the agencies that I contacted told me that they knew nothing about him. My father-in-law, who is a refugee in Croatia and who knew better than me the situation in

Brčko, sent me a message indirectly, saying that I should abandon hope that my husband is still alive. I don't know if they have some more reliable information about his fate; they only know that he disappeared and think that he has been killed. One thing is certain— it is already two years since anyone had any news from him, neither me here, nor his cousins in refuge in Croatia or abroad. The situation is further complicated by the fact that we are Moslem refugees, me here and others in Croatia, so that we can't directly phone each other and they can't send me an unambiguous message about his destiny.[7]

A lack of information and the impossibility of offering help to close relatives who remained in regions affected by war are a characteristic source of stress for all refugee women.

NATALIJA: "My daughter-in-law is very concerned about her parents, about whom she has had no information at all. Sometimes, as we sat down to dinner, she would start to cry, 'Look, I have everything here, while they in Sarajevo are surely starving to death. How could I eat peacefully when I know that they are lacking everything there?' My son told me that she's a little better now, because Sarajevo can be reached now by telephone from foreign countries, and she can hear her parents from time to time."

> MERIMA: All my relatives remained there, my sister, two brothers, my husband...I was terribly anguished for them. One day, I received the list of the people killed in Markale market. I did not dare to look at it. Finally I did and I was incredibly relieved when I saw that none of them were there. Then I began fearing that they might have been wounded, perhaps. I had to live all that, and there was nothing I could do to help them. In fact, I satisfied my need to help by sending them packages, medications, letters, words of support and by encouraging them to persevere.

NELA: "I could hardly face the fact that my dear ones remained in Sarajevo, in the part of the city under Moslem control. When my father died I had a nervous breakdown. I felt terrible because I was not there, to help him in his last days and to bury him. Since my mother and sister have left the city I feel much better."

Suffering caused by separation from the family was related to the destruction of a lifestyle which implied almost daily contacts and very close relations between parents and their grown-up children. Ana and Vesna, for example, pointed out that they missed their sisters, who had always lived with their families in the same city, and with whom they maintained regular contact. Nataša, Ana's sister, said the following in one of her touching letters that she sent from Mostar to her mother and sister in refuge. "Here I am, crying all the time because I'm especially sad today. It's my birthday, I'm 30 now and I say to B., 'Now my mother and sister would drop by for a coffee.' I can't explain to you how bad I feel. I'm here alone, everything that I have is here, luckily I also have my B., but that's not it. That's why I beg you to return as soon as possible."

In another letter she adds "The toughest thing for me is that you are not here...I stayed here because of B., and sometimes I get angry at him. Then I think, 'Poor is the one who does not have anybody close.' Simply, you don't have anybody to confess to. Only now I feel how much I miss you...I would be delighted if I could hear you over the phone."

Apart from their own suffering, women are additionally burdened by the thought that their husbands or children also suffer from forced separation and that they cannot help them at all. Metka describes the moment when she met her husband again after thirty-six months of separation. "He cried the whole night. He constantly demanded to see the pictures of our daughter, whom he had not seen for two years. I had the impression that he suffered terribly because he had been separated from our daughter."

Merima and Natalija had similar experiences.

MERIMA: "My husband is alone there and the loneliness kills him. He has not seen our children for two years, and they did not see him either. Then I sent him photographs so that he could see how much they grew up."

NATALIJA: "My husband is very ill and he suffers because our sons are not with us. He spends weekends by the telephone, hoping that they will call. He doesn't want to live anymore, he only hopes that he will die in their arms."

Disorder in the functioning of marriage and family relations

A long forced separation from family members ends up gradually producing a loss of optimism about marriage (Borjana, Tamara, Metka).

War and ethnic conflicts have put "mixed marriages" to the test. Even when families were not separated, the intensification of inter-ethnic intolerance could work to deteriorate significantly the relationship between a woman and her husband's relatives of a different nationality. Nataša wrote a melancholy letter during the time when the remaining Moslems were driven from the city of Mostar (during heavy fighting between Croats and Moslems). "I'm by no means surprised that there are so many divorces in mixed marriages. When times get tough, nobody wants to support the relatives of the other nationality."

The power dynamics within a family change when one of the members (usually the wife or a daughter-in-law) becomes completely dependent on the husband or his relatives because of evacuation or some such contingency. In similar situations even close relatives feel the need to demonstrate their power over the woman, who is "the first refugee," unprotected and without economic power. It is especially interesting that such behavior is characteristic of husbands and relatives who were originally from Serbia and who succeeded in finding a steady job. Marital relations become more and more disturbed and they "drift" towards the increasing mistreatment of the woman, who is not able to respond actively to exploitation and psychological abuse. Thus Sofija said, "My sister is here, in Belgrade, and she lives with her mother-in-law who came to safeguard the apartment of a cousin. They are making problems for her. She goes off to a village near Zrenjanin where she works as a hairdresser. She spends only weekends at home. She's completely in charge of two children, her mother-in-law and her husband...She's my special problem. On one side, I have my problem, on the other side, I have her problem."

Borjana speaks about the following situation:

> My friend married a man who is ten years older than her. They are both Serbs, refugees, here in Serbia. He works, she doesn't. She says that he annoys her very much. He compares her with the singer Lepa Brena,[8] and says she's not worth [the singer's] little finger. He's nervous when everything is not ready for him. Once, he said to her, "What would you like? It's me who buys you food and tobacco!" She excuses him by his illness. Even the child suffers. He behaves as if everything belongs to him, because he works, and he doesn't give her money even for the hairdresser. She says she can't recognize herself, because she looks so bad. She worked before, but she's now dependent on him, because it's him who's the breadwinner.

Parents are additionally burdened by the fear that their forcibly separated children may become distant to each other, or even to them. This anxiety is clearly and poignantly shown in a letter that Nataša's mother wrote to her other daughter, a refugee. "I would be happiest if you could come home, and this is dangerous and impossible now. But that day will come, although every day spent without you is like a year...Your sister also suffers because of you and your children, since, besides me, you two do not have anybody closer, and she has not forgotten you. She misses you terribly, because she doesn't have anybody closer than you and your children, especially in similar conditions."

Biserka's older son emigrated to Slovenia after being wounded and treated in hospital, while her younger son remained with her. She was also afraid that her sons might become strangers to each other, especially because there was a considerable age difference between them, which provoked strong feelings of jealousy. She said, "It happened already that the older son phoned and the younger one would pick up the phone and simply hand it over to me. Then A. said, 'What's happening with M.? Did he forget me?'"

A long separation between family members inevitably leads to some estrangement, either between spouses or between siblings and parents. When they finally see each other again, it usually becomes clear that this separation and exposure to different events has left traces, and that the re-establishment of the previous emotional closeness will take some time. For example, Olivera said, "I'm now with them...Thus, after thirty-six months of separation, my daughters got a ruined mother while I got two grown-up daughters. They got used to living without me; they have organized their life alone and my older daughter has taken over my role. We need a lot of time to bridge the gap that stands between us."

Women who were separated from their husbands for long periods (Merima, Borjana, Metka) were quite conscious of the possible emotional changes between spouses, and they feared for the future of their marriages. Metka's account, for example, reveals doubts about the future of her married life, in spite of their emotional closeness. Her Moslem husband does not want to quit Sarajevo. She lived with their child, separate from him, in the Serb part of the city. Metka thought that they should leave the city together and go live somewhere else. Metka saw her husband in August of 1994, after thirty-six months of separation.

> When I started to undress in order to go to bed, I asked my husband to turn off the light, because I felt like I was undressing in front of an unknown man. I felt a need to be courted again by my husband in order to gradually get close to him again[9]...He proposed that I return to him, with our daughter, and continue to live together. I said it would be best to go to some third place and start a new life. We both agreed to think it all over again. The next day, when I was

about to return to Grbavica, all his cousins were surprised. They asked me, "What are you going to do there, with chetniks?"...As to the future of my marriage, I began asking myself two questions: first, "Do I have the right to prevent the father from seeing his child?" and second, "Do I have the right to ruin my life by returning to that hell there, in order to preserve my marriage?"

Unlike Metka, who was unsure about the future and the destiny of her marriage, Tamara firmly decided that she would never return to Knin, which she and her children had left in 1991. "I don't know what I feel anymore—between me and my husband life has created a huge gap. I can't return to Knin and he can't come here. I don't feel anything special about Knin. I lived there only two years. I can't go back there; many people have been killed. My child can't live there."

However, some special circumstances, such as domestic violence, can be a crucial factor for a woman refugee deciding whether to quit a dissatisfying marriage in which she has been victimized. Thus Nedeljka, a housewife and 42-year old mother of two children, from the village of Bradina, near Konjic, decided in refuge to leave her husband with whom she had lived for nineteen years. He had been abusing her for years, and was a chronic alcoholic and idler. The experiences acquired in war and refuge made her feel like "another" woman. Having successfully coped with new duties and responsibilities, she became aware of her own capabilities. She became alive to the possibility of starting a new life and taking care of her children alone, without her violent husband.

The experience of the loss of close family members
"Nothing could be compared with the loss of someone close"

The loss of a family member is one of the most traumatic experiences of women in war. In the majority of cases, women were not immediate witnesses of these events. However, continual apprehension about the fate of a husband, children and parents, uncertainty about their destiny and finally the loss of a loved person provoke not only immediate but also retrospective neurotic and anxiety disorders.

The loss of her husband can be the crucial reason why a woman decides to leave her former home (Anka). This is a typical example of the desire to "burn your bridges."[10]

However, it was more frequently the case that women first left and only later came to know about the death of their husbands or other family members who had remained in the regions affected by war. Thus, in a sense, they benefited; they were spared from witnessing the sufferings of their dear ones, especially when murders were combined with torture and mutilation. Nevertheless, in similar cases, pain provoked by the loss was usually only exacerbated by details of a death they came to know of later.

STANA: "I felt really bad when I heard my sister-in-law asking her son-in-law (who is a Moslem, in the Green Berets) about the fate of my husband. By that time, my husband was so tortured that he was covered in wounds. The Moslem relative said that my husband was fine. 'He's in perfect condition,' he said. We were really glad about the news. We were waiting for some exchange of war prisoners and one day we heard that he had been killed. Nobody even knows the place of his grave."

If a woman experiences the loss of several close relatives in a short period of time, later losses affect her more than the first one, with which she seems to cope quite well. Suzana, Nadežda, Dragica and Sofija had similar experiences. They are women of different ages but they were all very close to their male relatives (especially to their brothers).

Thus Suzana said,

In June of 1992, after a skirmish with Moslems near Vrace, my husband disappeared...I don't know the details about my husband's death. He simply disappeared while he was on guard. I heard various rumors about his being captured or seen here and there, but until the present day he hasn't appeared. I'm sure he's dead. That's why I was only more bereaved by the news of my brother's death. He was shot and killed, on the front line, a year ago. He was the only brother I had; he was the youngest child in our family, still unmarried. A sniper shot him right through the heart, as he was about to enter the trench. I don't know why that event hit me so hard—probably I could never imagine that he might be killed.

Nadežda had a similar story. "I felt a terrible pain when I heard that my brother had been killed. He was in the Serb army. He stepped on a mine while going to bring water supplies. I lost several cousins in the war, but the death of my brother was the hardest thing for me to live through."

The pain women feel, caused by the loss of a loved relative, is only exacerbated by witnessing the suffering of their children and grandchildren who miss their fathers. In similar situations, women are expected to hide their emotions, and to conceal the very fact of death. Munevera speaks about the desire of her granddaughter to see her father.

> She was very close to her father. She's 5 or 6 now, and she has not seen him for two years. She constantly keeps asking about him. She says, "When is dad going to come home, to see how tall I grew?" She suffers terribly because of him. We tried to calm her down in various ways. There was a man who used to come to our house and I even told her that the man was her father. I wanted her to become close to him, but the girl immediately realized that I was lying. What afflicts me most is the idea that she doesn't even know that he has been killed and we don't even dare to tell her the truth.

Similarly to divorce, after the loss of husbands women experience strong feelings of guilt for having left them behind. Nada, a 35-year-old widow with two children who left the war region in 1992, said the following about her life as a widow: "My husband remained there, because he thought that the mess would not last more than a month and that it would be senseless to leave his country. Now I feel guilty for not persuading him to go with me, but, way back then, I didn't believe it would turn out this way. That's why I don't understand the women who feel guilty because their husbands are now together with them in refuge."

For the women who drew considerable strength from their emotional attachment to their (now separated) husbands, the death of the husband represents a real turning point in life.

SOFIJA: "Regardless of the fact that my husband was far from me, in the Moslem part of the country, I felt much more self-confident while he was alive. A letter means hope; it gives sense to life, it gives me strength. If I did not have my child I would not have had any meaning in life."

Apart from representing a change of family status and an irreparable emotional loss, the death of a husband also entails the loss of the husband's real or imaginary support. Women realize that they must rely on their own resources, and that they must manage all alone in order to secure the welfare of their children. Although the death of husbands only aggravates their overall life situation, they must find enough strength to face the difficulties of widowhood. The best advice to women was given by a young war-widow with two children, Nada, who managed to surmount her grief and adopt an active stance towards her life, said the following:

> In fact, we women rule the world. We give strength and guide the acts of men, although they play the role of bosses. Since the opinion of others is so important for them, they pretend to be the ones who are in control, who make decisions. In fact, women make the decisions even when they live with husbands, but they keep telling themselves that the truth is different, that the truth is the image of roles in marriage offered to the world, because men think that they are the ones who have to have power. Well, let them have it, if they are so keen on it. We women have a different role. Women are not usually conscious of it. They have to understand that they are strong enough and that decision making and guidance of our lives are not essentially affected by the absence of men, because, in the essence, we are those who decide, although we keep persuading ourselves that the image offered to the world is the reality.

Notes

1 Serbia and Montenegro.
2 *Srpska Demokratska Stranka* (Serbian Democratic Party) was the most popular party of Bosnian and Croatian Serbs in the period 1991–95.
3 A humanitarian organization of the Adventist Church.
4 *Šljivovica*, plum brandy, also known as *slivovitz*.
5 Jelena, a 27-year-old Serb woman, spent her first months as a refugee on the island of Brač (Croatia), where she shared refuge with other people from her region, mostly Croats and Moslems. She was pregnant, and her husband (child of a Croat mother and Serb father) remained in Mostar. Apart from her concern for her husband (who was arrested and interrogated several times), she feared for her own security because other refugees from her collective shelter knew that she was a Serb, although she declared herself a Croat in order to avoid possible harassment. Apart from that, she had no information at all about her parents, who remained in Tasovčići.
6 The United Nations Protection Force, the UN peacekeeping force in the former Yugoslavia.
7 Smiljka's case is somewhat similar to Jelena's (see 5). She is a Montenegrin, a widow, 45 years old, who had been married to a Moslem. He came to the Federal Republic of Yugoslavia as soon as war in Bosnia began. However, her son was abducted from the Belgrade-Bar train, together with a dozen Moslem passengers. In spite of an official investigation by republic and federal agencies, nothing is known about the fate of the passengers, although the event happened more than two years ago.

8 A Serbian version of Dolly Parton.

9 Marian Shelton, whose husband died in Laos in 1965, expressed herself with almost identical words. After ten months of separation, her husband seemed like a stranger to her. He appeared different from the man she remembered and he behaved like a stranger. She simply could not get used to the fact that this man, who had become a stranger to her, had a right to make love to her, just because he was her legal husband (Hayton-Keeva, 1987).

10 Psychologically, Olivera's case is somewhat similar, because she decided to join her children in refuge only after her marriage broke down.

CHAPTER 9

Life in refuge—changes in socioeconomic and familial status

"It's not easy, neither for those who come nor for those who receive them."

NATAŠA MRVIĆ-PETROVIĆ AND IVANA STEVANOVIĆ

Life in refuge brings women into a situation where they have to care for themselves and their children without any support from their husbands, who most often remain in the regions affected by war, or have been killed. A forced separation from a husband, or his loss, not only changes relationships in the family but also directly affects the role of the woman; she becomes "the head of the family," charged with caring for the remaining family members. Unlike similar examples from other wars—in Vietnam, Uganda, Cambodia, Mozambique, Somalia (Vickers, 1993; El Bushra, Lopez, 1993)—where armed conflicts produced significant changes in the economic role of women, in the case of the Yugoslav civil war women refugees were already economically emancipated and independent from their husbands even before the outbreak of war. This, however, does not mean that their position was enviable. The loss of a job and a regular source of income forces women to accept inadequate jobs in order to survive. Or, in other words, the gap between their previous and current status is so wide that it is hard to overcome it, regardless of the fact that women are already accustomed to working and caring for the family. In refuge, they often bear a heavier burden of physical work, to which they are not accustomed. In addition, their education and previous experience turn out to be insufficient for finding a suitable job in their field in the country of asylum, itself faced with an economic crisis and growing unemployment.

The absence of a more significant social support system for the social adaptation of refugees forces women to be responsible for improving existing conditions of life. These situations produce a widespread impoverishment of women refugees, to which they respond in various ways: by smuggling, by working in the "black market," by selling a part of their humanitarian aid or even by prostitution. Even if they succeed in finding employment, these jobs are usually precarious—temporary, unofficial, without social benefits and with insufficient and irregular incomes. Moreover, in such working conditions women are frequently exposed to mistreatment and exploitation. Therefore, attempts to integrate into the new environment bring women into a position where they can easily become victims of subtle forms of violence and exploitation which they must accept in order to secure the essential conditions for life.

Changes in the family role of women

There is a preponderance of incomplete families among refugee families. These families differ among themselves in their formation. The absence of the husband or father is very frequent. The absence can be permanent, due to the death of a husband or father, in which case we can speak of permanently incomplete families. On the other hand, there are temporarily incomplete families, created through the absence of a father or husband who is participating in war or who has become a refugee in some other country (Piorkowska, Petrovič, 1993, p. 133). A temporarily incomplete family can also be produced by separation between parents and children sent to a safe place for reasons of security.

The war in the former Yugoslavia especially separated mothers and children from their husbands and fathers. Data gathered by the Institute for Pedagogical Research in its survey of family status (which included 370 parents, mainly refugee mothers) also confirmed that the majority of refugee families are incomplete, most frequently due to the absence of the father. According to this survey, 92% of the respondents lived in complete families before becoming refugees. In refuge, this percentage fell to 50%. In 80% of the cases, incomplete families were caused by the absence of the father. Only in 8% was the mother absent. In 12%, families were considered incomplete due to the absence of some other member of the family (Joksimović, Milanović-Nahod, 1994, p. 32).

Changes within incomplete refugee families alter the woman's role in the family, especially in terms of economic roles (El Bushra, Lopez, 1993). Such a fate befell many of the women that we interviewed. They became "heads of households," regardless of their current marital status, charged with caring for the children and the sick. Most (forty) of our female respondents were married; the rest were widows (thirteen), divorced (two) or single (fifteen). Out of forty married women, only fourteen lived in a complete nuclear family in refuge. Twenty-two of them were alone with children, and they were forced to accept the role of sole breadwinner and protector of the family in refuge. Widows faced an especially difficult situation; ten of our respondents lost husbands in this war.

The death of a father or husband provokes especially serious and violent emotional reactions in women and children. Shock and disbelief are the first reactions to the news of a husband's or father's death. Mothers and children who have lost their husbands and fathers face increasing difficulties in their everyday tasks, and they react to the loss with anger and sorrow. This process usually ends with the eventual acceptance of this grief.

These symptoms aside, children often experience various physical and psychic troubles. The most frequent symptoms are sorrow and depression, fear of separation, withdrawal and hypersensitivity. Boys seem to suffer more when losing their fathers than do girls. The loss of a father means the loss of the role-model, a situation which can produce emotional and intellectual development disorders. The loss also produces various pedagogical problems. The woman, deprived of support herself, is faced with the problem of educating her children in harsh conditions. As Sofija said,

> Everything is easier when people are together. My husband and father were killed in this war. I have no place to go. I have no strength, even for my child. When you don't have any support the burden gets too heavy. The child keeps saying, "My father and grandfather are dead." That's all his life. What's left of his life?...I'm exploited in my workplace. Besides, my child demands devotion and care and I don't have strength. We are three families here, sharing the same room. I would like to have some peace, to live alone. The child has to start school but he doesn't have space to do homework. My husband was a Moslem and that's why I can't get anything from the funds for the children whose parents were killed in the war.

The previous example demonstrates that a mother cares for more than the strictly essential needs of her family—she strives to provide decent conditions for schooling and normal life. In the conditions of total impoverishment, the problem of supplying essential school material often seems insoluble.[1] Thus Nedžada said, "My daughter has to do tests in order to start school this autumn, but

I can't afford that. I don't have the money to buy her books and everything that is needed. I don't know what to do."

However, the need to educate children and the wish to offer them a better life sometimes motivates women to adapt to the new surroundings by any means possible, and to find a strength in that self-sacrifice. Some respondents (Merima, Goca, Emina) said that in their moments of deepest despair the thought of their children prevented them from committing suicide. The wish to see their families reunited one day, and to provide for their children as best they can, is the source of energy that kept many of the women going in refuge (Merima, Emina, Vesna, Gorica, Sofija, Nada). Merima spoke about that. "Without hope I would have been lost. My first source of hope is my children. I live for them, I want to offer them a good life, as much as I can, because they don't deserve to live this way. On the other hand, I have a hope that one day we will reunite. The main source of suffering in this war was the separation of families. Many people have been killed. In fact, mixed marriages were most affected."

Incomplete refugee families are inevitably changed from within. Frequently, lonely and insecure mothers increasingly rely on their children. In addition, they tend to over-control and restrict them. The acceptance of a child as an equal member of the family encourages him/her to mature, while, on the other hand, over-control thwarts his/her emancipation and adaptation capabilities in the new surroundings. Similar behavior leads to the child's isolation within the circle of the family, and in extreme cases, it can produce complete social isolation (Piorkowska, Petrović, 1993, p. 141).

There is another problem, that of insufficiently independent mothers who are suddenly thrust into new roles in refuge. They are required to face alone numerous existential and psychological problems. Refugee mothers are often nervous, depressed and tearful. They feel lonely, powerless and completely useless (Piorkowska, Petrović, 1993, p. 142). These women had always been taken care of. "First it was father, and then the role was taken over by husband or father-in-law," said Vesna. In her own opinion, she had never grown accustomed to taking care of herself and her family, so that, in a way, she was angry at her husband for leaving her to manage all alone.

The new role of the woman as family protector, apart from implying caring for herself and her children, also contains an additional problem in the situation of her elderly and ill parents. Gordana, Gorica and Borjana were in a similar situation. As Gorica said,

Right before the outbreak of hostilities I said to my mother, "Mom, you should go away, there's nothing for you here. Don't let me worry about you if I already have to worry about my family. You don't have to worry, you have a place to go." And she went off. However, when I came I saw that my brother-in-law was about to get her out of the house...Then I went to Kikinda, because my mother told me to find her a place in a home for the aged. I found it. They were charging 120 DM per month for room and board. I couldn't afford it so I took Mom with me and brought her into the house of my brother-in-law. Then, there we were, me in refuge, my mother sharing refuge with me. She did not become senile although she grew childish. If I prepared, for example, pancakes for the children, she would say, "But that's alright, a child is more important than a mother." She drove me mad.

Although caring for elderly parents represents an additional burden, it usually represents an additional encouragement for women if they are accompanied by a relative when they must deal with the painful experience of refuge and try to find their own place in the new social milieu. For example, Borjana said that her mother had helped her a lot when Borjana was ostracized by her colleagues at work simply because of her refugee status. "My mother accepts everything with a stoical peace of mind; she doesn't come out at all, she keeps herself busy, she crochets, for example, and thus finds an amusement. Sometimes, she goes off to visit my father in Vukovar."

It is apparent that women refugees are worried not only for the present but also for the future. They must learn to become self-reliant; they are the only ones who, in the new environment, must provide essentials for themselves, their children and their elderly parents.

Impoverishment
"The whole of my life was packed in a bag"

A sudden impoverishment is a general problem that women refugees are faced with. The need to escape the approaching war and evacuate children to a safe place required very quick, and often secret, preparations to leave. This meant that the majority of women could not bring anything with them, except clothes and, perhaps, savings. Such were the experiences of the women who left their homes in the period between April and June 1992, immediately after the outbreak of the first hostilities in Bosnia-Herzegovina. Caught by the new situation and cut off from their homes, they could not return. From temporary guests at their relatives' and friends' homes, they soon became true refugees.

The experiences of other women who left besieged towns in Herzegovina and central Bosnia, from the end of 1993 to the beginning of 1994, are even more tragic. It is clear that saving their own lives and the lives of their children was the main motive for deserting their homes; the transfer of property was simply unimaginable. Olga quit Mostar illegally with her two juvenile daughters, and without any of her belongings, after being expelled from her apartment by the HOS. Stana's experience was similar; she simply walked out with her daughter from the besieged town of Hrasnica (which has a predominantly Moslem population). She took only a shopping bag and her wallet, pretending that she was off for shopping. Having walked for twenty-two kilometers, Nedeljka succeeded in reaching the Serb-controlled region with her two daughters. She said that she passed the barricades easily because, as she discovered later, she looked like a Croat woman from her village who worked in the local grocery shop. Jelena, a 21-year-old refugee from Čapljina who was pregnant at the time, got out of the besieged city accidentally with a Moslem woman from her neighborhood, after trying several times to flee the city. She said, simply, "I took my husband's jacket and a blanket and tried with her to get away for several days."

The danger of being exposed to immediate war operations made women refugees leave their homes with the most elementary belongings to bring with them to shelters and refuge. All the women's stories were very similar. Jana, who by pure chance escaped the massacre in her village of Sijekovac in March 1992[2], decided right after that event to leave for Belgrade. All she had was a plastic bag with clothes and a half loaf of bread. Zorica, a 19-year-old student, was also lucky to escape the massacre of Serbian civilians in the village of Čemerno, in October 1992. Her house was burned down, and she left for refuge with her mother and brother. All she had was a bag with the most necessary belongings. Vera from Tasovčići, a 64-year-old housewife, went off to a shelter. She intended to stay at home, but as the Croatian paramilitary units invaded her village she had to leave her house, separately from her husband. His fate remained unknown to her. She said, "As the shelling began we went to a shelter. We thought we would stay there only two hours. All I took with me was a plastic bag."

Some women (Gordana, Nela, Vida) who succeeded in leaving the besieged cities with their families spoke about a dramatic escape. They left on the spur of the moment, accidentally and unprepared, passing check-points by pure chance.

Husbands or parents often remained in order to safeguard jobs, apartments, houses and valuable items. As it turned out, the communication breakdown and the siege of cities, combined with the growth of the war into a large-scale conflict between three nations (Serbs, Croats and Moslems), prevented those who had not left immediately from leaving the war area afterwards. The women who decided to stay (alone or with their husbands) in the regions affected by war in order to preserve their property, became impoverished in the war. They either had to spend their savings on food and medication on the black market (Svetlana, Olivera, Stanislava[3]) or their apartments were sacked and/or destroyed (Senka, Olga, Snežana). Moreover, the women who left besieged cities a year or two after the outbreak of the civil war with only temporary permission to leave, could not bring any valuable items with them. Valuables would have been taken away at check-points, apart from creating an air of duplicity about their "temporary" permits. As Olivera said, "I couldn't preserve anything, I left everything behind. I couldn't take anything with me, because I asked permission for two days. That was the only way to leave Sarajevo, although I did not have, and still don't have any intention of returning."

Svetlana had similar experiences:

> We couldn't let our daughters leave with bags, because in that case they would have known that they were about to leave. We sent them off with a bagful of clothes. I think it was the hardest moment in my life...Later on, we also wanted to leave but we didn't know how to do it. We finally succeeded because my husband obtained a certificate that he's mad (he's an invalid), and I could accompany him as his guardian. We were granted a one-year permission to leave: "a displacement from the war zone because of illness."

Leaving a besieged city (illegally or through the Red Cross) was often paid for by a family's last savings. This was the experience of Lepa and Dragica. Dragica, a retired woman from Zenica, could not immediately move out of the town at the beginning of the war, as she was recovering from an operation for breast cancer. Until June 1994, she had been continuously trying to leave the city. She said, "I had a small sum of money and I gave it in order to leave Zenica." Having retired in 1993, Lepa had been attempting throughout to leave Sarajevo legally; she even tried to concede her four-room apartment to the Bosnian state in order to get permission to leave. When everything else failed, she had to find a private "connection" for an illegal exit in September 1994. Marina, who escaped from Tuzla in June 1994 with two children and her husband (who was exchanged as a war-prisoner), said the following about her exit. "When I came to Serbia I couldn't believe that I remained alive with children. Many families had been killed in mine fields during exit."

If somebody, after a long time spent in constant fear and worry, finally succeeded in saving him- or herself, then the exit itself represented a source of joy. It turned out, however, that as a refugee the person would have to invest additional energy in order to surmount new problems, regardless of his or her fatigue and sufferings, and with no essential existential means.

Impoverishment even accompanied the families who succeeded in taking something more than the most essential clothes and savings. It turned out that, in the long run, the value of material property decays in the conditions of refuge. Sometimes this was due to inadequate housing, sometimes it had to be sold at any price in order to secure survival, while sometimes it was lost in transport or stolen by thieves. Mirjana, from Slavonska Požega, sent her child off to Belgrade as early as June 1991, while she herself transferred property piece by piece from time to time. However, the property could not be easily stored in new premises, and that was a problem. Biserka had to sell her furniture and electrical appliances taken from her house in Sarajevo, because her brother-in-law refused to keep them in his garage. In relation to what women had before the war, any saved property was only a "drop in the sea."

Women in refuge are forced to spend their savings and gradually sell the items they took with them, due to certain factors: the loss of regular income, insufficient material help in their new environment and the impossibility of securing a steady job. The result of this is further impoverishment. It was usually the main reason for women to seek accommodation in collective shelters, after previously having lived in rented apartments or with relatives and friends. Thus, Nela said that the deep economic crisis and hyperinflation in 1993 forced them to spend all the savings they had, although her husband worked and they lived in a friend's vacant house, for which they had to pay only regular costs. The friend also gave them clothes and bed linen, yet they had to sell the only valuable item they had (a car) in order to finance the education of their son. Nedžada, her mother, and her sister with two children spent a month in a hotel (paid for by a friend). Later on they had to ask for accommodation in an Islamic community center. The people they got acquainted with in the center gave them mattresses, bed sheets, an electric stove, children's clothing and so on. Thus, only after a certain time did women become conscious of the real dimensions of their tragedy. At that point they often became desperate and resigned; they generally felt that they could not change anything and nobody could say how long their insecure condition would last. Mirjana, for example, said, "This status is worse than fear. There, I feared for my life, I thought that I might be killed. Here, I fear that I won't survive because of insecurity, uncertainty."

Impoverishment affects women in a way which makes them feel incapable of fulfilling obligations which they as mothers and, often, as the only protectors, have towards their children. They experience the situation as their failure to fulfill their role as mothers.

OLIVERA: "I feel terrible because I'm not even capable of providing essentials for myself, let alone for my children, who are expecting that from me, because I had always been able to work and earn and I always knew how to find a way out of every situation. Now I feel helpless and my daughters have to help me to adapt to this new life."

VIDA: "I'm here in refuge with two juvenile children. I felt most terrible last autumn when my son fell ill. He had pharyngitis. He had a high temperature and I couldn't even buy him medication because I didn't have the money. He begged me to buy him only two tablets of antibiotics, and I couldn't help him."

The inability to provide help for dear ones is an additional source of pain and the key factor that can push a woman to accept almost any offer in order to earn some money.

Aggravated conditions of life

Housing. The majority of the women we talked with (thirty-four, in total) were accommodated in various collective shelters in Bogovađa, Niš and Belgrade. The rest lived in the houses of relatives, in rented apartments or in rooms that were allocated to them as emergency shelters. A certain number of women were interviewed on other premises, in the regions affected by war.

Although there were individual differences in opinion about the quality of accommodation in collective shelters, negative opinions prevailed. Criticism most frequently focused on the number of persons sharing a room, poor nutrition and the attitude of the official personnel towards refugees.

The conditions of accommodation, especially in collective shelters, was deemed unsatisfactory. A particular problem was accommodation in collective rooms, without any possibility for each family to have their own space. Also, our respondents mentioned poor food and bad hygienic conditions in collective rooms and lavatories. The majority of women came from urban areas (sixty-five), while only four had lived in villages. Since most of the women had a high standard of living and good housing, they could hardly be satisfied with the quality of the refugee summer camp housing[4] or with the conditions in collective shelters. Since they had limited means, women were not able to buy the most necessary items to partly compensate the negative effects of unsatisfactory accommodation. Or, as Emina said, "I went to see my husband's cousins in Obrenovac, but they kept persuading us that they were in difficulties too. They found me a room to live in. I still had two or three checks left, and I used them carefully. It is a terrible story, I could not believe that it happened to me. It was filthy. I was on the edge of a nervous breakdown; had I not had my child I would have committed suicide...My child saw bread on the TV, he demanded bread, he cried."

Nadežda, a 43-year-old woman with two children (one still young) said the following about her life in a collective shelter. "It was really hard in the collective shelter. There were nine of us sharing the same room—me with my two daughters, and six members of other families. Now, the situation is better—there are only four of us. The biggest problem is that there is no cooperation and solidarity between refugee women, but jealousy and envy."

Similar negative conditions affect students. Since most of them are alone in collective shelters, without close or distant relatives, they have more difficulty in adapting and find it harder to concentrate. A serious psychic state does not encourage girls to devote themselves to learning in such conditions (Branka, Ljiljana, Sandra, Jovana, Sanja, Zorica). While Jovana (a 20-year-old student of political science) said that she would prefer to start working because it is hard to study in these conditions, Sandra (a 27-year-old student) and Zorica (a 19-year-old student) want to finish university and strive towards their goals. Sandra said, "I'm alone here in refuge. I study and contact mostly my peers. Collective shelter is filled with problems: rooms are overcrowded, several families live together, there are no appropriate conditions for learning. But I can deal with that. I worry most about my [family], especially my brother and father who are at the front. It has already been a month since I received the last news from them."

She is a good student and passes her exams regularly (although she could not prepare for her last exam because she was too worried about her brother). Zorica said something similar. "I'm already two years in refuge. I did not have any problem in adaptation. I adapted well to the new surroundings, I worked sometimes in a café. I study regularly. I'm satisfied with accommodation although I share my room with three other girls."

Sandra and Zorica shared a goal, to finish university. That is what "pushed" them forward and forced them to adapt to new conditions and a new environment. They saw studies as the best way of joining their generation and escaping the horrors of war (Zorica was an eye-witness of the massacre in the village of Če-merno).

However, similar examples are rare. At the very beginning of her girlhood, Sanja had to face the harsh realities of refugee life.

> Here I'm overcome by worrying how to survive...This war has upset me completely; I did not have any documentation about the finished high school, except the final diploma. Due to incomplete documents I could not enroll in the group that I wanted, and I enrolled finally in wood-engineering as a part-time student. However, I don't feel a genuine wish to study, although I was a very good pupil in high school. I don't have proper working conditions here. Besides, the studies themselves are very expensive, and I don't have money at all.

The transfer to a collective shelter frequently comes after personal funds for private accommodation are exhausted, and after hospitality has run out. That was the case of thirty women from our sample. However, there were also examples of a girl who, after fifteen days spent in a friend's apartment, had to sleep several days in parks before getting admitted to a collective shelter (Ljiljana, a 22-year-old student from Sarajevo).

Housing conditions in the homes of relatives were not always satisfactory. It happened that several families shared the same apartment. Emina, for example, said that there were nine of them at her aunt's apartment. Nedeljka shared a room-and-kitchenette apartment with twelve people, while Zorica had to squeeze in with fifteen people sharing a two-room apartment. Yet another problem for refugees was the temporary character of most solutions. Senka, for example, changed eight apartments before she and her children finally moved to live with her mother. A certain number of women (Jasna, Sofija, Slobodanka, Dobrila) lived in rented apartments for several months or even a year before they came to collective shelters. Two women (Desa, Stojanka) went to live with their relatives in other regions of Bosnia-Herzegovina, but were forced to move to Serbia because of the spread of military actions.

There were very few women (Svetlana, Natalija) who were still accommodated by their relatives when this study was conducted. Even in these cases, where relatives showed a maximal solidarity with the families of refugees, it is evident that women were very conscious that their presence represented a burden for their hosts. Natalija said that she offered to pay rent for the apartment where she lived, but her relatives refused, and she pays only utilities. Natalija added, "We feel really good here. We have a special apartment. I always had good relationships with my brother and his son (where we live now). When his son studied in Sarajevo he lived with us. However, every little trifle from my apartment is dearer to me than anything else here. It's hard for me to adapt. My sister-in-law is good and she says that I can use everything I want, but I still use only a few drawers that she conceded me, and thus we live."

Vidosava, a 65-year-old widow, who lives alone in a rented apartment, commented that "It's thanks to the help of my daughter who lives in Germany that I can live here. I feel terrible here, because I'm alone. However, I can't go to Germany because all of us have moved there, and she has to have a bit of personal life also. But these days, my second son has found another accommodation as well as a job, so that he can take over her burden a bit."

Material conditions. Unsatisfactory material conditions additionally burden women refugees, especially when they have to take care of their children or elderly relatives with whom they share refuge. The majority of the women we talked with (thirty-nine) were previously employed but had to leave their jobs because of the war. They were especially handicapped by the fact that they could not claim their rights in the regions where they worked, nor could they find corresponding jobs in the Federal Republic of Yugoslavia.

While trying to earn some money, women frequently accepted jobs below their professional level; Nedžada, who had finished high school, and Nela, who had finished law school, both started working as janitors. For the moment, Nedžada works as domestic help, and also cleans apartments and baby-sits. As Stana said, "Here I tidied apartments, and that's all that I could find to make some money. Believe me, eight months I wore one summer dress after I came here; I did not have anything else to wear. My daughter had an operation on the spine; it's because of her that I worked. I wanted to buy her something. She was in hospital six months."

The women were mainly employed in the private sector, where they work "black market," undeclared and without welfare, or in state-owned enterprises, where they were hired through student employment agencies. They had no steady jobs because they were refugees without citizenship. Twenty women, in total, worked or work even now in similar jobs. Faced with dramatic poverty, women are forced to accept the jobs which are offered to them, although they are inadequate and poorly paid. Our respondents' professional activities included acting as "help" at various apartments, caring for the old and the sick, baby-sitting, working in private cafés or doing various types of agricultural work. Eight women cleaned apartments, while some others gave up (Maja, Nadežda, Stana, Sofija) because they could not bear the effort. Only six women (an administrative and an economic technician, a lawyer, an economist and a dentist) succeeded in finding jobs in their professions (or jobs that were somewhat similar, such as actuaries or sales personnel, etc.). However, this statement is valid only for the regions of Belgrade and Niš. In some cities the influx of refugees was several times larger than the number of inhabitants, and there was high unemployment or only seasonal work (for example, in Herceg-Novi). In such places the situation was different, and women with an academic education had to accept jobs as janitors or waitresses in restaurants and cafés, in order to provide essentials for their families.

The jobs that women perform do not offer much of a chance to earn money and make a decent life. Also, the women who are hired by private employers or through student employment agencies are faced with uncertainty and lack of job security. Moreover, they frequently must accept extra jobs, and are subject to great exploitation and face the possibility of being exposed to various forms of blackmail. Therefore, even when they perform their jobs, women refugees are exposed to various forms of arbitrariness; their work is undeclared and they have no regular income or welfare, and, since their work is undeclared, they are not included in pension plans. Thus, as Sofija said, "I am a dentist. Presently I'm working in a private office. I do everything; I'm a doctor, assistant, worker. They exploit me...My work is not declared, I have no pension plan. I work on Saturdays, too...my child remains alone, because kindergartens are not open on Saturdays."

In spite of exploitation, humiliation and bad working conditions, work represents a particular therapy for women, especially for those who have a chance to work in their profession. Many women in our study pointed out that work brought them back to life. They also said that finding work would help them to feel like human beings, giving them some goal in life (Borjana, Vesna, Anka, Gordana, Stana, Metka).

Gordana and Emina spoke about different forms of mistreatment they were exposed to while working with private employers or in private apartments.

GORDANA: "The boss was flattered when I brought drinks and coffee to his friends. He said to his friends that he had a woman working in his firm who has an MA in economics and who prepares him coffees."

EMINA: "I was employed by a woman. I had to tidy her apartment. Every time that somebody came to see her she used to say, 'Well, I have a woman here from Tuđman and Izetbegović.' She was nasty. At the beginning, it did not hurt me much but later on I felt uneasy, stigmatized. Her mother died in my arms, I did everything in her house. She let herself go with me. I hear that she's now helping refugees and says that I don't need help, because my husband is here and because, according to her, he should have been at the front."

The difficulties attendant upon securing the material well-being of the family—especially in those situations where a woman has to manage alone and stabilize her economic status in a new environment—make women suitable objects of economic exploitation and various forms of sexual blackmail.

Exposure of women refugees to sexual harassment
"If we have lost everything, we didn't lose our dignity"

The unfavorable economic condition of refugee women is conducive to the possibility of sexual harassment by the powerful. Employers, landlords, directors of collective shelters and Red Cross officials sometimes abuse their positions in order to blackmail and harass refugees. Jasna, a 37-year-old woman with two children reported that, "In my refuge, I have been insulted, unfortunately, by the activists of the Red Cross. There was the abuse of official position and there were some humiliating sexual offers."

Branka had a similar experience. "Some women were blackmailed by men. Men occupy all the key positions in different institutions (hotels, collective shelters, etc.) and, of course, they use their positions in order to make women sleep with them even for some small favors."

The situation is only more complicated if women refugees have problems opposing such treatment because they are handicapped by their age, their material and marital status and their ethnic affiliation.

The situation of unprotected women in collective shelters, where they themselves or their young relatives can be attacked, is especially difficult.[5]

Branka, a 23-year-old student from Sarajevo who was alone in a collective shelter, reported a typical example.

> When I came here I was skinny and rather exhausted. One day a waiter served me breakfast three times. Then he started to court me, to hug me, to pinch me. He tried that with every woman here. Perhaps he thought that, because we are refugees, we would do anything in order to get some money or food. Since I remained aloof, it happened that sometimes he did not serve me dinner or supper although I came in time...When I fell ill, my friend went to order a dish for me. I didn't get it, and the waiter said that it was that way because I wasn't fond of him.

If alone, women refugees were exposed to sexual harassment and violence even when they shared a collective shelter with men of the same nationality. It is clear that even in the conditions of refuge, the patriarchal pattern of male domination over women maintained itself, outside of the restrained circle of family. Similarly to the mechanisms of violence in the family (Konstantinović-Vilić, 1985; Mrvić 1993), women refugees receive a "message" that men have a "legitimate" right to apply violence against them. In similar circumstances, the presence of spirit, emancipation or a willingness to appeal for help can be the deciding factor in the success of a defense. The following example about Moslem refugees accommodated in the Islamic community center in Belgrade is illustrative. According to Munevera,

> We are all women here, although there are a few men. He was already here with his family when we came. He always acted as if he

could do whatever he wanted, as if he owned everything. We tried hard to avoid conflicts with him. He had already been here for a couple of years, with his wife and a 24-year-old son. The son harassed a little girl (my daughter's stepdaughter), who was with us here (she has left now and went off to Germany to join her mother). She was too ashamed to complain to her mother or to her aunt. When I heard about that I went to see the man. I told him what his son was doing and ordered him to keep him away from the girl. Then he started yelling at me, saying that was none of my business, and so on. He then hit me on my neck; I fell. I could hardly move; I could hardly reach the bed. I'm an old and very ill woman and he might have easily killed me. When I came back, I put some bandage on my neck and when my daughter came back she saw me. I couldn't hide what happened and my daughter immediately called the police. I don't know what they told him but he didn't dare to beat me anymore. Then one day the mufti also came, but there was not much effect from that—he only said that T. would soon go away and that we should remain patient for a couple of days. Indeed, T. went off soon afterwards.

Poverty, fear and the impossibility of working or providing essentials for their families can force women to engage in extra-marital relations with men who can provide them with a certain material security. Concerning this, there was no difference between unmarried, formally independent women and married women with juvenile children who demand care and protection. The only difference is that mothers with juvenile children decided to engage in similar relations mainly in order to provide food for their children. The common characteristic of these women is that they are all alone in refuge, without parents or close relatives. It is a characteristic phenomenon which follows all wars[6] and could be found among women in the regions affected by war as well as among women in refuge. Apart from the degradation of women and their reduction to the objects of prostitution, they were exposed to systematic humiliation. Frequently they were involved in a sociopathological and criminal milieu that was bad for the mental health of these women, and very difficult to leave. Of course, a similar environment also affected children who grew up in unfavorable conditions.

In our research, accounts which demonstrated engaging in extra-marital relations with men exclusively for the reasons of material security were rare. Thus, the report of Gorica, a 48-year-old widow who came to Serbia with her 9-year-old son, is extremely illustrative.

And there [in the village of Perućac] my child was hungry. I worked in other people's houses. It was really impossible. I was working like a dog all the time. I thought I would go crazy. One night, at half past ten my child said, "Mother, I'm so hungry I can't sleep." His stomach was growling, really growling. In such moments, there's nothing you wouldn't do, as a mother...Other women managed somehow, they would go down to the village and bring something. Women managed in various ways, including prostitution. Thus, one finds a guy, the other goes to the café, and so on. Myself, I also lost some dignity. I found a widower, who called me to come to live with him in Vojvodina. March 15, I went to see him and he told me, "Forget everything. You have nothing in Sarajevo, neither husband nor child. It's all gone." Yes, women had to put up with everything. Some even remarried. I know a woman who remarried; she left her husband although he's still alive in Zenica...Our women, then, lost their dignity, and the women who went to Perućac are really poor and unhappy, I mean, the women who used to go to bed for ten eggs. It's all sad, but I don't blame them. They had to do it. There's no other way when your child says "I'm hungry."

Because of the hard conditions of life, women refugees become susceptible to more than various kinds of blackmail and sexual and other harassment. They are also forced to live in a criminal demi-monde. This makes them the possible victims of various kinds of crime, or connects them to, for example, smugglers and criminals whom they have to hide. A similar situation is also present when a woman works "in the black," without papers, or when she has to deal with disreputable landlords and similar characters.

Gordana, who worked for some time as a professor, said that she and her parents were cheated when they rented an apartment.

Cousins from France sent us some money through a woman from Pančevo. I couldn't believe that somebody could manipulate me so badly. She [the woman from Pančevo] did not give us the money, but she proposed instead to find a flat in Pančevo that she would pay in advance for a year (she also wanted to put some of her things there). However, she cheated us as well as our cousins. She returned to France and left her old husband with us, so we had to take care of him. We renovated the apartment and she reappeared a month later and began insulting us. She submitted an account to our cousins, and she pretended that they still had to pay her some additional money. It's in refuge that I met for the first time similar characters. Later on, she even tried to get us out of the apartment... I couldn't stay in the school because salaries were too low. I started working in a private enterprise. I earn just enough to pay the rent. My boss is a psychopath. We were forced to deal with some dubious

characters...These are people of the lowest kind. All my life
I worked with normal people but now I have to deal with delin-
quents, because they have power.

Emina, who had to find an apartment for her and her child, con-
curred. "The landlord's son was a thief. He used to bring home the
items he had stolen. Once police came and began questioning me,
'Why am I here? What is my nationality? Where is my husband?' and
so on. One evening, the landlord's son was killed by the members
of his gang and my child saw it all."

Faced with the hard facts of living as refugees, with insufficient
means, women are obliged to "work it out" any way they can in
order to secure the means of existence for themselves and for the
people who depend on them. Blackmailed or humiliated by those
on whom they immediately depend, in collective shelters or at
their jobs, women have numerous difficulties in adapting to their
new environment, in which they are considered second-class citizens.

Notes

1 It turned out that refugee parents explained the poor scholarly success
of their children by the lack of necessary books and school material,
which was directly related to the overall economic situation of the refugee family (B. Popović et al., 1993. pp. 9–23). If they are not successful
in school, refugee children face many more difficulties in adjusting to
the new social environment. That is why refugee parents strive to provide them with appropriate clothes, books and material, in order to save
their children from being "singled out."
2 At the time of the event she and her three children were visiting her
cousins in a neighboring village.
3 Stanislava, who spent the whole war in the Serbian community of
Grbavica (Sarajevo), said that she spent all her savings and sold all her
jewels in order to buy food and send packages to her close relatives who
remained in the Moslem part of the city. Later she herself was supported
and thought about moving to Serbia because she had nothing to live on.
4 A good number of collective shelters are children's summer vacation
camps.
5 It is typical that the women themselves remarked that the personnel
from collective shelters treated single women with children differently
from women with complete families. Thus Borjana, who was in a collec-

tive shelter in Belgrade with her son of 7 and her mother, said several times that her friends Ana and Blaženka were still protected because their husbands were with them. This holds true even despite the fact that refugee husbands are generally despised because of their refusal to go back to the front.

6 There are widespread examples of women who, in order to survive, engage in extra-marital sexual relations with men of an inferior social or educational level (El Bushra, Lopez, 1993). The confession of A. Bach-huber, who during World War II worked as a typist in the German military headquarters in Berlin, reveals dimensions of the degradation of women in war conditions. At the end of 1944, she lived for some time with a driver who had helped her to flee occupied Berlin and go to Munich. During their time together, he, among other things, acted as a pimp for his friends. As soon as she gained some independence, she told him about her decision to leave him, and he replied, "Of course, the Black guy did his job and now he can go away." He thought that because he had helped her to leave Berlin, he had the right to dispose of her body and life as he saw fit (Hayton-Keeva, 1987).

CHAPTER 10

Social acceptance and the difficulty of adapting to a new environment

NATAŠA MRVIĆ-PETROVIĆ

Having survived the myriad threats to their life that endangered them in the war zone, having abandoned their homes and separated from their close relatives, in refuge women are faced with new ordeals. It becomes necessary to quickly adapt to the new social environment. A state of unrealistic euphoria, produced by the fact that they and their children have survived the immediate danger, is soon replaced by sober disillusionment. Soon it becomes evident that their expectations differ from reality in the new social surroundings.

The ability to adapt to life in refuge is highly personal. However, it has been observed that the lack of ability to cope with real-life problems is significantly tied to poor social adaptation, poor economic status and conflicts in the workplace, the family and the immediate social surroundings (Kaličanin, Lečić-Toševski, 1994; Kapamadžija et al., 1990). Thus, refugees can be labeled as a "vulnerable group," because they are exposed to the prolonged effects of various psychosocial stressors: forced separation from spouses, parents and children, inadequate housing, poverty and existential insecurity, strained communication with the new social environment, serious illness of the women or their children or persons they take care of, and so on.

It is quite clear that the most successful integration will be done by independent persons who are interested in adapting to the new social environment and who have overcome the trauma of forced migration and separation from (or loss of) family members. It would also be justified to suppose that complete families and women who share refuge with direct or lateral relatives of approximately the same age will adapt more successfully than old or lonely women, or women with dependents. In the first case, the problems of life in refuge are "shared" among several persons. In the second case, women must assume the unduly heavy burden of responsibility and family care. Moreover, women are especially vulnerable to new stressful events when they are ill or pregnant, or when their children or further dependents are seriously ill. In such cases, women need additional emotional and material support, both from the individuals in their immediate social surroundings as well as from the competent humanitarian organizations and social services.

Statistical data and results from previous research on refugee families suggest that, except for the most pressing survival needs, the needs of refugees are not adequately met. Most frequently, attention has been drawn to the realization of the right to work and the development of specialized programs for the satisfaction of specific needs of refugees (*Porodice izbeglica u Jugoslaviji*, 1993). Since women with juvenile children make up the majority of refugees, it is obvious that those programs should first of all take into account the specific integration needs and abilities of women refugees.

In a situation when the material resources of the host community (Serbia and Montenegro) are seriously reduced by an economic crisis and international sanctions, it is difficult for the host country to cope with a flood of refugees. In the Federal Republic of Yugoslavia, which is burdened by the necessity to provide for a large number of refugees,[1] there is a serious gap between the needs of refugees and the objective possibility of their satisfaction. That is why refugees are forced to look for additional solutions in order to ensure their own survival.

Emancipation of women in refuge

A new challenge, stressful even for stable and emotionally mature persons, is especially difficult for those women who have been educated in the patriarchal spirit, which denies women the ability to make decisions. In refuge, deprived of the support of their husbands and parents, they feel that they are not able to cope alone with the difficulties that they are exposed to. This, in turn, only increases their insecurity. A situation like this can easily lead to the development of hysteria or depression. Very frequently, women refugees feel resentment towards their new environment or feel bitter about their husbands or relatives who "don't help them enough." Under this hides their inability to adapt to the new surroundings and assume the responsibilities they have never been taught to assume. In a situation like that, it can happen that women "choose illness" or become completely uninterested in their children (El Bushra, Lopez, 1993; Kaličanin, Lečić-Toševski, 1994).

Two examples (Emina and Vesna) demonstrate that this was largely the case with women who married very early, as senior juveniles or immediately upon coming of age.

EMINA: "I did not learn to make decisions for myself and manage all alone. First it was my father who made decisions for me and then it was my boyfriend (husband now). Every time I had to make a decision I would ask him."

VESNA: "Ever since I was born my father took care of me. Later on, my husband and father-in-law took it over. I did not get used to earning my living. In a way, I'm angry at my husband because he left me alone to take care of me and my children, and I didn't get used to it."

Some fragments of Nataša's letters to her sister reveal her feelings of helplessness. "You don't know how lucky you are. At least you know that your husband is by your side and that nothing bad will happen to him. You know how strongly I am attached to B. It seems that I can't do anything without him..."[2]

It turned out that these women largely built their identities as wives and mothers. In these cases there is a danger that they will become dependent personalities who will sacrifice their talents and abilities and thus gradually lose themselves.

In such instances, women take separation from, or loss of, a husband as a subsequent loss of identity and social status. This is aside from emotional tension, which appears as a natural consequence of the experience. That is why Vesna hoped that the arrival of her husband would resolve the bulk of her problems and why Jelena was desperate because her husband did not see any way out of their difficult situation. Similarly, Nataša expected that her husband would make decisions alone about their common destiny, with which she would comply.

Unlike the above examples, the experiences of other women (including those who married very young, as did Blaženka,[3] Nedžada or Nedeljka[4], or who lost husbands, like Anka or Suzana) demonstrate the contrary. The personal strength of some women and their independence (previously acquired or "won" in new conditions) represented the key elements of autonomous decision making and were essential preconditions for the successful overcoming of war-related trauma. Their experience encouraged them to make some vitally important decisions alone (El Bushra, Lopez, 1993). Thus Borjana said that her experience of war and refuge made her incredibly strong. Before the war, she thought that she would never make decisions by herself and was afraid to emigrate with her children. She became completely prepared for that, because she realized that she had to live and make all her decisions by herself. Besides, she thought that earlier she would have put up with being beaten by her husband but now she would never allow him to treat her that way.

Women who lost their husbands still managed to find strength to continue to live, after a period of depression. It is as if troubles and suffering "fortified" them in a way and made them more prepared to cope with new problems. Anka, a 38-year-old widow with two children, said, "I have nothing to say. I have to manage all alone and cannot expect assistance from anyone. As soon as I came here, I went to the National Bank (I worked in the Sarajevo branch), and they instantly found me a job of the same kind as I had before. However, since I don't have Yugoslav citizenship, I am formally engaged through the Student Employment Agency."

Nada, a 35-year-old widow with two children, had a similar story. "After my husband's death, I spent two months in depression but I refused to take sedatives, because I wanted to face all that alone. But then I realized I had to find strength and continue to live, not so much because of me but because of my children. I didn't feel very sorry for myself. I rather felt sorry for him, because he wasn't there anymore and because my children remained without a father."

Nedžada, a 38-year-old widow with one child, said briefly, "I just can't go back to Brčko. My husband was killed and now I have to think how to get the best possible life for me and my child."

The decision to try refuge acts as the breaking point for some women, who then clear up their relations with their husbands after long-lasting marital discord in the pre-war period, and start an independent life. This is clearly demonstrated by Nedeljka's example. It was in refuge that she decided to end her 19-year marriage with her violent alcoholic husband. As she said, she came to understand that war, in which she lost everything but from which she saved her children, represents an occasion to start a new, independent life. The ability of women to make autonomous decisions in the moments that represent turning points in their lives has significantly contributed to their successful adaptation to new social surroundings. However, regardless of their internal strength, women refugees encounter hostile attitudes in their new social environment, which renders their social adaptation much more difficult.

Acceptance and lack of acceptance in the new environment
"When you say you are a refugee, they look down on you as if you have AIDS"

A lack of acceptance in the new environment leads to apathy and disillusionment. Our interviewees (Slobodanka, Olivera, Ana, Mirjana, Borjana, Jasna, Jovana, Tatjana, Vida, Branka, Svetlana, Julijana, Ranka and Nedeljka) complained that non-refugees frequently asked them what they were doing in Serbia (especially if their husbands had remained in other areas). Refugees were frequently reproached for making the situation in Serbia even more difficult. They were told that they were responsible for everything bad happening in it, that they were unjustifiably given priority in employment, that they were taking others' jobs and that they were given everything for free. Blaženka: "They all look at us with suspicion." Branka: "They just love to tease us." Mirjana: "They treat us as if we have AIDS." Ana: "We are even guilty if we happen to be made-up and have clean hair."

The new environment demands refugees to be discreet, to renounce their religious or ethnic identity and to humbly accept their changed social status. This is especially visible in language (with the use of *ijekavica*[5] and the Bosnian accent). Although it is not as widespread, intolerance is often displayed against the young refugees as well. Thus, Ivana, a 17-year-old highschool student, said, "My professor of biology once said that she was proud of her Belgrade accent and that she did not want to spoil it. As she said that, she looked at me and I felt lousy. She gave me a lower mark than I deserved just because I once said something in *ijekavica*."

Jovana, a student from Croatia, talked about her last year of school in Zemun. "They were particularly irritated by my accent. At the beginning they were just joking but then they began threatening me, such as 'Why don't you adjust to us? If you want to speak Croatian, why don't you go to Croatia?' or 'What are you waiting for here? Why don't you go where war is?' and the like.

I took it the hard way, because I was very depressed and just couldn't adapt."

Adults as well had problems with their accent. Thus Vida said, "I tried to avoid talking on the street or on the bus so that people would not realize that I'm from Bosnia, because they immediately would begin to comment about refugees. It's best to remain silent, not to beg for anything and not to let yourself lose dignity."

Since they represented a marginal social group and were unable to protect themselves, women refugees were made scapegoats for everything bad that happened to the domestic population, from purely local problems to the overall political situation in Serbia. Employed women refugees are reproached for taking away jobs from other people, even when they have accepted jobs that do not correspond at all to their educational status (such as workers in fast-food restaurants, or janitors). Thus, as Nedeljka said, "I was insulted in a fast-food joint in Niš where I occasionally worked. They called me 'refugee bitch.' Once I had a similar experience in a bus, during ticket control. When I showed my refugee identification card, I heard some women behind me saying 'Refugees are all we needed now!' while others were cursing."

Nela, for example, was insulted when she came to the premises of the local Red Cross to pick up her parcel. Her husband was waiting for her outside in their Volkswagen Golf. Nela heard people reproaching her, saying "Shame on you, you drive a Golf and demand assistance from the Red Cross." The car was the only property that they saved from Sarajevo.

The most successful tactic for overcoming the stress provoked by hostile attitudes in the new social environment turned out to be ignoring the problems and adopting an active stance in order to enhance self-esteem (Kaličanin, Lečić-Toševski, 1994). In our survey, we found examples where women instinctively reacted in that way (Nada, Vida and Tijana), thus avoiding conflicts.

The anti-refugee stance of a woman's environment can produce some unwanted negative emotional reactions in women. Verbal assault and provocation may trigger aggressive responses or reinforce their need to affirm their ethnic identity. Jovana, for example, said, "And then, out of spite, I decided to speak *ijekavica* whenever I could and I did not want to back down. I don't understand how they can't understand what I've been through and how many of my friends were killed while they were living normally here." Merima also addressed the issue of affiliation and identification.

I never declared myself as Moslem before. We always declared ourselves and our children as Yugoslavs. It is only here that I began feeling some ethnic element in myself, because, if these women here think that this is something important for them then neither am I going to renounce my identity. I don't want to renounce my parents who educated me to love everybody and it's for them that I declare myself as Moslem now. When this war ends, I will declare myself differently. It's important that people remain human. I would like to say that I am Bosnian.

Unfortunately, much more frequent than the previous types of self-assertion is the situation in which women become introverted. They suffer so much from the rejection of their new social environment that they actually give up their efforts to overcome the hostile attitude of their surroundings.

Hostility towards refugees is quite visible when the case of non-Serb women is examined. The majority of these women came to Serbia because they lived in so-called mixed marriages or because they wanted to save their children. Arriving in a place a woman knew would be hostile towards the members of her ethnic group was always accompanied by fear for her personal safety or the safety of her children. This is how Blaženka, a Croat, explains it. "I came to Serbia because of my children. They are Serbs and their father is Serb as well. I thought they would be better off here. I used to love this country and this city. I wanted to remain with my father-in-law, in Bosanski Petrovac, but he told me he could not protect me from others, because I'm a Croat."

Thus women in refuge were sometimes forced to hide or misrepresent their ethnic affiliation. Jelena, a Serb refugee from Mostar, recounted the story of her sojourn in a refugee camp on the island of Brač (Croatia).

We had to register in Brač...The worst of all was that everybody knew that I am a Serb from the village of Tasovčići, which was ill-famed as being a chetnik stronghold. When we wanted to register, we did not have any documents and they said they would check all data. I said I was Croat, because Serbs couldn't get refugee status. We were accommodated in hotels where the majority of refugees were Croats and Moslems...I became fearful, because they indeed began checking all data and soon afterwards harassment began.

Nedžada, a Moslem, left Brčko (Bosnia) and came to Serbia together with her mother, sister, 7-year-old daughter and 12-year-old nephew. She came on the invitation of her husband's best friend, who is a Serb. Nevertheless, she experienced tension and fear when deciding to come. "After we had come to Belgrade, we were afraid because we were of different ethnic origin and we didn't dare ask openly for the Islamic community. Still, one day, while walking in Kalemegdan city park, my mother asked an elderly lady, a Serb, about the community and the woman took her straight to the mosque and the mufti. Likewise, for several months I did not dare call my child by her real name when she was with other chil- ·dren, because I feared ethnically motivated harassment and vio- lence."

Non-Serb women refugees turned out to be a handy object of harassment in the street, in the workplace or in refugee shelters. These women in particular, because of their pro-Yugoslav attitude or the "mixed marriages" they were living in, did not hate Serbs. Nevertheless, they were forced to passively endure these racial at- tacks. However, the women who shared refuge with their hus- bands (Ana, Blaženka and Emina) felt more protected than the women who lived alone with their children (Nedžada and Mer- ima).

Harassment is by no means exclusively limited to non-Serb refugees. It also affects women who are stigmatized, provoked or ostracized for various reasons (for example, because of their po- litical ideas or because their husbands dodged the draft or re- mained in enemy-controlled territories). Such a situation is most exploited by persons from the women's immediate social sur- roundings (relatives, other refugees in collective shelters, class- mates and colleagues, etc.), to let out excessive patriotic feelings and thus establish at least some domination over the refugees. As Snežana said, "My relatives, who first offered me shelter, could not understand that my husband had remained in the Moslem- controlled part of Sarajevo. They told me, 'It would have been bet- ter for him if he had tried to escape and even got killed than to stay there. Why don't you join him? You should leave the children here and join him.'"

Exposure to the continuous stress of rejection can lead to or worsen depression. It may significantly reduce or even make im- possible the adaptation of refugees to their new environment, where they are seen as unwanted guests. Merima's experience is especially illustrative.

I even had a couple of arguments with women here who think they can tell me everything just because I am of different ethnic origin. I really have nothing to do with this war. I did not want it and I did not help initiate it. It happened to me that people tell me, "You don't have any rights here, your rights are there, in Alija Izetbego-vić's Bosnia." Everything happening there becomes quickly reflected here and me, being in a minority, I have to shut up. Thus, it happened to me several times that I was so tense that I vomited or dehydrated. I grew terribly anxious, I began shivering. I just felt terribly unsafe and I just want to get out of here although I have a couple of great friends who want to help me out.

Borjana, too, had similar experiences.

My husband was seen as guilty because he did not run to Vukovar to fight...While I was working in the shop, I received intimidating phone calls and I was threatened and insulted because I am a refugee. Once, I was even set up by my colleagues. They said that because of my negligence and poor organization somebody stole twenty pairs of socks. "My husband would get killed for me and my children, and where's your husband?" They used to say this to me over the phone. Colleagues began avoiding me; they didn't want to go to lunch with me. I was completely boycotted and I am sure that I would never experience something like that in Croatia. Harassment was especially aggravated after the fall of Vukovar: "What are you doing here? You are a traitor! Others have liberated you"...and the like. I was on the verge of a nervous breakdown and I had cramps in my throat and neck. My mother had realized that and she went to talk to my boss. He summoned a meeting where he said he wasn't interested in where my husband was but only how good a worker I was. Afterwards, a group of women began socializing with me.

Rejection by relatives

Women refugees generally had bad experiences in refuge, regardless of whether they were accommodated in collective shelters or with their relatives. Usually, women refugees would spend the first days after their arrival with their relatives or friends or in private apartments. Later on, after the first conflicts with relatives or the first signs of the shortage of money, women would move to collective shelters.

Negative experiences with relatives were especially distressing, because refugees had significant expectations regarding them—expectations that were unfulfilled, or not fulfilled in the expected degree. The situation of women refugees was aggravated if they were not alone. Women were often in charge of their children and/or parents, responsible for the specific needs of the old and ill, obliged to provide for children who needed schooling, and so on. In that case, the welcoming relatives found themselves providing for several people. Moreover, the impossibility of finding regular jobs made it impossible for women refugees to contribute significantly to the needs of the host families. The women refugees that we talked with mainly assisted in housekeeping and partially participated in paying food costs. The most important problems, however, were related to the following two facts.

- Women refugees left their homes temporarily, hoping and indeed anticipating that they would soon return;
- The deep economic crisis in the Federal Republic of Yugoslavia, aggravated by the UN-imposed international sanctions, profoundly affected the domestic population, which was unable to cover its own most elementary needs.[6]

Temporary refuge gradually became permanent emigration, with ever-smaller chances of repatriation. This was a double burden for women refugees in the new country. On one hand, women refugees in general did not have sufficient means to secure the livelihood of their families without being assisted by their relatives. On the other hand, refugees quite clearly became an additional burden for the host families. These families, although they initially demonstrated great sympathy for refugees, gradually became torn between the moral obligation to assist refugees and a material and/or emotional inability to do something about that. The extremely difficult economic situation in the Federal Republic of Yugoslavia in 1993 (characterized by enormous inflation) only worsened the situation.

Frequently, some unforeseen condition, like the death of the host, made refugees unwanted guests in their new-found homes. As Emina's experience demonstrates, relatives were sometimes not ready to provide for several persons simultaneously. "My husband's aunt threw us out of her apartment after three months. I don't know how I would react if I had nine people hanging around in my home. In a way, I understand the aunt's reaction."

Sometimes it even happens that there is a split within the host family concerning sentiment for the refugees. For example, one relative may treat the woman refugee in a fair and sympathetic manner, while other members of the host family react in quite a different way. Sara, a 19-year-old refugee from Zenica, left her parents in the city and came to refuge alone. She recounted the experience that made her seek accommodation in a collective shelter.

The aunt's son-in-law was most unpleasant towards me. Once he told me, "You didn't come here to go to school but to work." I was running all over the place to get the necessary documents issued and I contacted even the Ministry of Education, because I did not take my certificates with me. I bought books secretly and asked a cousin of mine to help me come here [to the collective shelter]. I have succeeded in maintaining correct relations with my aunt, but when I go to her place I usually leave before 3 p.m., that is, before her son-in-law comes home.

Being at the mercy of close or distant relatives can lead to deteriorating relations, but it also can produce some very negative effects on the psychological equilibrium of refugees. They are disillusioned about the anticipated warm welcome in the new country, impoverished, despised by their new neighbors, often burdened with their own psychological problems, concerned for their own survival and for that of their children; the final straw occurs when women refugees do not encounter the much needed sympathy of their relatives. Jelena related the difficult moments that she had to pass at a distant relative's house, when, due to her pregnancy, she could not find other accommodation.

My cousin is an older man and an alcoholic. I was alone with him in a huge house. He used to tell me terrible things, like "Your husband is an *ustaše*, just like you and your mother. So what are you doing here?"...When I wanted to take a shower, he would say, "Why do you take a shower every day?" He used to tell me that his ex-wife had had arguments with my mother-in-law because she is a Croat...I was waiting to give birth every moment. My husband was away and I couldn't go to my folks. My cousin told me that my husband had told him that I would stay twenty days and he began pressing me to go to my mother's place. I wanted to go to the Red Cross and ask them to find me any kind of accommodation. I was crying all the time...When I told my husband about the harassment I was exposed to, he couldn't believe it and said, "You're only imagining that. He only says that when he's drunk." However, when he himself spoke to him, he realized that the cousin meant what he said and so we left. First we went to Novi Sad to see my folks and then we moved to Belgrade, to my aunt's place. After a week, I gave birth. The first fifteen to twenty days in the aunt's place were fine, but then she also began to mistreat us. For a month and a half she did not enter my room to see the baby. We spent three months in her place and we just didn't know what to do. My husband became heavily depressed and one night he started banging his head against the wall. Yet we were paying for everything and we were bringing in all our food. We left her place in the coldest winter. It is so hard for me to recount now...We were unemployed and our savings were at the end. The aunt has a five-room flat and she lives alone in it. My husband did all kinds of jobs, he used to paint walls in –13°C. He slept on three chairs.

Merima, a sensitive woman, could perceive the gradual change of attitude towards her and her children. This is how Merima tried to explain such changes. "We spent five months in a house belonging to some distant relatives. At the beginning, we felt really nice and they were kind and warm. However, as time went by, they began seeing us as a burden, and we felt the same way. I felt they were expecting us to make some sacrifice as well, to suffer a bit and feel the way they felt."

Even when they were accommodated by their own or their husband's parents, women refugees became unwanted; as married women they did not belong in their parents' house anymore, even when they were forcefully separated from their husbands. Interestingly, those women who were socialized to accept the patriarchal idea that through marriage they had "broken" with their original family and gone to the husband's family had much less pain in accepting such treatment. Thus Vesna, who with her children left her parents' house in a village near the city of Priboj and came to Belgrade, said without any bad blood, "Leaving home hit me real hard, but, then again, I couldn't remain there anymore, because as a married woman I'm not a part of the family anymore. These are the ideas of my country, and I accept them as being normal."

In contrast with her, Senka was seriously hurt by the fact that her parents and her in-laws rejected her. She had fled with her two children to Belgrade, where she has a number of close relatives.

My late father reproached my husband for not joining us in refuge and for having sent us to be a burden for them, with their two small pensions. "What does he think, your husband? There are so many people who went to refuge!" The criticism became particularly bitter when my husband phoned me and said he would remain there. Anyway, I never got along well with my father, who's an alcoholic. So, arguments began almost every day, and it was so bad that my 10-year-old daughter once ran away from home because she couldn't stand that continuous pressure and harassment. Then we moved to my in-laws but they were not delighted either because they thought we didn't belong to them if their son, my husband and the father of my children, was not with us. From March to August we were in their place. At the end of August, they had to approve our [continued] stay in their place, but a week before the beginning of school they refused. They said I belonged to my parents as long as my husband was not with us. They also refused to give me the money to help my husband get out of Sarajevo (which he had been trying to do for more than a year). Even now, my in-laws behave as if we were dead.

Senka's story suggests that the war and the economic crisis only exacerbated the already strained relations between some young spouses and their parents. It is, however, hard to forget the fact that women came to refuge mostly to safeguard the lives of their children, and thus close relatives should have had more sympathy and understanding.

The lack of life prospects
"You belong neither here nor there"

Women see life in refuge as something "in between," a situation when one is at the same time close to one's family and friends and yet so distant from them, because there is no way of helping them. In conditions of refuge, people do not plan for years ahead but live from day to day, without real opportunities of settling down and starting a new life.

The amount of time spent in the new environment is one of the key determiners of a successful adaptation and reorganization of life. However, adaptation is seriously hampered by poverty and the lack of appropriate housing and permanent employment. These factors very often go hand in hand with other discouraging elements. This is particularly the case with the so-called mixed marriages and with non-Serb women (Merima, Metka and Nedažda). However, it is important to remember that this is not an absolute rule. In our sample, the pro-Yugoslav women (Ana, Senka and Blaženka), who with the breakup of the Socialist Federal Republic of Yugoslavia lost their true country, firmly believed that only abroad they could start a successful family life.

The decision to emigrate was mostly determined by the fact that those women had lost their homes and country forever. On the basis of the news they received from their former homeland, they were convinced that the environment where they had lived had changed so much during the war years that they could no longer return. The testimonies of Merima (from Sarajevo), and Metka and Ana (from Mostar), are very illustrative in this respect. Merima commented on this loss of a homeland.

Judging by the letters from my husband, I can see that Sarajevo is not the city I knew. Some new people came and grabbed the power. My husband says he simply cannot live any longer in that ambience and is convinced that our children will not have any future there. I think we should emigrate, in order to protect our children...On the other hand, we don't see our place [in Serbia] and the same goes for Croatia or some other ethnically pure territory in the former Yugoslavia. The only solution for us is to emigrate, so that we can send our children to school and start a new life...I live in an ethnically mixed marriage, and that's why, when we had to leave Sarajevo, we didn't know where to go. We had some distant relatives in Serbia and that's why we decided to come here. However, we don't see any prospects in Serbia or Croatia.

METKA: "I walked across the Brotherhood and Unity bridge, to Baš Čaršija and back, without seeing anybody I knew. That completely defeated me. I felt as if I never lived in that city. I'm convinced that I could by no means continue to live there. There are some new people walking in the city and the whole ambience has become completely redneck."

ANA: "My place of birth is completely destroyed and I can't go back. My national feeling is that I'm an ex-Yugoslav (my father is Serb and my mother is Moslem) and I just feel I don't belong here. That's why I want to emigrate. Perhaps I will succeed in joining my sister there."

Even when there was no problem from "mixed marriages" and the like, women refugees like Senka and Snežana, for example, believed that emigration was the only solution. In Serbia, they said, they feel rejected and insecure and cannot find permanent jobs and settle down. Senka said, "I feel I don't belong here and I am just waiting for my husband to leave Sarajevo and emigrate to Canada with him (we have all the documents needed)."

SNEŽANA: "The process of the revision of refugee status is going on in Serbia and perhaps they will tell me to repatriate. How could I return when now it's more insecure than ever? I would prefer to emigrate, but my husband cannot join me here and cannot have a passport issued."

Emina simply said, "We don't have any future in Serbia. You can't get a job, citizenship or passport. I hope we will get out of here and go somewhere. Perhaps we will return to Mostar."

In the case of younger or middle-aged women the decision to emigrate was very often motivated by the wish to go somewhere where life, employment and child rearing would be easier. Thus Nedžada said,

My mother says she would never leave Serbia, because she already has a couple of good neighbors who will look after her and help her if she falls ill, and, besides, my sister wants to stay with her. Me, however, I would like to emigrate. I can't find a decent job here. From time to time I work as maid or janitor or something of the kind, but this is not the future. We can't even get citizenship. We are not nationalists; two of us who are younger would even convert to Orthodoxy only if it would mean something, but I'm not sure that this would help.

According to the information we gathered later, eight of our interviewees emigrated legally to the United States, Canada, and Australia. Only one of them (Maja) decided to move to another city in Republika Srpska (Bosnia), where her husband had found a permanent job. The remaining women tried to extend their refugee status and remain in Serbia. They did not see any future in their old cities, devastated by war. According to the objective criteria, as well as according to their subjective feelings, they are the innocent victims of the civil war in the former Yugoslavia. That is why they believe they have the right to ensure a secure and safe life for their children, and to spend the rest of their lives in peace.

Notes

1 According to data published in the *Bulletin of the Commissariat for Refugees of the Republic of Serbia*, the number of refugees by the middle of 1992 was 426,519, while the biggest figure was reached in the spring of 1993 (655,000). The average refugee could be described as female, aged 30–45, mother of two children, of Serbian ethnic affiliation, with secondary education and formerly employed (*Porodice izbeglica u Jugoslaviji*, 1993).
2 As OXFAM research demonstrated, the feeling of helplessness and insecurity in women in war is the main reason why women remain in dissatisfying marriages or enter extra-marital relations with socially or educationally inferior men (El Bushra, Lopez, 1993). Similar reasoning can be found in women who tolerate lasting family violence in peacetime.
3 Blaženka, who left Zagreb together with her three children, explained how she made the decision herself, against the wishes of her husband who, although a Serb, thought they should remain. "When I arranged travel with a friend of mine, the same evening I packed the bags and the

next morning I told my husband that I was leaving with the children and that he could join me if he wished."

4 Nedeljka, a mother of two, who endured family violence for years, said that although she was always submissive, she decided to leave her village against her husband's will. She did not regret at all that she had to leave the house that she had been investing in for years. All she wanted, she said, was to get her children out of the village.

5 *Ijekavica* is a dialect used by Croatian and Bosnian Serbs, different from the speech of Serbs from Serbia.

6 According to official statistics from 1993, almost 66% were unable to take their savings or valuable items with them. On the other hand, 56% of host families had an income that could barely cover their own survival needs.

CHAPTER 11

Strategies of support and help

SLOBODANKA KONSTANTINOVIĆ-VILIĆ

History teaches us that there are always wars and that their effects know no boundaries. Wars produce victims, destruction and hopelessness. While men fight for the realization of political and military goals, thus demonstrating their power, women and children suffer and lose in every battle. In war, women and children form the majority of the civilian victims, those who are uninvolved with the beginnings and maintenance of wars. Civilians are exposed to various forms of physical, psychological and sexual violence. Women are the unwilling victims of wars—all wars—regardless of whether conflict is inspired by religious, ethnic or nationalistic motives. Women are physically tortured, raped, psychologically abused by threats, intimidation, blackmail and insults. The overall situation of war represents for women a high level of violence and fear, especially fear for their own survival and fear for their children and close family members. Some new situations created by war (the loss of family members, their recruitment into armed forces, separation and the necessity of refuge) demand that women adopt new, more active roles and engage in independent decision making. Life in war demands more of women, and consequently they become stronger and more decisive. However, suffering in war produces feelings of helplessness, hopelessness and depression. This happens especially when women have difficulty in coping with the fact that they have lost all or a big part of their former lives, which means that they must start anew. War is a major stressor for women because of the alterations and losses it brings.

Although every war has demonstrated that violence does not only devastate material wealth but also human souls, it is only during the last few decades that there have appeared organized professional and paraprofessional assistance for war-affected persons and refugees. This form of social assistance implies giving information, counseling and emotional support. It can also be defined as a social network, wherein beneficiaries feel loved, accepted, cared for and appreciated. Such a social network implies also the active participation of its beneficiaries, as that is the only way to activate natural defense mechanisms based on instincts of self-preservation.

These support networks cover many areas. Psychological assistance is offered by professional teams composed of psychologists, psychiatrists and social workers. Expert medical and psychiatric help is necessary for those women and girls who were victims of rape in war, as they are frequently in a state of shock produced by the traumatic and stressful events they have survived. Expert psychological and psychiatric help must be given to those women who, after their experiences in war and refuge, have become emotionally unstable and upset. Their instability, in turn, deeply affects their attitude towards their children, who very frequently are abused or neglected. Expert teams also set up special work programs for refugees and organize educational assistance.

Aside from professional help, paraprofessional assistance, offered by individuals, humanitarian organizations and host families, is significant in helping women overcome war trauma. Women and children come from the war zones to a new, unknown, social environment where their accommodation consists of collective shelters or the homes of their relatives or friends, who are also very often faced with poverty and existential insecurity. A common trait for all such situations is that nobody knows how long the war will last, or how long they will be a refugee. That is why paraprofessional help in the form of socializing, cooperation, conversation, encouragement and personal empowerment has the same importance as expert professional help. In fact, it became apparent that paraprofessional help was efficient in other crisis situations as well, such as the prevention of suicide. This form of assistance is provided in centers with mixed personnel (where usually paraprofessionals are the majority of the personnel, while the core staff is composed of the experts who organize programs). There are also centers mainly composed of paraprofessionals, where professionals appear as consultants or coordinators (Kapamadžija et al, 1990). Paraprofessional help has numerous advantages (constant contact, immediate and quick action, a larger number of participants, etc.) and that is why it is necessary to include these types of group when working with women who have survived war violence.

While carrying out our research on violence against women in the war in the former Yugoslavia, we at the same time acted as a paraprofessional group for victim support. While talking to refugee women, we complied with our feminist principles of intervention in a situation of violence, without offering any prefabricated solutions or unrealistic expectations. Through conversation and regular meetings, we tried to encourage and empower women to seek their own ways out of the situations they were in. Past experience demonstrated that women who had actively confronted experiences of war and refuge finally emerged as reinforced and more stable. For example, one of our interviewees (Nada) told us that she hadn't wanted to take any sedatives because she wanted to consciously face her husband's death, all the horrors and all the ensuing problems she had to put up with in war and refuge.

In the course of our research, paraprofessional help and support to women refugees was also provided by the feminist organization Women in Black and the hotline SOS Phone for Women and Children Victims of Violence.

Our investigation of violence against women in the war in the former Yugoslavia was carried out in 1994, a period in which the consequences of the civil and ethnic war had already begun to appear. At the beginning of our interviews, we encountered women who did not want to be reminded of their losses, their moments of anguish and terrible scenes. These were usually women refugees who did not come to Serbia immediately after the beginning of the war. Still, those too who left the war zone immediately after the outbreak of hostilities and who still had some family members there felt reluctant to talk about their experiences of war violence. They feared that cooperating with us might in some way negatively affect those who had remained. This reaction was understandable and expected from women refugees, because they had lost all their confidence in others. At the beginning of our conversations, they most often stated that they had not experienced any violence, by which they meant physical or sexual violence. However, later on, their attitude changed. They gained confidence in us and began manifesting a desire for cooperation. In the course of our interviews, they expressed their opinions, made suggestions and actively participated in countless other ways. When asked about what kind of assistance they needed most, our respondents most often replied that they would be delighted if the domestic population would accept them with more sympathy and understanding, to make them feel like equal human beings and not like "second-class citizens."

Conversations that focused on the kind of help they needed in order to successfully adjust to the new conditions of life were a precious source of information about their social status and their chances in the new environment. Women from collective shelters came from various regions of Croatia and Bosnia-Herzegovina and all had lived in various conditions in their homeland. It was quite natural for their needs in refuge to differ. Nevertheless, all the women said that it was very important to them how their new environment accepted and evaluated them, because emigration to a new country entailed a profound change of socioeconomic status. It was very important to them, they said, when somebody understood them, offered them moral support and helped them forget their dark experiences. They wanted somebody to pay them visits, listen to them, socialize and talk to them, so that they could see that all humans "are not bad, after all." That, they said, would greatly help them reintegrate into society and thus overcome their difficulties and dilemmas. Women refugees had the hardest time when they were treated as "things," when they were derided, despised, humiliated, blackmailed and socially isolated.

Our interviewees proposed the addition or amendment of various forms of assistance and support, which may be classified in the following way:

— Organization of specific work activities;
— Provision of accurate information about family members who remained in the war zone or emigrated abroad and assistance in establishing relationships with them;
— Social acceptance, socializing and moral support in their new social environment;
— Better housing or an improvement of the conditions in existing accommodation;
— Various forms of material help.

These forms of assistance and support should be supplemented by some assistance in the establishment of various forms of women's self-organized associations. After the period of adaptation, new possibilities for female initiatives must be sought. This conclusion is bolstered by the fact that in the course of time refugee families in Serbia have become more complete, because by and large, male family members have joined their families already in refuge. In the course of our study we found some forms of autonomous women's associations. For example, there is one collective shelter near Belgrade where women have succeeded in organizing themselves and thus making a slightly better life for themselves and their families. There were fourteen families in the shelter, with fifteen women and twenty-seven children. Every family had a separate room, while the kitchen and dining room were collective. Every week, two women were on duty and they did all the housework for all the families. Food was prepared for everyone with products obtained from a small collective farm—a patch of land that surrounded the center, where the women grew vegetables. They also used the humanitarian aid ration of flour to bake their own bread and cakes. Moreover, they also raised pigs and asked various humanitarian organizations to find them hens as well.

A second form of self-organization is more appropriate to urban environments, and it consists of establishing house-councils in collective shelters for refugees. The house-councils of collective shelters publicly consider all problems that might appear, and assign concrete responsibilities and duties, with particular individuals being charged with hygiene, maintenance, house repairs, and so on. All activities unfold according to the previously established schedule, and there is a committee which deals with the complete documentation about the humanitarian aid received. This form of self-organization has been recently applied in some collective shelters in southern Serbia.

Organization of particular work activities

The majority of women were willing to work, not only because of the economic effects, but also because work would help them overcome the feelings of helplessness, absurdity and social isolation. The following examples illustrate this point.

RADA: "It's no good to isolate us. We should be helped in our efforts to get back to normal life. I would like to work. I have seventeen years of work experience and just cannot be imprisoned between four walls."

BORJANA: "While I was working, I felt like a human being. I had a goal in my life and I tried hard to earn my living."

MILKA: "It would be best to find some work for women refugees, because it is pointless just to sit here and receive food. Although I am retired, I would like to work at something, be it crocheting, if nothing else. When you don't work the day seems endless."

When they spoke about the possibility of employment, women mentioned, however, that employment should be commensurate with their education and previous work experience. In refuge, women most often work as maids or farmhands and receive very low wages. Women with higher education and women who, prior to the war, held managerial positions have the hardest time, because they cannot find appropriate jobs and are very dissatisfied with manual labor. "I tried to do physical jobs but I couldn't manage because my heart could not endure that," said Sofija, a dentist. Maja, a former clerk, said "I am not physically fit to earn my living by doing housework. I would never refuse a job that is remotely similar to the one I had before, but here I can find only physical jobs." "It is awful when you are educated and yet have to make coffee in some stupid firm," added Gordana, a former economist, who, prior to the war, had worked as a sales manager.

Family regrouping

It was easy to observe the suffering of women because of family members who had remained in the war zone. This was especially visible when women talked about what they considered as the most necessary forms of assistance. Some women found it easier to cope with social isolation and the lack of employment than with doing without information about their family members. Very frequently, our respondents pointed out their need for reliable information about loved ones who had either remained in the war zone or emigrated elsewhere. They were also particularly interested in any methods of getting in touch with them.

Social acceptance, socializing and moral support

All our interviewees desired social acceptance, and, indeed, considered it necessary in order to avoid feeling like "second-class citizens." Here are some examples.

VIDA: "A kind word and an occasional visit is what matters most. Everything else is insubstantial."

MARINA: "I think that it is most important to talk to us and offer some support."

JASNA: "One has to socialize and talk with people to realize that all people are not bad."

BOSILJKA: "We need somebody who would listen to us and not only criticize."

DANICA: "We need some conversation and comfort so as not to feel isolated from the society into which we would like to integrate."

Better housing and material assistance

Inadequate housing and the lack of material help (including medications, clothing and shoes) were considered by our respondents to be major reasons for their poor emotional state. They thought that assistance in solving these problems would significantly contribute to their ability to adapt to the environment.

The authors acted both as a group of researchers studying violence in war and, simultaneously, as a female support group. We tried to socialize with the refugees as much as we could, to talk with the women about their problems and their needs in refuge and to encourage them to seek solutions on their own. Unfortunately, the objective conditions did not offer many opportunities for a favorable solution of the existential questions and problems of our interviewees. However, we tried to empower and encourage; we hoped they could persist in their everyday battles, become aware of their personal value and strength, overcome bad feelings and, thus, perhaps find a way out of the situation. The results of such cooperation and socialization did not miss. A group of our interviewees intensified their efforts to obtain refugee status abroad and now live as immigrants in far better conditions and with much broader perspectives than they had before. Among the women we socialized with, there were students who have succeeded in obtaining better housing and a better learning environment, which significantly stimulated their further work and education (Branka, Zorica). Also motivating was the inclusion of female refugee volunteers into the work of the SOS Phone for Women and Children Victims of Violence (Branka, Lepa, Zorica, Senka and Merima). They declared that they felt "reborn," reinvigorated and accepted for the first time since they had come to Serbia. For the women who felt a need to do some handicraft and thus "fill in" their free time, the feminist organization Women in Black procured the necessary material (Merima: "Many women felt alive again when they could do some handwork.") On their part, our interviewees responded to our efforts by giving us small gifts, inviting us to birthday parties and collective visits to the theater, among other things. This represented quite a lot of progress and was seen by us as a sign that they were beginning to return to their earlier lifestyles.

While trying to assist and encourage the women in refuge, and to offer them some precise help for satisfying their needs, we realized that the possibilities of assistance were very limited. From 1991 on, when the first refugees came to Serbia, not much was done to help the women among them, although there were some programs for social and psychological help. The majority of the programs of refugee assistance focused on the problems of employment, accommodation and distributing the most elementary materials. This assistance basically means dealing with the essentials, nothing more. It is unrealistic to expect that something significant will change in the near future. That is why women refugees must fight for their status in this society. They are required to find their own solutions for their difficulties, and to ensure their survival and the survival of their children. This is, in fact, the major difference between the refugee situation in Serbia and other countries. On that account, it is even more important to support and empower women refugees here. As one energetic woman refugee, who became a widow while she was in refuge with her two children, put it, "Women refugees have to understand that their experience is different from the experiences of the domestic population and they must not expect to be understood, because it is impossible. They have to struggle, but peacefully, and avoid unnecessary conflicts. I think I was greatly helped by the fact that I did not pay attention to anti-refugee remarks. I have just pushed all that aside and tried to adapt to the new environment."

Feminist groups and humanitarian organizations can do a great deal to further animate women refugees, to snatch them away from the monotonous routines of collective shelters. Organizations can do much to constantly draw the attention of the competent public authorities to establish better collective shelters and raise the quality of life in refugee camps.

The social component of our relationship with the women who came to Serbia fleeing the war goes on, although the research is finished. They stay with us and we socialize, talk, pay visits, encourage and empower each other. We constantly encourage them to do something for themselves and their children which will alter the monotonous course of everyday life or which will, at least temporarily, make them forget their unsolved problems. Time will show how much we succeeded in channeling a part of our positive energy to them, and if we have succeeded in stimulating others to assist us in our efforts.

Conclusion

Violence against women exists in peacetime, but it continues even more drastically in war. First of all, war increases the imbalance of power between the sexes. It widens the gap between the man who has social power and the woman who is deprived of it. Women, as a rule, are not armed; in contrast, men, when armed, become more "mannish" and powerful. In war, moreover, women are deprived of the minimum of protection that they normally enjoy as citizens and members of the subdued "second sex." The mechanism of protection is paralyzed during war, so that women are protected neither by the state nor by "their" men. Their fathers, husbands and sons are often unable to safeguard "their" women, especially when the men themselves are arrested, tortured or killed. Additionally, sometimes the men have left to fight and can protect women only abstractly. This form of protection usually means little more than an exchange; the women belonging to "the enemy side" will be victimized in the same way as their women were victimized.

Women, as a rule, were completely deprived of the opportunity to decide about this war. They, however, were the ones who had to pay most dearly for the warlike decisions of "their" men. They had to suffer simply because of their own or their husbands' ethnic affiliation. Women of all nationalities were used for the achievement of male political and military goals. They were not only deprived of protection and left alone to face destruction, fear, sexual, physical and psychic violence of the enemy, but were often abused by those who, in the patriarchal society, were traditionally expected to protect them (for example, their own husbands).

Although considerable progress has been made in the matter of the international legal recognition of rape as a war crime, many of the effects of war that women have been forced to undergo are still not recognized as war crimes. Forced impregnation and war-related family violence, for example, are still not prohibited by international law. Women of all the belligerent ethnic groups had to endure violence, which means that all perpetrators, regardless of their ethnic affiliation, should be punished. Unfortunately, the existing system of witness protection for women who were victims of rape in fact discourages possible witnesses. This means that many cases of rape remain unreported. That is why it is necessary to grant immigrant status to women witnesses and to protect them from being deported to their country of origin. Meanwhile, until a permanent criminal tribunal becomes established, it is necessary to ensure adequate funds for the normal functioning of all services of the Hague Tribunal. Better guarantees must be offered that the procedures for the protection of rape victims will be truly followed.

In the impossible conditions imposed by war, women were left alone to cope not only with violence but also with full responsibilities for home and family care. These and similar conditions, in fact, forced many women to choose the most discreet form of prostitution, relationships based on provision and protection (which remained most in accord with the male definition of female chastity). Even as refugees, women were sexually harassed and abused and were forced to engage in prostitution in order to survive.

Suffering produced by the forcible separation from family or by the loss of family members was also a consequence of the totality of war violence. Equally likely to occur was a forced change of habitation, a loss of property and regular income, a change of socioeconomic and family status and an alteration of usual lifestyle. Women who had structured their identities as mothers and spouses and who had never been encouraged to make decisions on their own were faced with new obligations imposed by war, which represented an additional psychological burden for them.

Women have a very hard time when they have no information about their family members and close relatives. They suffer considerably when separated from their children (be their children minors or adults) and their husbands, parents, brothers and sisters. Worrying about the destiny of their relatives becomes a necessary part of their lives, at the expense of a personal quest for the solution to the problems of life in refuge. Some women only come to know about the death of a husband or relative some time after the fact. Knowing they did not witness the death does spare women a great deal of suffering, but it only temporarily alleviates the emotional loss. A husband's death represents a profound and durable change of the already established family system. It also means a definitive absence of a psychological support that had made the women stronger and more motivated to cope with the problems of life in refuge.

Women refugees have to face new forms of violence as part of their integration into the new environment. Separation from, or the loss of, a husband means that these women have to accept a greater obligation towards their children and other persons with whom they shared refuge. This inevitably changes their family functions and their relationships with their children. In a stable economic situation, a woman can deal more easily with war traumas that she has experienced. However, the fact that women were left alone, helpless, impoverished, in difficult conditions, with almost no chance of improving their condition (no matter how hard they worked), made women susceptible to sexual blackmail and all kinds of exploitation at work.

Women also found difficulty when attempting to adapt to the conditions of life in refuge. Social adaptation was rendered more difficult by inadequate housing, a lack of money, existential insecurity, difficulties in communication, and the serious illnesses of the women themselves or of their children and families. Moreover, they are faced with misunderstanding and even ostracism to further multiply the obstacles facing them. For women whose ethnic origin differs from the ethnic majority in the host country (i.e. women living in so-called mixed marriages), it was even harder to adapt. They were exposed to aggravated harassment in their immediate social environment. Not infrequently, the insults came from the refugees living with them in the same collective shelters. That is why many women refugees do not see their future in Yugoslavia.

A society that accepts refugees should be more interested in offering an adequate (not only material) support to, in particular, single-mother refugee families. This point is especially valid because the majority of women refugees from the former Yugoslavia are by their age, level of education and previous professional experience quite able to compete with the local labor force. Employment in their own fields would represent a major step towards the integration of women refugees into the new social environment. Aside from making them economically independent, appropriate employment inevitably improves their social and psychological status. Women of the former Yugoslavia had to undergo various and destructive forms of violence in a war they were not asked about and which they did not support. That is why they have a moral right to demand, both from the host country and from the international community, conditions for a better life for them and their children.

Who are the women who have spoken?

1. ANA: 36 years old, married with two children, Yugoslav; economist. She went to Serbia with her husband and children. She was interviewed in a collective shelter. She emigrated to Canada together with her family.

2. ANĐA: 24 years old, single without children, Serb; shop clerk. She was interviewed in the war zone.

3. ANKA: 38 years old, widow with two children, Serb; economist. After her husband was killed she fled to refuge with her children. She lived with them in a collective shelter while her mother and brother remained in the war zone.

4. BILJANA: 19 years old, single without children, Serb; no profession. Mentally retarded, she lived in refuge with her mother in a collective shelter. Her brother is also a refugee, but in a different place.

5. BISERKA: 46 years old, married with two children, Serb, married to a Slovene; clerk. She lived with her entire family in a rented apartment.

6. BLAŽENKA: 27 years old, married with three children, Croat, married to a Serb; typist. She went to refuge with her family, while her parents and in-laws remained in the war zone. They lived in a collective shelter and are now in Australia.

7. BOJANA: 28 years old, single with one child, Serb; clerk. She was alone and lived in a rented apartment.

8. BORJANA: 32 years old, married with one child, Yugoslav; economist. She went to refuge with her child and her mother while her husband remained in the war zone. She was accommodated in a collective shelter. She moved to Canada, together with her child and husband.

9. BORKA: 62 years old, married with one child, Serb; house-wife/farmer. She was accommodated in a collective shelter after having left her home area with other members of her family.

10. BOSILJKA: 30 years old, married with two children, Serb; economic analyst. She lived in refuge with her husband, children and in-laws, while her relatives remained in the war zone.

11. BRANKA: 23 years old, single, without children, Serb; student. She lived alone in refuge in Serbia before her mother joined her. While in refuge, she began and completed a degree in electrical engineering, *cum laude*. She emigrated to Canada with her brother.

12. DANICA: 41 years old, married with one child, Serb; accountant. She lived in a collective shelter together with her child, while her husband remained in the war zone.

13. DESA: 46 years old, Serb; tram driver. She lived in a collective shelter together with her two children. Her husband and sister-in-law remained in the war zone.

14. DOBRILA: 62 years old, divorced with two children, Serb; retired. She lived alone in a collective shelter while her children were also in refuge somewhere else in Serbia.

15. DRAGICA: 60 years old, married with two adult children, Serb; retired. She lived with her sister in a collective shelter.

16. EMINA: 28 years old, married, Moslem; chemical technician. She lived in refuge with her husband and their two children. They found private accommodation afterwards. Her mother, sister and son-in-law remained in the war zone, while all her in-laws were in refuge as well. She came to refuge with one child and gave birth to the second one some time later.

17. GORDANA: 38 years old, married with one child, Serb; economist. She lived in refuge with her child and mother. She was in private accommodation. Her husband, brother and other relatives remained in the war zone.

18. GORICA: 48 years old, widow with one child, Serb; clerk. Her husband was Slovene and her son was killed. She lived in a collective shelter together with her child.

19. IVANA: 17 years old, single without children, Serb; high-school student. She lived with her sister in a collective shelter. Her parents joined them later.

20. JANA: 35 years old, married with three children, Serb; housewife. She went to refuge with her children. When interviewed, she lived in a collective shelter with one child, while her husband and other two children remained in the war zone.

21. JASMINKA: 38 years old, married with three children, Moslem, married to a Serb; architect. Her husband, together with her

mother, remained in the war zone. We interviewed her while she was in a collective shelter. Afterwards, she emigrated to Canada with her children.

22. JASNA: 37 years old, married with two children, Serb; architect. She lived in a collective shelter together with her children and parents, while her brother and his family were also in refuge but not in Belgrade. Her husband remained in the war zone.

23. JELENA: 26 years old, married with two children, Serb; shop clerk. She lived in refuge with her husband and children. All her family was in refuge as well, while her husband's family remained in the war zone.

24. JOVANA: 20 years old, single without children, Serb; student. Her brother and parents remained in the war zone, while she lived alone in a collective shelter.

25. JULIJANA: 38 years old, married with one child, Serb; clerk. She lived with her child in a rented apartment, while her mother, husband and other relatives remained in the war zone.

26. KATJA: 55 years old, married without children, Slovene, married to a Serb; retired. She lived with her husband in a rented apartment.

27. LEPA: 56 years old, married with two children, Serb; legal expert. She lived in a collective shelter with her daughter, while her son was also in refuge somewhere else in Serbia. Her husband remained in the war zone. In refuge, she joined the SOS Phone for Women and Children Victims of Violence in the city of Niš. Since her daughter emigrated to Canada she was considering joining her husband in the city of Doboj, Bosnia.

28. LJILJANA: 22 years old, single without children, Serb; student. She lived alone in a collective shelter. Her brother was also in refuge, but lived in another place. Her father remained in the war zone.

29. MAJA: 38 years old, married with two children, Serb; clerk. She was interviewed in a collective shelter. Some time after the interview, she returned with her children to join her husband.

30. MARINA: 33 years old, married with two children, Serb; pharmacist. She went to refuge with her children, husband and in-laws. They lived in a collective shelter. She found a job in a private pharmacy.

31. MERIMA: 46 years old, married with two children, Moslem, married to a Croat; professor. Her husband remained in the war zone together with her family (parents, sister and two brothers). She had been accommodated in a collective shelter, but afterwards she emigrated to the United States together with her children.

32. METKA: 37 years old, married with one child, Yugoslav, married to a Moslem; legal expert. She was interviewed in the war zone, where she remained with her parents and her child. Her husband and other relatives lived in the Moslem-controlled part of Sarajevo.

33. MILENA: 23 years old, single without children, Serb; agricultural engineer. She was interviewed in the war zone, where she lived.

34. MILEVA: 52 years old, married with three children, Serb; professor. She lived in a collective shelter together with her daughter, while her son emigrated together with his family. Her husband remained in the war zone.

35. MILICA: 21 years old, single with one child, Serb; worker. She came to Belgrade only to give birth and immediately after she returned to her family which had remained in the war zone.

36. MILKA: 64 years old, married with two adult children, Serb; retired. She lived in a collective shelter together with her daughter, son, sister-in-law and grandchildren.

37. MIRJANA: 45 years old, single with one child, Serb; legal expert. She came to refuge with her mother, two sisters and their children, while one sister remained in the war zone. They all lived in collective shelters.

38. MUNEVERA: 60 years old, widow with two adult children, Moslem; housewife. She is Nedžada's (44) mother.

39. NADA: 35 years old, widow with two children, Serb; social worker. Her sister and parents remained in the war zone and she lived with her children in private accommodation.

40. NADEŽDA: 43 years old, widow with two children, Serb; worker. She lived with her children in a collective shelter. Her brother's and sister's families were also in refuge, while one sister remained in the war zone.

41. NATALIJA: 67 years old, married with two grown-up children, Serb; housewife. She lived at her cousins' place, while one of her sons had emigrated.

42. NATAŠA: 34 years old, married with one child, Yugoslav, married to a Croat; nurse. She lived in the war zone where she wrote a series of letters to her sister Ana. She emigrated with her family to Canada. Eventually, she, with her family, lived in the same city as her sister and her family.

43. NEDELJKA: 42 years old, married with two children, Serb; housewife. She lived in a collective shelter with her children, husband, sister and mother.

44. NEDŽADA: 38 years old, widow with one child, Moslem; textile technician. She lived in a collective shelter together with her

child, mother, sister and niece. Some of her relatives remained in the war zone while others emigrated.

45. NELA: 43 years old, married with two children, Croat, married to a Serb; legal expert. She lived with her whole family in a rented apartment.

46. OLGA: 34 years old, divorced with two children, Yugoslav; legal expert. She lived with her children in private accommodation, while her parents remained in the war zone.

47. OLIVERA: 45 years old, married with four children, Serb; chemical technician. Having spent two and a half years with her husband in the war zone, she decided to join her children, who lived in refuge in a collective shelter. Her mother and husband remained in the war zone.

48. RADA: 37 years old, married with two children, Serb; economist. She lived in refuge with her children and her sister, while her parents remained in the war zone. She lived in a collective shelter.

49. RANKA: 34 years old, married with one child, Serb; economist. She lived with her entire family in a rented apartment, while her brother remained in the war zone.

50. SANDRA: 27 years old, single without children, Serb; student. She lived alone in a collective shelter, while her entire family remained in the war zone.

51. SANIJA: 76 years old, single, without children, Moslem; housewife. She was alone in refuge. She had a sister who remained with her family in the war zone, while her brother emigrated with his family.

52. SANJA: 19 years old, single without children, Serb; student. Her parents remained in the war zone and she lived in a collective shelter with some distant relatives.

53. SENADA: 61 years old, married with one adult child, Moslem, married to a Slovene; housewife. She is the mother of Metka (32).

54. SENKA: 36 years old, married with two children, Serb; playwright. After two and a half years of waiting, her husband succeeded in leaving Sarajevo, after which they left for Canada.

55. SLOBODANKA: 49 years old, widow with two children, Serb; worker. Her son and husband were killed in the war and she lived in a collective shelter together with her daughter.

56. SMILJKA: 45 years old, widow with two adult children, Montenegrin, married to a Moslem; economist. Her youngest son was kidnapped from a train in Republika Srpska. While in refuge, she lived in private accommodation and had a couple of cousins in refuge in other parts of Serbia. She later emigrated to the United States.

57. SNEŽANA: 36 years old, married with two children, Serb; economist. She lived in refuge with her children and her sister, while her husband and her parents remained in the war zone. She moved to Canada.

58. SOFIJA: 39 years old, widow with one child, Serb; dentist. She was married to a Moslem and at the time of interviewing lived in a collective shelter together with her child. Her sister and her family were also in refuge but lived elsewhere, while her mother remained in the war zone.

59. STANA: 39 years old, widow with one child, Serb; worker. She lived with her child in a collective shelter. One of her sisters remained in the war zone while the other one was in refuge as well.

60. STANISLAVA: 48 years old, single without children, Serb; clerk. She remained in the war zone while her relatives lived in the Moslem-controlled areas of Bosnia.

61. STOJANKA: 54 years old, married with three children, Serb; housewife. She lived in a collective shelter together with her husband and two children, with one daughter also in refuge with her family, although not in the Belgrade region. The relatives who remained in the war zone were all killed.

62. SUZANA: 38 years old, widow with two children, Serb; economist. Her brother and husband were killed in the war, while her sisters with their families remained in the war zone. She came to refuge with her children and lived with them in a collective shelter.

63. SVETLANA: 46 years old, married with five children, Montenegrin; clerk. She came to refuge with her husband in order to join her children who had already been accommodated in a collective shelter. She and her husband spent some time with relatives and afterwards returned to Višegrad (Bosnia).

64. TAMARA: 35 years old, married with one child, Serb; technician. Her husband, parents and in-laws remained in the war zone, and she lived in a collective shelter together with her child.

65. TATJANA: 40 years old, married with two children, Serb; accountant. Her mother, husband and brother remained in the war zone, and she lived in a collective shelter together with her sister and children.

66. VERA: 64 years old, widow with two adult children, Serb; housewife. She is the mother of Gordana (17).

67. VESNA: 33 years old, married with two children, Serb; clerk. Her sister's and her sister-in-law's families were also in refuge, while her husband and her in-laws remained in the war zone. She lived with her children in a collective shelter.

68. VIDA: 40 years old, married with two children, Serb; teacher. She lived in a collective shelter with her children and her mother-in-law. Her husband remained for a while in the war zone and then joined them. She earned money by selling fruit in the market.

69. VUKOSAVA: 65 years old, widow with four adult children, Serb; retired. Her son and daughter-in-law remained in the war zone while her other children went to refuge. She lived alone in a rented apartment.

70. ZORICA: 19 years old, single without children, Serb; student. Her parents and brother remained in the war zone, while she lived alone in a collective shelter. During her refuge, she passed several exams at the Belgrade Law School and worked occasionally in a café.

A sample of their stories and letters

Sofija

My husband and father were killed in this war. I have no place to go. I have no more strength left. I think a woman must have a support. I was energetic and brave when I was in Sarajevo and now I can't even recognize myself. I feel terribly weak, both mentally and physically. When you don't have any support the burden gets too heavy. My child keeps telling me all the time, "My father and grandfather were killed." That's all his life. What's left of his life?

I am a dentist. Presently I'm working in a private office. I do everything, I'm a doctor, assistant and worker. They exploit me. Besides, my child demands devotion and care and I don't have enough strength left. We are three families here, sharing the same room. I would like to have some peace, to be alone sometimes. The child has to begin attending school but he doesn't have the necessary space to do homework. My husband was a Moslem and that's why I can't get anything from the funds for the children whose parents were killed in the war. He was killed in the city, in the Moslem-controlled part of Sarajevo, in a café, on February 21, 1993, and I was informed seven weeks later. He worked in the Central Power Station and his Serb colleagues informed me about his death. My father, who was still alive at the time, heard it as well but he couldn't believe it. I have received a death certificate with no explanation whatsoever. The people from the Central Power Station said he had been killed accidentally in the café. Later I realized how that could have happened. It was our son's birthday that day and he must have celebrated the event in the café, when a fight occurred. My father was killed on our balcony.

We never cared about ethnic origins. We did not have any problems, we had a superb marriage and we got along very well indeed. Had we had an occasion to make big decisions, all this would have never happened. People living in ethnically mixed marriages had the hardest time. My mother calls or writes me from time to time.

I took sick leave from April 2, 1992, in order to go somewhere until the situation became normal again. There were rumors that the sovereignty of Bosnia-Herzegovina would be proclaimed on April 6, 1992. The ambience was really hot and we were all afraid. I left my home to see a colleague, I took some clothes with me and I remained there two years. Now, here, my work is not declared and I have no pension plan at all. I work on Saturdays too. On the other hand, my child remains alone, because kindergartens are not open on Saturdays. I even tried doing physical jobs, and I couldn't stand that because I have heart problems.

Regardless of the fact that my husband was far from me, in the Moslem-controlled part of the city, I felt much safer when he was alive. A letter means hope; it gives sense to life, it gives me strength. If I did not have my child I would not have any meaning in life. My sister is here, in Belgrade, and she lives with her mother-in-law who came to look after a cousin's apartment. They are making problems for her; she goes off to a village near Zrenjanin where she works as a hairdresser. She spends only weekends at home. She's completely in charge of two children, her mother-in-law and her husband. I used to blame my brother-in-law for having left Sarajevo but he says he will defend Serbia if necessary. My sister is my special problem. On one side, I have my problems and, on the other side, I have her problems.

As the older daughter and as a sister, I always had the main role to play. Everybody turned to me for support. I had responsibility for my parents and for my baby sister, who always had frail health, same as her children. I always was the pillar of the family. Now, when I myself am in a terrible situation, I'm still expected to assist my sister and their children, but I don't have enough strength. There is no act of violence that can be compared to the loss of a dear one. The only thing that matters is to be together. Everything is easier when people are together.

Olivera

When the war began, I was ready to leave Sarajevo immediately. My husband did not agree because he had heard that there was mobilization going on in Serbia and he thought that there were ways of avoiding mobilization in Sarajevo. He did not want to take up arms at all. Besides, he thought that we had to remain in the city and thus save our house. I just can't forgive myself for not leaving immediately with the children. You know, I was taught to be always by my husband's side. I thought, "What would happen if he had to go to fight and then got killed? Would my children tell me that I had left him to manage everything alone and get killed?" And he, indifferent as men mainly are, did not even understand that we had to take the children to a safe place. It was a bloody mess; there was shelling, people were being taken away and killed, girls were being raped. Once, my younger daughter, aged 15, came home, all desperate and said, "I'd rather be killed than raped." Then I lost patience and said to my husband, "We have to move the children out immediately. Our daughters are young and pretty. I can be beaten, raped or even killed, but I can put up with everything and continue to live, because I have them. But they can't deal with that; just think what they would become if somebody raped them. Their life would be ruined." Thus, we decided that they should leave.

After the children had left we lived a real hell. They used to forcibly enter whenever they wanted and search our flat. Once, four Moslem soldiers (my daughter's schoolmates) pointed their guns at me and said, "And where is your daughter?" I replied that she had left at the very beginning of the war and they asked ironically why she had left and where she had gone. Then they said they knew that my older daughter was an instructor in a detention camp for Moslems. I was astonished because it was not true at all and because the lie had hurt me profoundly. Later on, my husband was taken prisoner. The first thing they asked him was the whereabouts of our daughters. I just can't imagine what they would have done with them had they been around. We irritated them, because we were a very respectable family, very distant from others. I was always well dressed, made-up, wearing silk only. My father-in-law was an officer and was killed by Moslems. He was a respectable officer and that's what irritated them; they just couldn't forgive us, and that was an additional reason for being afraid for my children.

Separation from children was the toughest thing for me in this war. I couldn't stand to be without them any longer. During the last month I spent in Sarajevo, I only vegetated. I cooked but I didn't eat; I didn't go out; I took no interest in anybody and I couldn't read or work at anything. I took a bath six times a day, because I was sweating all the time. Once I went to see a doctor in order to get permission to leave Sarajevo. I told him I couldn't stand it anymore. I said, "The day I even stop bathing, I will commit suicide, because the sorrow for my children tears me apart."

I think they blame me now, because they had to live so long without parents, alone. They don't blame their father, because it was me who always decided about everything in the family and they think that I should have persuaded him to leave Sarajevo immediately, all together. They don't say it, but I feel it, and I feel very bad about it. I am with them now. I couldn't save anything there; I left everything behind. I couldn't take anything with me, because I asked for permission for two days. That was the only way to leave Sarajevo, although I had not, and I still don't have, any intention to return. That's how, after two years of separation, my daughters have gotten a ruined mother and me, I have gotten grown-up daughters. They've got used to living without a mother. They have organized their life in a way that the older one has taken over my role. We need a lot of time to bridge the gap between us.

When I had to leave Sarajevo I was searched in a tobacco shop/improvised customs-office. I had to take off my clothes in front of three men, Moslems. There was also a woman who performed a gynecological examination on me. As I stood there naked, a thought came to me, "That's it, they will rape me, but I will survive; that will be my last suffering and then I will go to join my children." No suffering on that road would be difficult for me, because I had my goal, to finally be with my children.

I came here expecting that I would be accepted decently. However, I found myself being treated in a rough, humiliating way by the officials, the director of the collective shelter and even my cousins who reproached me for not having left Sarajevo earlier. And I am a stranger for my children as well. I feel terrible because I'm not even capable of providing essentials for myself, let alone for my children, who are expecting that from me, because I had always been able to work and earn and I always knew how to find a way out in every situation.

Now I feel helpless and my daughters are the ones who have to help me adapt to this new life. Instead of me giving them support it's me who needs their assistance. I was always well dressed and made-up and now I'm happy that the Red Cross gave me a pair of coarse shoes of the kind I never wore before.

I'm full of fear. When I go on the street I always have the impression that somebody's tailing me, that he will shoot at me or attack me in some other way. The things I've been through just cannot be recounted. One has to live it to understand it.

Zorica

Sometime around October 10, 1992, my parents and I went to my grandma's house in the village of Čemerno, because life in Sarajevo became too dangerous. That was my father's idea because during the Second World War, the village was not attacked at all. This time again, the village was full of Serb soldiers. Since the village is high in the mountains we could easily see Sarajevo, Breza and Visoko. In fact, the village was a Serb military stronghold from which they fired upon Moslem positions. It was believed that the village was rather safe, so that there were many refugees. Our cousins were accommodated in the house next to ours, some fifty meters away.

My father would go to the front line during the day and he would be back in the evening. I felt safe because my parents were with me and, besides, there were many Serb soldiers around. However, suddenly a large number of soldiers were transferred, so that only some thirty soldiers remained in the village. Still, nobody thought about the possibility of a Moslem attack. In fact, a couple of days before the attack, a cousin of mine told me that we should go away, because Moslems would come. Although she slept with her clothes on, with a suitcase in her hand, I continued believing that this would not happen.

One October morning, though, I was awaken by terrible shooting. Father, who had just returned from his duty, grabbed his gun and left the house to see what was going on. We others (mother, brother and grandmother) took a look through the window and saw a group of Moslem soldiers shooting at our cousins and setting their house on fire. Then they came to our house. In terrible panic, we all ran to the cellar while father got out of the house and hid in the nearby forest. I thought it was our end. I shivered by my mother's side and my brother cried silently. We heard them entering the house, shooting randomly and looking for something. I understood they were looking for a lighter or matches or something similar to set the house on fire. They cursed and protested because they couldn't find anything of the kind. I understood they were in a hurry but would return later.

Finally, they got out of the house and we swiftly ran to the forest. There we met my father and a cousin who was wounded. We spent almost four hours in that terribly cold forest and I still shiver when I recall that. The birds shrieked terribly as if they anticipated something. The cousin cried because of the wounds, and my brother cried out of fear. We didn't know where to go and what would happen with us. During the whole two years, not until this year could I forget the horror we experienced in the forest. When we realized that the Moslem soldiers had left the village, we returned. Some five to six hundred Serb soldiers were already there. Soon, the buses for evacuation came. Father put me, mother and brother into the bus and this is how we came to Belgrade. We took few things with us, because our house had burnt as well, so that we could barely fill a suitcase.

We first reached the city of Loznica, where we spent five days in a sports hall. Afterwards, we were transferred to the city of Niš. During the next two months, we were all together except father, who had remained at the front, in my aunt's house. There were fifteen of us in a two-room flat. Mother and brother returned to Sarajevo while I have remained in Serbia. I was transferred to a collective camp for refugees. I've finished high school and begun to study at Belgrade University.

Lepa

When the war began I was living with my family (husband, son and daughter) in Sarajevo. I held a very responsible post in a state agency. At the beginning, there were no big problems, except insecurity and tension. However, from July 1992 on, ethnic hatred began gaining place—I realized that among my colleagues, who were all highly educated persons. They kept telling me that I should stay in Sarajevo and publicly renounce my Serb origins. That's when I began worrying about the fate of my family. My daughter had a Moslem friend, long before the beginning of the war, and he continued to come to our home and that scared me even more. There was a shortage of food at the time and he always used to bring us something, coffee most frequently, because Moslems were given everything. My daughter and me, we refused everything from him but he kept insisting and we were afraid to refuse. We heard that there was mobilization going on, so a couple of days before the mobilization order arrived my son had gone secretly to our country house where father was already waiting for him. Later on, he joined the Serb forces. Had he not done so, Moslems would have mobilized him and sent him to the front. That's how many boys from Sarajevo were killed.

I remained in our flat with my daughter. I couldn't leave the city because I was still employed. I was constantly supervised and controlled. They used to read the letters that I received and sent. A Moslem neighbor used to come to my place every now and then, asking me where I was going, whom I was receiving, etc. She used to tell me that I should tell my children to return to Sarajevo, that we all should remain in the city but renounce our Serb origins. Once she told me that all Serbs should have been killed, that Belgrade should be bombed, and when I replied that my children were in Belgrade, she asked me why I had not told them to return.

I found it increasingly difficult to cope with constant tension, shelling and hiding in cellars. I was constantly treated unequally, humiliated and reproached for being a Serb. When they began making food lists at my workplace, I was omitted because I am a Serb. In my building I was the only person without electricity and running water, just because I am a Serb.

Therefore, I decided to leave Sarajevo and I thought I would be able to do it legally. I applied for the September 1993 convoy. By that time, I had already met the retirement conditions and I finally retired in March 1994 and began waiting to leave Sarajevo. From April 1994 on, I went several times to the place where the convoys were leaving from but my name was never on the list, so I decided to demand an official explanation. I went to the police headquarters where I was told to ask some people, in fact, ex-criminals who had become policemen. They asked me plenty of questions but never gave a straightforward answer. They just kept repeating "We'll see, you have to wait, it's not so easy, you know," and so on. I told them where I had been employed and I also mentioned that I had been working in the "new state" but it did not help at all.

I was not physically abused, but the constant waiting, the fear that they could break into my flat and evict me, because I was alone and unprotected—it all affected me profoundly. I couldn't sleep at night and was thinking all the time about a possible way out. Once, when I went again to the police (I don't know which time it was) to ask why my name was not on the list, one of the Moslem leaders told me that I could not leave Sarajevo, in spite of the fact that I had offered our four-room flat (according to their rules, the authorities would let people leave Sarajevo if they renounced their apartments). That's when I came to know that I had a police record, because my husband was out of Sarajevo and because my son was fighting on the Serb side. That really scared me, because my anonymity was therefore lost.

From that time on, I couldn't find any peace at all. My political imprisonment began and my freedom was taken away. I couldn't go anywhere without reporting to the guard who stood in front of my house. Then I began secretly and intensely to collect information about how to leave Sarajevo illegally. I took a serious risk but I couldn't wait any longer. I succeeded in finding a connection and was very cautious to cover all traces. The day I finished all the preparations I told my neighbor and my guard that I was going to attend a birthday party and that I would remain there all night. That's how I succeeded in leaving Sarajevo.

I will never forget how scared I was that night. A Moslem man led me through one part of the no-man's-land and I had to cross the other part alone, not knowing if the field was mined, where the guards were, would they fire without warning, etc. Still, everything worked out smoothly. I reached Serb-controlled territory, from which I was transferred to Serbia.

Merima

On May 2, 1992, we left Sarajevo by plane, through the Children's Embassy. Up to that time, although the city was shelled and there was a curfew and the snipers were active in all parts of Sarajevo, I worked all the time but it was not until I sat on the bus taking us to the airport that I realized that there was a war going on. When the partition of Sarajevo began, when the nationalistic parties became active, we knew that some parts of the city belonged to Serbs and some to Moslems, but neither I nor my friends took it seriously, because Sarajevo was unified, people of different ethnic origins were living side by side, all over the city. I lived in a part of the city where Moslems were the majority. I was born there and that's where I worked as well. But at the beginning of the conflict the whole city was surrounded by tanks and nobody could get out of it. The shells were falling from the surrounding hills and no matter where you were, in what part of the partitioned city you happened to be, you ran a serious risk of being wounded or killed. Before the war we joked about what part of the city belonged to whom, but it was only a joke.

Therefore, we were shocked when the first barricades appeared. Everything stopped, including the public transportation system. That day I did not go to my job. Quite simply, I was shocked, I was out of my mind. A couple of days later, we resumed our jobs and forgot the incident. On May 4, the Moslem holiday of Bairam, I heard shots in the city. Never before was the holiday celebrated in that way. We were appalled, we could hear the shots on a beautiful, sunny day. I remember it quite clearly. We went to pay a visit to my parents; my father was still alive at the time. When we returned, I began preparing a cake. Our neighborhood was without streetlights and I took it for a bad omen, for our street had always been well lit.

When we reached our home I realized that my daughter had gone out with friends. When I heard shots, I immediately went out to bring her home. She had gone out for a walk with her friends in the neighborhood. I took her home, but, all in all, I did not panic much, because people sometimes used to shoot during the big holidays, Christmas and New Year, so we thought that it was the same thing and that it would stop soon and we went to bed peacefully.

The next morning I went out to buy some bread and milk and I saw armed men all over the place. Those were the neighborhood boys that I knew. I just froze. Some time later, on April 5, there were those barricades so we could not go to work and I was filled with some unspeakable fear. However, on April 6, the citizens of Sarajevo began marching towards the Assembly of Bosnia-Herzegovina, in order to try to topple the authorities because nobody wanted that war, that's what I think. There was a huge crowd and we, my husband and I, took both of our children with us. That was great! That was something I will always remember—all that crowd which came in support of Zdravko Grebo and other progressive people. We wanted to topple the authorities who were indeed nauseating and unable to reach any common agreement. That was all terrible—the girl who had been killed on the Brotherhood and Unity bridge, all the people who walked empty-handed towards the Assembly. I don't know the girl's name, she was from Dubrovnik.

We were all anxious but we felt strong as well because we believed that Sarajevo could not be divided so easily, because 50% were ethnically mixed marriages, because there were so many people who did not pay attention to your name but only to what kind of person you were. The majority of my friends were Serbs and Croats. Within my circle of friends nothing had changed.

There were a couple of discussions at my work but I did not experience any harassment.

However, when the barricades appeared, when the shells began falling, we were all shocked and people stopped discussing politics, probably out of fear. When we reached the Assembly something (a sixth sense that I always feel?) made me tell my husband that we should leave the place immediately because something terrible would happen. And my son said, "Yeah, I think I see someone in one of the windows up there." So we returned. The first thing we did was to turn the TV on. We saw that there was almost no one in front of the Assembly and that some people were lying on the ground. It was then that we realized that something had happened, that someone had been shooting from the Holiday Inn hotel, that the crowd had dispersed and that our effort to topple the authorities had come to nothing. The very instant I realized that, I grabbed a couple of things and brought them to our cellar. I did that semiconsciously, like in a trance, led only by a wish to protect my children. I was vaguely aware that war had begun but, still, I kept persuading myself that it would only last a couple of weeks before things returned to normal.

We brought down a children's bed and some covers and pillows. Neighbors began organizing guards in order to discourage burglars. In fact, people were completely taken aback. They did their rounds without knowing why they were doing it and whom they were supposed to be protecting themselves from. And on top of that, they were completely unarmed. Yet there was a multitude of armed guys walking around, there was a curfew and the shells began falling all over the city. I was terribly afraid for my children. The cellar we were in, in fact, presented no shelter at all. It was an ordinary cellar in an ordinary apartment building. And we were all there, Serbs, Moslems and Croats, all together. Nobody understood what was going on, because, in the position we were in you just could not know anything, indeed. All you knew was that you were enclosed and that you could not go out as you wished. Still, the sound of trams passing by gave us some hope that things were not as bad as they were looking. And we managed somehow to go to work. Yet, people really panicked. There were rumors all around, but me, I did not know how long the whole thing would last. It was complete chaos. We were buying food, any food, just to have something in stock—flour and sugar and the like.

I continued going to work until April 30, although not regularly because it became too dangerous. There were snipers and I had to travel nine kilometers every day, leaving my children behind, not knowing whether I would return at all. The authorities introduced obligatory job attendance measures but they were not enforced regularly.

I feared for my children all the time. As for the decision to leave Sarajevo, I really can't say that it was my decision. It just happened spontaneously. My best neighbor—a cheerful, witty woman who didn't let fear overwhelm us—decided to get her daughter out to Montenegro. That made me think that I too should do something with my children. I phoned the Children's Embassy and asked them to put my children on the evacuation list. They said I could come the next day and make an arrangement. I felt relieved but I felt worried at the same time, because I hadn't yet prepared anything. I just wanted to send the children out for two weeks or so, until the shelling stopped. Children, as they are, just wanted to continue to play outside of the house, as if nothing was happening. That drove me crazy, because the shells were not choosing their victims. In fact, there were some military headquarters in our vicinity and they were probably aiming at them.

I spent a night packing bags for my children, hesitating whether I should go with them or not. I feared that if I refused I wouldn't be allowed to leave the city afterwards. Then my husband and me agreed that I should leave the city with the children and return when things settled down. I left with three bags. I remember it quite clearly, it was the evening of the first of May.

When we were about to leave, the neighbors looked down on us in a way that made us feel guilty. As if we knew something they didn't know; you're getting out and don't know what to tell the people with whom you've spent days in the same cellar. Then there was a feeling that you were leaving your beloved city and heading for the unknown. And you just cannot explain to your neighbors that you are getting out only because of your children.

Then we arrived at the Children's Embassy. There was a huge crowd, mothers, children and pregnant women—all of them had been waiting the whole night for the bus to arrive. Finally, we entered the bus. I remember thinking if I would ever return to the city. My husband could not get out, and, in fact, we didn't even think about that, because they didn't let men go out. The only ones allowed to leave were women and children. We just didn't realize in time what kind of war it was.

It took us two hours to reach the airport. Normally, the distance would take ten to fifteen minutes. Then we boarded the plane. Since it was the first time my children had taken a plane I told them they should buckle up, but then I realized that we had boarded a military helicopter which had no seats at all–which meant that we would sit on the floor just like sardines. It was only then that I realized quite clearly that I was leaving the city to which I would return God only knows when. We arrived in Belgrade. I wanted to phone my husband but the lines were cut. I spent a week without hearing from my husband, before the line was established again. I heard that all my family was alive but that something sad had happened, my father had died. My mother died a year before the war and my father was still alive when I left Sarajevo. He was ill; he had a benign tumor which later turned malignant. He never wanted to take shelter. Today, it's a year since he died. I saw him in April last time. He looked at me as if he would never see me again. [She cries.]

I was born in Sarajevo and that's where my origins are. [She cries.] However, judging by the letters from my husband, I can see that Sarajevo now is not the city I knew and loved. Some new people came and grabbed the power. My husband says he simply cannot live any longer in that ambience and he believes that our children will not have any future there. I think we should emigrate, in order to protect our children. He wants to get out but it's impossible for the moment. I don't dare to initiate anything from here, because, if something happened to him, I would blame myself for the rest of my life. I think he will get out as soon as he can.

We don't see our future in Serbia and the same goes for Croatia or some other ethnically pure territory. The only solution for us is to emigrate, so that we can take our children to school and start a new life. The hardest thing for me is that my husband has remained alone there. Loneliness and separation kill him. It's been two years that he has not seen his children, so we sent him pictures lately, to see how much our children grew up. [She cries.] I'm doing my best to be their mother and father at the same time, but it doesn't work. We were a family that always held together. After work, we would run home. He never went out alone, to a café for example, with his friends, without bringing me, and I always did the same. Now, we are brutally separated, and I feel guilty for leaving him behind. However, I hope that we will be soon together again. On the other hand, I saved our children from the horrors of war. Many children in Sarajevo starved and lost their limbs. I sent parts of my humanitarian parcels to Sarajevo.

What I'm going through here is a terrible mental harassment, because I was deeply affected by every massacre in Sarajevo. When that shell fell on the Markale market I went out of my mind, because I was born near the cathedral. I had a terrible fear that some of my family were killed. One day, I received the list of the people killed in the market and I did not dare to look at it. Finally, I did it and I was incredibly relieved when I saw that none of them were there. Then I began fearing that they might have been wounded perhaps. I had to live all that, and there was nothing I could do to help them. In fact, I satisfied my need to help by sending them packages, medication, letters, words of support and by encouraging them to persevere.

However, one has to endure all that, because I can't see an end to it. Without hope I would have been lost. My first source of hope are my children. I live for them and I want to offer them a good life, as much as I can, because they don't deserve to live this way. On the other hand, I hope that one day we will reunite. The main source of suffering in this war was the separation of families. Many people were killed. In fact, mixed marriages were most affected. We didn't take sides. I live in an ethnically mixed marriage, and that's why, when we had to leave Sarajevo, we didn't know where to go. We had some distant relatives in Serbia and that's why we decided to come here. However, we don't have any prospects in Serbia or Croatia. I never declared myself a Moslem. We always declared ourselves as Yugoslavs and that's how we declared our children as well. It's only here that I began having some ethnic sentiments, because, if these women say that this is something important to them then I wouldn't like to renounce what's mine. I don't want to renounce my parents who educated me in a very humanistic spirit and taught me to love all people. It's because of these women here that I declare myself as a Moslem. And when the war is over, I will say something different. What matters most, in fact, is that you are a decent human being. I would like to say that I'm Bosnian.

I left all my dear ones there: a sister, two brothers and my husband, and I am alone here. I would like to talk about what I've been through, about my experiences here. We spent five months here at the house of some distant relatives. At the beginning, they were very nice, warm and hospitable, but as days went by we realized that they were beginning to consider us as a burden. I felt we should assume some responsibilities as well, but my daughter fell ill and spent a month in bed. Her veins were bursting and she had to receive infusions. That happened immediately after our arrival here. The illness was an obvious consequence of the stress she had suffered because she had never had anything like that before. During her illness, I worried a lot and had significant weight loss. After her recovery, I tried to somehow prettify our room. A friend gave me some embroideries, we put some pictures on the walls, in order to make the place feel like a home. Now, they have grown accustomed to the place we are in. However, it's me who suffers the most, and the children have somehow accepted it. I cook, I do my best to make them feel at home. However, every time I watch the TV news I remain appalled. And, besides, every other day I hear the women here commenting about me. I even had a couple of arguments with women here who think they can tell me everything just because I am of different ethnic origin. I really have nothing to do with this war. I did not want it and I did not help initiate it. It happened to me several times that people told me, "You don't have any rights here, your rights are there, in Alija Izetbegović's Bosnia." Everything happening there becomes quickly reflected here and me, being in a minority, I have to shut up. Thus, it happened to me several times that I was so tense that I vomited or dehydrated. I grew terribly anxious, I began shivering. I just felt terribly unsafe and I just wanted to get out of here although I have a couple of great friends who want to help me out. I just fear I can't stand all this anymore. I just can't watch the news, hear the comments, etc. I just try not to watch the news but cannot resist. I just want to know what's happening there, but when I see what they were saying on the news, I just leave the TV room. I know that war is war and that many people have lost everything they had. Perhaps that's why they became aggressive and intolerant, but I don't want to be a part of that game. I refuse to hate; I refuse to be taken in by this madness. I just want to preserve good energy in me in order to help the people who have remained there. The war will come to an end and we just have to find strength to endure all this.

Mirjana

It happened in Slavonska Požega where I lived. At the beginning of July 1991, I brought my child to my husband's relatives who lived in Belgrade. I thought it would be a temporary measure. After I brought her there, I used to spend two weeks with her and then come back to Požega.

On the day of the Croatian declaration of independence, the local chief of police came to my neighbor's flat. My neighbor was a member of the most popular Croatian nationalistic party, so that pretty frequently we could hear Croatian nationalistic songs that he and his guests were singing in his flat. Our balconies were side by side and one evening the crowd in the nearby flat got quite drunk. It was the time when clashes in Knin had already begun and I feared that my neighbors might react and do something terrible to my child. That was the immediate reason for bringing my daughter to Belgrade.

We used to travel there pretty frequently. After the summer holidays I wanted to bring my daughter to Belgrade. I heard that the army (the YPA) had surrendered. Every evening we could hear shots, because Croats had surrounded the military barracks. We used to go to shelters every day. In the shelters, Serbs and Croats did not talk to each other. We were always near the stairs. Had we not gone to the shelters they would have considered us spies or traitors and would have searched our flat.

At that time, I was the head of the juridical department in a company. One day I was drinking coffee with typists, mainly Croats, when an ex-worker dropped by. He was wearing the uniform of the Croatian Guard. Some time before, we had initiated a law suit against him and the suit was not finished. He ordered me to come to his office and told me that the suit must be finished the next day. I said that it was up to the court to decide when the suit would finish, to which he replied "not to kid around with him." I told him not to threaten me or else I would go to see the manager, which I did. He was also wearing the same uniform. He said he would see to it that I was no longer harassed. I asked not to be sent to the court this time. I participated in meetings of the administrative board where everybody, except Serbs, wore a uniform and had a gun. I felt terrible. I said I did not want to go to the court because I was afraid and the others criticized my behavior.

My mother lived in the Serb-controlled area. Before the first big attack of Croatian forces in that region, my boss and other Croats told me that there would be an attack and a "cleansing of the terrain" in the area. I said that then my mother would probably be killed as well and they said that she would be safe if she went into hiding. When I returned to Croatia, after having brought my daughter to Serbia, they asked me how many chetniks I had brought with me. I asked "Where?" and they said "To your country." I said there were already enough chetniks so I didn't need to bring any more. Now, when I recount this, it all looks like a joke, but I felt terribly afraid then. My boss told me that I had to explain why I had brought my daughter to Serbia and that I would be very suspicious if I went frequently to Serbia. He also told me not to go to see my mother and especially not to bring her any food because it would be a way of assisting chetniks.

Once I was returning from Belgrade and the YPA was withdrawing from Slovenia. I drove alone and was very afraid. As soon as I crossed the Croatian border they forced me to give a ride to an unknown man. I protested, but it was useless. Once I even had to give a ride to a member of the Croatian Guard. I just can't describe the fear you have when you have to cross all those checkpoints.

If you were preparing for a trip, you had to be very careful so that nobody could see what you were doing. Thus, I was once discreetly preparing a trip to Belgrade. My neighbor's flat was so situated that she could easily look at my garage. The next day, at work, she asked me, "Boss, tell me, what were you doing last night in your garage?" She obviously was charged to stalk me.

Once on the road, you have to pass hundreds of checkpoints. On the occasion when I was taking away my child with me, they searched all the car for weapons. They told me several times in my workplace that I was playing a double game, that I couldn't hold a managerial post and they did not trust me at all. I wanted to go on vacations, but my boss did not allow me to, saying that we Serbs caused him serious difficulties. He also said that Serbs could not be allowed to hold managerial posts.

Once, a hundred armed men came to arrest a colleague of mine, a Serb, who allegedly had weapons at his home. We were all terribly afraid, thinking that they had come to arrest us all. We thought they would round us up. There were rumors that the first step of the operation would consist in throwing hand grenades into our houses. The survivors would be then taken away to form a living shield in front of the military barracks, which, at the time, were under Croatian siege. I just did not know what to do because my daughter was still little and I did not know to whom I could entrust her. I spent many sleepless nights. There were always rumors that something would happen over the weekends. I was not a member of any Serbian nationalist party. They always had information on what would happen next. I was angry at them, because they did not tell us anything. There was not a single day without a Serb house or a shop being blown away. I felt completely helpless because the authorities did strictly nothing to protect us.

You feel uneasy. You see yourself as a hypocrite, and still you have to take care of yourself. When Croatian forces performed the "cleansing of the terrain" in the village where my mother lived, our first neighbor, a Croat and a member of the Croatian Guard, was killed. It happened quite frequently that Croats killed each other in combat, because they wore different uniforms, and afterwards they would say that Serbs had killed them.

The Croatian Guard was accommodated in the school that my daughter had to attend. There were beer-cases reaching up to the ceiling. There were rumors that the YPA was shelling the school. The Guard was also accommodated in hospitals. My enterprise was turned into a bomb production facility and you can imagine how I felt knowing to whom the shells were destined.

That period was filled with unremitting, sharp fear. If you go shopping, you feel afraid. You are afraid all the time. I was shivering when going to my daughter's school to see when the classes would begin. Once I wanted to travel to Gradiška, to see my sister, and they told me not to go there alone because I am a Serb. All Serbs were proclaimed traitors.

Still, this refugee status is worse than fear. There, I feared for my life, I thought that I might be killed. Here, I fear that I won't survive because of poverty and insecurity. What annoys me most is the way people look at you when you say you are a refugee. People envy us because they think we are given everything we need. We have submitted a petition to stay in the collective shelter. You don't have a job, you don't have a home and you don't even know whether you will stay in this country or not. When the Greeks had sent some humanitarian aid, my child went to see what was happening and the lady official who works in the distribution unit here pushed us away and said "Do you perhaps need a camera to record what's going on?" I came here to save her life from Croats, and look what Serbs are doing to her! [She cries.]

Nada

When the war began, I spent a month in a cellar. The shells were falling all the time. When I finally got out with my children, I wanted to stay two weeks here, just to get away temporarily from the shelling. My husband had remained, because he thought it could not last more than a month, and, anyway, that it would be senseless to leave his country. Now I feel terribly guilty for not persuading him to get out with me but neither did I believe at the time that things would turn out this way. That's why I don't understand the women who feel guilty because their husbands are with them in refuge.

After my husband had died, I spent two months in deep depression but I didn't want to take any medication. I wanted to face it all alone. That's when I understood that I had to find strength and continue to live, not so much for myself but for my children. I didn't pity myself. I only grieved because of my husband and because my children would grow without a father. I had a perfect marriage. I have always been a self-conscious and strong person. I think the education I had received from my parents helped me to overcome the crisis. But perhaps my profession has helped me most of all. I'm a social worker and I have learned to help people to overcome their problems. I found strength in myself and I think every woman can do the same. I try to absorb the energy that's all around me. So, I will steal a bit of your energy [she turns to the interviewer].

In fact, we women rule the world. We give strength to and guide the acts of men, although they play the role of bosses. Since the opinion of others is so important for them, they pretend to be the ones who are in control, who make decisions. In fact, women are those who make decisions even when they live with husbands, but they keep telling themselves that the truth is different, that the truth is the image of roles in marriage offered to the world, because men think that they are the ones who must have power. Well, let them have it, if they are so keen about it. We women have a different role—a role that women are not usually conscious of. They have to understand that they are strong enough and that decision making and guidance of our lives are not essentially affected by the absence of men, because, in the essence, we are those who decide, although we keep persuading ourselves that the image offered to the world is the reality.

When I start talking like this, the women I socialize with do not seem to understand. They can't understand it and say I'm philosophizing too much. The majority of the women refugees that I know are depressed and keep telling themselves that they can't do anything without their husbands. My sister-in-law, for example, said the following when I told her that my husband had been killed, "God forbid that anything similar should happen to me! What could I do alone, with these two children?" And I replied "How could you say that? Are you aware of what you've just said?"

I'm greatly helped by the possibility to work and to have a job the status of which is rather similar to the job I had before, although I'm not employed in my profession. Women refugees have to sympathize with each other; they have to understand that their experience is different from the experiences of the domestic population and don't have to expect to be understood, because it's impossible. They have to struggle, but peacefully, and avoid unnecessary conflicts. I think I was greatly helped by the fact that I did not pay attention to the anti-refugee remarks I could hear every other day. I have just pushed all that aside and tried to adapt to the new environment.

Milica

My house was at the beginning of the street and the youths usually gathered at the end of the street. On our way to the meeting point we usually called each other, waited for our friends to come out and then continued together. I have known him for years. He was 22, a Croat, and he had gone several times to the front, but I did not pay much attention to that fact. That night, I found him at his house. I called him and he came out. We continued together, talking. But, as we walked through the dark part of the street he suddenly put his hands on my mouth. He then called two men who grabbed me and dragged me into a car. They covered my eyes with a band, stuffed my mouth with a piece of cloth and began beating me on the head, so that I don't remember what happened afterwards.

When I woke up, I realized that I was in a field near my village. I looked terrible, every bit of my body ached. I was sick. It was a terrible feeling that could not be described, something insipid and sleazy. I realized what had happened to me. I came back home; I was shocked when I saw myself in the mirror. My mother called me while I was in the bathroom, but I did not want to come out immediately. I heard her asking behind the door, "How was your evening?" "Fine," I replied.

I did not know I was pregnant, because I had my regular periods even until the fifth month after the rape. I did not have a medical examination immediately after the rape, because I feared that it might become known. Sometime in the fifth month I went to see the doctor, because I realized there was something happening with me. In my town abortion is performed only until the third month, and after that, you can do it, provided you have money and connections. I was poor. I did not succeed.

I was ashamed to give birth in my town, so I decided to go to Belgrade. I gave up my baby for adoption. The ambience in my town is such that if you are not a whore, if you don't break marriages, if you are not scum, you can't survive. You don't realize where you live until something happens to you. Only then you can see who's your real friend. I could not accept my baby because it would have always reminded me of the thing that happened to me. I think it would have killed me.

Emina

Here's how we decided that me and the child should leave. First, I didn't want to quit my job (I worked in the YPA), although my colleagues told me that I should quit and be with my child. I was always very conscientious and could not even imagine missing a day of work. However, one day, having finished my work, I really became afraid because I couldn't return home. There was no transportation at all, nobody wanted to drive because snipers were active in the city and it was very dangerous. So, a colleague gave me a lift. He told me, "If they hit me, you just jump out and run. But don't come to work anymore, stay with your child." When I came home I saw my husband and child crying. The hall was full of suitcases and bags. My mother cried at me, "What the hell are you doing at your job anymore? Don't you see your child? Are you nuts or what?" Then we went off to my sister-in-law's home. From there we went to board a helicopter and we never returned to Mostar.

So, we jumped into the helicopter and after forty minutes we were in Belgrade. When we landed in Batajnica airport, there was a marvelous welcome ceremony for pilots and soldiers. I thought that's how it would be all the time. We were accommodated at my husband's aunt's place. I think 90% of refugees had bad experiences with their relatives. After three months, she had thrown us out of her apartment. On the other hand, I don't know how I would react if I had ten people buzzing around in my flat. In a way, I can understand the way aunt reacted.

The army offered us help, but I was still feeling comfortable at my aunt's place. I lost seventeen kilos in a few weeks. My eyes are constantly filled with tears, and I can cry anytime. I loved my husband too much; he remained there and there were no letters from him. My sister was in Macedonia with her two children and she returned to Mostar, where she was arrested in the Croatian part of the city. I cursed the day when I came here, but then I began thinking about the child and I realized it was better this way. I went to see my husband's cousins in Obrenovac [near Belgrade], but they kept persuading us that they were in difficulties too. They have found me a room to live in. I still had two or three checks left, and I used them carefully. It is a terrible story; I could not believe that it happened to me. It was filthy. I was on the edge of a nervous breakdown; had I not had my child I would have committed suicide. I did not get used to making decisions by myself and I don't know how to manage alone. First it was my father who decided for me, and then my boyfriend (now husband). I always asked him when I had to decide on something.

Once my child saw bread on the TV; he demanded bread and he cried. The landlord's son was a thief. He used to bring home the items he had stolen. Once police came and began questioning me, "Why am I here? What is my nationality? Where is my husband?" etc. One evening, the landlord's son was killed by the members of his gang and my child saw it all. We had to leave the place. I asked my aunt if we could come to her place but she refused, because her husband wanted to have his peace.

Then I found accommodation in the collective shelter. Although it was terrible, I was happy because I wasn't afraid anymore. That's where I made a very good friend. I began working for a woman, tidying her apartment. Every time somebody came to see her she used to say, "Well, I have a woman here from Tudman and Izetbegović." She was mean. At the beginning, it did not hurt me much but later on I felt uneasy, stigmatized. Her mother died in my arms, I did everything in her house. She let herself go with me. I hear that now she's helping refugees and says that I don't need help, because my husband is here and because, according to her, he should have been at the front.

In November 1992, my husband sent me a letter. I had him swear on our child that he wouldn't go to fight, because in our family, we are all mixed, Croats, Slovenes and Moslems. There was only one line in his letter, "I love you all, and I hope I will see you soon." That brought me down completely. I expected a long letter, something that I would read and reread for days. Finally, my husband came in December. He had troubles at the frontier. I was awaiting him for days and days. When he finally appeared he looked as if he had been in a concentration camp. During the first two hours we didn't say a word. I was crying and he was kissing the child. The child was afraid of him, because she was only seventeen months old when we left. My husband began working and then we began looking for an apartment although we were unable to afford it. We didn't have any marital relations properly speaking while I was in the collective shelter, because he couldn't live with us. It all can be recounted now with a couple of words, but those were terrible days. I became depressed again.

I suffer a lot because of my sister and mother. I am so burdened with care for my sister—will somebody kill her? What could they do to the children? I felt terrible when my mother-in-law returned to Mostar and I was unable to send anything to my sister. My flat

(I got it immediately before the war) was sacked and ruined so that nothing was left. The grave of my parents was hit by a shell. I feel sad because nobody did anything for us—people who felt like Yugoslavs. We don't have any future in Serbia. You can't find a job, you can't have citizenship, a passport. I hope we will emigrate. And one day, I hope we will return to Mostar.

A couple of days ago I had an abortion. I am really desperate because I wanted to give birth, but it would be impossible since we ourselves barely survive.

Nataša: letters from Mostar

June 26, 1992
Dear Mom and Ana,

Mostar is utterly destroyed. There are no bridges left, except the Old Bridge which, also, barely holds. Mahala, the Harbor and the Old City do not exist anymore—they are all turned into a huge pile of burnt trash and nothing can be done about it except to flatten the ground and start building again. Quite simply, everything is destroyed. Here's how it happened. First they would break into shops and flats, sack them and eventually set them on fire. We could do nothing but watch those innumerable trucks, loaded with spoils, heading for Nevesinje and further. There are so many things I would like to write to you that I don't know where to begin and where to end.

Maybe you will find it strange that I have decided to remain here, and not to go to the sea. Well, quite simply, once you feel how it all looks like, when you see all those people hidden in cellars, getting terribly close to each other, regardless of nationality, you just cannot leave. You know how strongly I was attached to B., and I found it terribly hard to leave him when I knew that as soon as he stepped out of the building he could be killed, for there was a sniper at Duma shooting at us all the time. Most important of all is that I know that my child is safe and that he was cared for as much as I would care for him.

I'm glad you are safe too, although I know it must be hard for you, especially for Mom, because she would not have endured all this. Simply, you better not fall ill, because only the wounded are admitted to hospitals. As for our flat, our skyscraper was hit by nine shells. The neighbor's flat was hit, so that our windows broke. The church was burned. I thought they were targeting the church, but on June 14 (the day I will never forget) they fired at the sky-scrapers, one by one, with anti-armor shells that blow away half a balcony at once. I'm terribly embittered because they've caused such havoc. And what they have done to the decent Serbs living here!!! You can't buy anything here, there's nothing coming in except humanitarian aid so we stand in lines, waiting to be given something to eat and it's so terrible and humiliating. You get up at 3 a.m., go to the church, join the line there stretching up to the park, and the same thing happens every day. Without that, the war would not be necessary: we would all starve to death. And if somebody were to have something to sell, there wouldn't be a place for that because the green market is destroyed. It's not true that Croats have destroyed it, I can guarantee that, because I was watching it burn and I saw where the shells were coming from. Frankly, sometimes I wish the same thing would happen in Serbia so that some people could see how it feels to sleep in cellars and wait to be given something to eat.

Perhaps it would be different if we had electricity. There was no electricity for twenty days and the few steaks I had in the refrigerator, I had to throw them away, just like others did. You can imagine how terrible it was. By the way, during the last thirty days we've eaten only canned food. You know that I'm not much of a carnivore, but still, I would like to *see* a piece of meat, let alone eat it.

As I write this letter, I cry all the time. Today, I feel particularly bad. It's my birthday, I'm 30 now, and I said to B. that if my mother and sister had been here they would have come for a coffee. I can't explain to you how hard it is for me. I'm alone here, everything of mine is here. Fortunately, I have B., as he is, but that's not it. That's why I beg you to come as soon as you can, because you are not so much safe there either.

The worst is that the phone isn't functioning and I can't call you. There are some rumors about a mobile phone station so that we will be able to use phone booths again, but we won't be able to reach Serbia.

Your Nataša

July 22, 1992
Dear Mom and Ana,

This is my second letter. I hope you've received the first one, which I sent a month ago. I am well, at least physically. Psychically, I am completely down. I shiver all the time and have palpitations—

the old trouble of mine. I just can't believe that all this is happening. It all looks like a bad dream from which I will wake up. I am most grieved by the fact that you are not here. I wrote you a lot in my last letter. I remained here because of B., and sometimes when I get angry at him, I say to myself, poor is the one who does not have anyone. You simply have nobody to open your heart to. It's just now that I feel how much I miss you. Dear Ana, I wouldn't know how to tell whether you should come or not. The situation changes every day. I don't even dare to write you. Most of all, I would like to phone you all. Mom should by all means come to see the flat.

Ana, I went up to your flat. I wish I hadn't done it at all, especially because I felt terrible when an unknown woman opened the door and when I saw your bedroom. I don't remember how I entered and how I exited the flat. I felt terrible, thinking all the time you would show up. I took only your fur coat and a lamp, the few things I could grab, for we are ordered not to take anything from the flats.

I write to you what first comes to my mind. There's nothing left of Mostar. Today, I went down to the Old City (I wish I hadn't). All we need is a caterpillar to flatten the ground. Everything is destroyed. I wrote you in the last letter what in fact happened. Those reserve troops are to blame. This, you must believe me. Ana, don't watch that TV news. You know how I was on that point. It's them who have destroyed Mostar and all the bridges. You can believe me, I was here all the time. And that fuel tank that exploded, it's all the army's [paramilitary] work. Now everything seems peaceful, except that they are still somewhere around Podveležje where they can shell us from, which they do from time to time. Just for fun, they drop a shell or two in the middle of the city and kill civilians as they please. Lately, many people were killed and crippled. You just go out, relax a bit, and then there is a shell coming out of thin air. Worst of all, we all have got used to it and just wait for something to explode. You ask me about the possibility to come to Mostar. I would recommend to mother to come while you, Ana, please wait a bit and see what the others will do.

My son is a big boy now. He grew some twenty centimeters. He's a child but he's aware of everything. The last time I heard him over the phone he asked me if I had something to eat. He sounded so tearful. During the last four months, I saw him twice. I go there, I see him, feel better but I feel worse when I come back. Please, send me a letter. Tell me how you are, what you are doing, what the children are doing (last night, I saw them in my dreams). I feel so bad when I want to see somebody that I cannot see, especially when people here say that those who have gone to Serbia will never return to Mostar. Dear Ana, if you see K., tell her that her flat as well has been taken by some unknown people. Had I only known what would happen I would have taken your and her key, in order to give them to the people I knew, who could have put their names on the doors. Well, now, we can only guess what they have stolen. They came under the pretext of looking for a sniper, and then searched the flat and stole what they wanted. All right, I don't know what more to write you. There are many things I would like to tell you but not to write.

Say hello to your children and say that their auntie's thinking a lot about them. I love you so much and, please, come as soon as you can.

Your Nataša.

August 3, 1992
Dear Mom,

The shells continue to fall. They come suddenly, so that every day there are a dozen dead and wounded. Sometimes I think that without my child I would swallow a pill and disappear, because nobody needs a life like this. You can't go out to the street, fearing that a shell might fall anytime. Besides, everything is closed, there's nothing you can buy, except some vegetables in the green market. Mom, I see you long to come here. I understand you, but you also must understand me. The city, as it is now, makes me so sick that I would gladly go to some village and never return. All that happens here is terrible. I hope it will come to an end. Mom, please, if you think of coming here, do it right now! Everything will be much more difficult later. Mom, once again I tell you to come, because I just cannot cope with all this. I keep on saying to B. that all his relatives are here while I have no one left. It's so terribly hard sometimes. This one can go to see his mother, that one his sister, while me, I can't even go to see my father's grave. We are still not allowed to go to the other side. Imagine, it's the fourth month that aunt J. does not know anything about her family. No trace at all. She's going nuts. All right Mom, that will be all for this time. Try again to send me a letter. Love,

Your Nataša

November 11, 1992
My dear Ana,

There's nothing new in Mostar. Everything is as it was described in my previous letters. The shells keep on falling, people are killed, etc. We too are in a difficult situation. B. is on the waiting list; almost everyone recruited, and enterprises don't work. B. is not recruited yet and says he won't go until he receives an order, but believes he won't answer it. He really is an intelligent person—he keeps saying that this is not his war. Indeed, you just have to see who did take up arms and you'll understand everything. Whenever I hear people theorizing about this war I just say, "Well name me just one university-educated person who has taken up arms and gone to Podveležje." Of course they don't answer, simply because such a person cannot be found. My dear Ana, I know how hard it is for you, but patience please, all this must pass one day. When we take a look at our cousins I want to vomit. I see that you suffer in that temporary accommodation and your uncle and aunt don't do anything to help you. I'm ashamed to say that I have cousins in Belgrade as well. But, let it be, their turn will come one day as well. Love,

Nataša.

December 4, 1992
My dear Ana,

Days pass by as usual. You sit in your home and wait for the shells to fall then you run to the cellar, and the same story goes on and on. I'm constantly at home, B. began working, which means that I remain alone and fearful all day long. Mom must not leave the flat vacant, so she remains there with the auntie most of the time. Every now and then I go there and bring her what she needs, as much as I can. Generally, we are not hungry. All our life can be put in just one sentence. Then, I miss my child terribly. He grows up and it seems to me that I will never compensate him for the time that he passed without me. I see you are having troubles, too. If I tell you that you can come then it means that you really can come, and I keep telling you not to believe the news and be intimidated by it, because that's their goal. Of course, I believe what you wrote about those ex-detainees and it all must be true. But, then again, only I can tell you the truth and you must believe me. I feel stupid for having to persuade you in every letter. Believe me that no one will do you any harm here. Of course, as for your return, it would be stupid to do it now, because there's still some shooting going on and, besides, schools are still closed, and Mostar kids are not going to school. But I believe that peace in Bosnia-Herzegovina is impossible until all the exiled return to their homes. That's why I beg you not to believe the news. When we see what stories they are telling you, we cannot believe that people like you can believe them. You asked me if refugees from Serbia return to Mostar. Yes, they do, but they are mostly the women whose husbands had remained in the city. Love,

Nataša

February 8, 1993
My dear Ana,

There are very few Serbs in Mostar, and they are constantly afraid of being taken away. The other day, there were clashes again, some soldiers were killed so they wanted an exchange: fifteen killed soldiers for fifteen Serb civilians. So they came to our neighborhood and picked up the Serbs. Sometimes I feel sad because you're not here, but it's better this way. Imagine that, besides shells and other terrible things, you would also have to worry, will someone pick you up at once. That would be terrible. I couldn't stand that.

Your Nataša

March 3, 1993
My dear Ana,

Everything is as usual here. I won't write anymore about the shells and the horrors we live. All that is going to stay for some time and there's nothing I can do about it. The alert siren is my only music, it sounded today as well, and I just began crying, not out of fear, but out of some anger. I thought, "I would like an A-bomb to fall, wipe us all out and thus terminate our suffering." But it was a moment of weakness. Don't be afraid, we will persevere, and you, please don't worry, and take care of yourself. You know you have trouble with the stomach and worrying can only aggravate it. I believe everything will settle down. B. continues doing his job. Mom is as usual. She comes to us every Monday and remains until Friday, and then goes off for the weekend. It is true that I'm afraid of being alone but I still reproach her for coming to our place—you know her, she wants to please everyone. Still, I feel safe when Mom is around. It's war out in the streets and I don't have to tell you what I'm afraid of.

On the other hand, I'm glad that Mom is not alone as well. You never know who might knock on your door and take you away, God knows where. Everything's possible these days. Love,

Your Nataša

May 15, 1993
Dear Ana,

I fear B. might be recruited, since he already skipped twice. I'm going out of my mind. I must have mentioned your name a hundred times. Thank God that you are not here now. You don't know how lucky you are. At least you know that your husband is by your side and that nothing bad will happen to him. You know how strongly I am attached to B. I feel I would be completely lost without him and today, when we separated, I felt betrayed by all. Everybody's gone somewhere to save his life and I wonder why we have remained. Love,

Nataša

May 30, 1993
Dear Ana,

C. came to see us yesterday. He told us how all the Moslems were taken away from the Velež football stadium and I felt I would go insane. I immediately thought that Mom had been taken as well. Reportedly, the hostages were soon allowed to go but their property was sacked. Quite simply, Mom does not want to go anywhere, and makes me worry a lot. I feel guilty when I'm not with her, and when I am at her place, I cry for my child all the time. What would he do if something happened to us? Mom sits down there and looks after things, as if they were important now! B. has finally realized that we cannot stay here anymore but we first have to obtain passports.

Your Nataša

June 20, 1993
My dear Ana,

My worst fears came true. B. received a special assignment order today. I just pray for him to be refused going to fight tomorrow! Ana, I don't know what to do anymore. I just want to go to a beach and swim until I drown. I can't take sedatives anymore for I am all swollen. I cried so hard yesterday because you couldn't reach me over the phone. I waited for you until 2 a.m. Mom simply cannot use her brains. Moslems are being taken away every day. Mom says that it doesn't happen in her neighborhood, which doesn't mean it wouldn't happen. In my neighborhood, the entire population of one skyscraper was taken away. I just can't live only with Croats and this little boy says he won't move anywhere without his grandparents and begins to cry immediately. He would be ready to go anywhere but only with his grandparents. It's only now that I feel afraid. They do terrible things to their Croats who are with Moslems and there is no reason why they should not do the same to me. B. and I have definitely decided to leave but we wait for the right moment to do it.

I love you. Nataša

June 25, 1993
My dear Ana,

It's Friday and they have to decide today whether B. is going to remain in his job or be sent to the army. I am completely numb. Strangely, I am angry with him as well, so I cried all day long. He just doesn't dare to do anything. If my health was better I would go somewhere alone. I can't explain to you how I feel. I have no ethnic consciousness at all, yet I feel as belonging to all. I feel I couldn't bear to see B. wearing a uniform. Otherwise, Mostar is hell, as usual. I pity the Moslems who have remained. They just wait for somebody to knock on their door and take them away. That's what's happening now, ethnically mixed marriages are probably next. I'm so afraid. There's plenty of news about the people who were killed. Two men from my building were killed as well. I just don't know what will happen with Mom. She doesn't want to go anywhere. I don't know what I would do if she was taken away. I think I would swallow a handful of pills, and, anyway, that's what I am thinking of sometimes. This is not life. You know that I'm oversensitive and this is too much for me. Love,

Nataša

Bibliography

Arnautović, D., Lj. Kasagić, and D. Pajević (1988). *Vojna psihologija* (Military psychology). Belgrade: Vojno-izdavački novinski centar.

Bojanin, S., and V. Išpanović-Radojković (1994). *Adolescenti i stresovi rata* (Adolescents and war stress). Belgrade: Institut za mentalno zdravlje.

Bojić, M. et al. (1982). *Narodzooslodilački rat ižrevolucija u Yugoslaviji* (The national liberation War and Revolution in Yugoslavia). Vojno-Istaijski Institut.

Brownmiller, S. (1975). *Against our will*. New York: Simon and Schuster.

——(1994). Making women's bodies battlefields. In *Mass rape: the war against women in Bosnia-Herzegovina*, ed. A. Stiglmayer. Lincoln: University of Nebraska Press.

Chinkin, C. M. (1993). Peace and force in international law. In *Reconceiving reality: women and international law*, ed. D. G. Dallmeyer. New York: Asil.

Ćirković, S. (1964). *Istorija srednjevekovne bosanske države* (A history of the medieval Bosnian state). Belgrade: Srpska Književna Zadruga.

Copelon, R. (1994). Surfacing gender: reconceptualizing crimes against women in times of war. In *Mass rape: The war against women in Bosnia-Herzegovina*, ed. A. Stiglmayer. Lincoln: University of Nebraska Press.

Ćorović, V. (1920). *Crna knjiga* (The black book). Belgrade and Sarajevo: n.p.

——(1940). *Istorija Bosne* (A history of Bosnia). Belgrade: I. Đurđević.

Cvijić, J. (1902). Antropogeografski problemi Balkanskog poluostrva (Anthropo-geographic problems of the Balkan peninsula). *Srpski geografski zbornik* 4, no. 1.

Dedijer, V. (1966). *Sarajevo 1914*. Sarajevo: n.p.

——(1987). *Vatikan i Jasenovac* (Vatican and Jasenovac). Belgrade: I. Đurđević.

Državna komisija FNRJ (1947). *Izveštaj jugoslovenske državne komisije za utvrđivanje zločina okupatora i njihovih pomagača Međunarodnom vojnom sudu u Nirnbergu* (The Report submitted to the International Military Tribunal in Nurenberg by the Yugoslav Commission for the War Crimes of the Occupying Forces and Their Collaborators). Belgrade.

Đurđev, B. (1959). Prilog pitanju razvitka i karaktera tursko-osmanlijskog feudalizma (A contribution to the understanding of the history of development of the Turkish Ottoman feudalism). *Godišnjak istorijskog društva BiH* 10.

Ekmečić, M. (1953). *Istorija naroda Jugoslavije* (A history of the Yugoslav people). Vols. 1 and 2. Belgrade: Prosveta.

El Bushra, J. and E. P. Lopez (1993). Development in conflict: the gender dimension. In *Report of an Oxfam AGRA East workshop held in Pattaya, Thailand, February 1–4, 1993*. Oxfam.

Faludi, S. (1991). *Backlash—the undeclared war against American women*. New York: Anchor Books.

Fischer, E. (1994). War, women and democracy. In *Test the West: gender democracy and violence*. Vienna: Austrian Federal Ministry of Women's Affairs.

Gelsthorpe, L., and A. Morris, eds. (1990). *Feminist perspective in criminology*. Philadelphia: Open University Press.

Hayton-Keeva, S. (1987). *Valiant women in war and exile—thirty-eight true stories*. San Francisco: City Lights Books.

Hornaj, K. (1987). *Neurotična ličnost našeg doba* (The neurotic personality of our time). Titograd: Pobjeda.

Institut za socijalnu politiku (1993). *Socijalne službe u zaštiti izbeglica* (Social services in the service of refugees). Belgrade.

Jackson, S. (1978). The social context of rape: sexual scripts and motivation. *Women's Study International Quarterly* 1.

Joskimović, S., and S. Milanović-Nahod (1994). *Teškoće učenika u izbeglištvu* (Learning difficulties of pupils in refuge). Belgrade: Institut za pedagoška istraživanja.

Jovanović, B. (1997). The International Tribunal in the Hague and rapes of Serbian women. In *Women's rights and social transition in the FR Yugoslavia*, ed. V. Nikolić-Ristanović. Belgrade: Women's Studies Center.

Jugoslovenski Crveni krst i Institut za socijalnu politiku (1993). *Izbeglice i lica koja traže azil* (Refugees and asylum seekers). Belgrade.

Kaličanin, P., and D. Lečić-Toševski (1994). *Knjiga o stresu* (A book about stress). Belgrade: Medicinska knjiga.

Kapamadžija, B., M. Šovljanski, and M. Biro (1990). *Osnovi medicinske suicidologije* (The handbook of medical suicidology). Belgrade and Zagreb: Medicinska knjiga.

Komesarijat za izbeglice Republike Srbije i Crveni krst Srbije (1994). *Izbeglice u Srbiji* (Refugees in Serbia). Belgrade.

Konstantinović-Vilić, S. (1986) *Žene ubice* (Women murderers). Niš: GRO Gradina.

Lather, P. (1988). Feminist perspectives on empowering research methodologies. *Women's Studies International Forum* 6: 569–581.

Lerner, G. (1986). *The creation of patriarchy*. New York: Oxford University Press.

MacKinnon, C. (1993). Comment: Theory is not a luxury. In *Reconceiving reality: women and international law*, ed. D. G. Dallmeyer. New York: Asil.

——(1994). Turning rape into pornography: postmodern genocide. In *Mass rape: the war against women in Bosnia-Herzegovina*, ed. A. Stiglmayer. Lincoln: University of Nebraska Press.

Mihailović, N., and Z. Petrović (1997). *Odgovornost za štete nastale u oružanim sukobima na teritoriji prethodne SFRJ u periodu od 1990. do 1995. godine* (Responsibility for the damage resulting from the armed conflicts in the territory of the former Yugoslavia from 1990 to 1995). Belgrade: NIU Vojska.

Mrvić, N. (1993). Policijska intervencija u slučaju nasilja u porodici (Police intervention in cases of family violence). *Bezbednost* XXXIII, 3: 458–463.

——(1993). Žene ubice–žrtve dugogodišnjeg porodičnog nasilja (Women murderers–victims of long-lasting family violence). *Zbornik Instituta za kriminološka i sociološka istraživanja* 1–2: 270–280.

Mujović, R. (1995). *Medunarodni faktori u gradanskom ratu i krizi u Jugoslaviji* (International factors in the civil war and crisis in Yugoslavia). Podgorica: Pravni fakultet.

Niarchos, C. N. (1995). Women, war, and rape: challenges facing the suffering or international tribunal for the former Yugoslavia. *Human Rights Quarterly*, 4: 649–690.

Nikolić-Ristanović, V. (1989). *Žene kao žrtve kriminaliteta* (Women victims of crime). Belgrade: Naučna knjiga.

——(1993). Nasilje u braku: teorijski okvir i rezultati istraživanja (Marital violence: a theoretical framework and the results of a survey). *Sociološki pregled* 1–4: 27–41.

——(1994a). Feminist research as a process of empowering: an example of research on violence against women in war. In *What can we do for ourselves?* Belgrade: Center for Women's Studies.

——(1994b). Feministička kritika epistemologije i metodologije kriminološkog istraživanja (Feminist critique of the epistemology and methodology of sociological research). *Sociologija* 2: 165–179.

——(1994c). Nasilje nad ženama u uslovima rata i ekonomske krize (Domestic violence against women in conditions of war and economic crisis). *Sociološki pregled* 3: 409–419.

——(1996a). Domestic violence against women in conditions of war and economic crisis. In *International Victimology*, eds. C. Sumner, M. Israel, M. O'Connell, and R. Sarre. Canberra: Australian Institute of Criminology.

——(1996b) War and violence against women. In *The gendered new world order: militarism, development and the environment*, eds. J. Turpin and L. A. Lorentzen. Routledge: New York.

——(1998). The protection of war rape victims before the international criminal tribunal for the former Yugoslavia. *Temida* 2: 13–21.

Nikolić-Ristanović, V., ed. (1997). *Women's rights and social transition in the FR Yugoslavia*. Belgrade: Women's Studies Center.

Piorkowska-Petrović, K. (1993). Neki problemi izbegličkih porodica u novoj sredini (Some problems of refugee families in the new environment). In *Deca, položaj izbeglica i škola*, B. Popović et al. Belgrade: Institut za pedagoška istraživanja.

Queffelec, J. (1985). *Les noces barbares*. Paris: Gallimard.

Rejali, D. (1996). After feminist analyses of Bosnian violence. *Peace Review* 3: 365–371.

Šabanović, H. (1956). Početak turske vladavine u Bosni (The beginning of Turkish rule in Bosnia). *Godišnjak istorijskog društva BiH*, VII.

———(1958). Bosansko krajište (Bosnian frontierland). *Godišnjak istorijskog društva BiH*, IX.

Sandher, H., and B. Johr (1992). *Befreier und befreite* (The liberator and the liberated). Berlin: Kunstmann.

Seifert, R. (1994). War and rape: a preliminary analysis. In *Mass rape: the war against women in Bosnia-Herzegovina*, ed. A. Stiglmayer. Lincoln: University of Nebraska Press.

Smiljanić, N. (1997). Law, war and the female body. In *Women's rights and social transition in the FR Yugoslavia,* ed. V. Nikolić-Ristanović. Belgrade: Women's Studies Center.

Smith, L. (1989). *Domestic Violence: an overview of the literature*, London: Home Office research and planning unit report.

UNHCR (1993a). *Porodice izbeglica u Jugoslaviji* (Refugee families in the Federal Republic of Yugoslavia). Belgrade: Visoki komesarijat Ujedinjenih nacija za izbeglice (UNHCR) i Institut za socijalnu politiku.

———(1993b). *Socijalne službe u zbrinjavanje ugroženih izbeglica.* (Social services for helping vulnerable categories of refugees). Belgrade: Visoki komesarijat Ujedinjenih nacija za izbeglice (UNHCR) i Institut za socijalnu politiku.

Stiglmayer, A. (1994). The rapes in Bosnia-Herzegovina. In *Mass rape: the war against women in Bosnia-Herzegovina*, ed. A. Stiglmayer. Lincoln: University of Nebraska Press.

Vickers, J. (1993). *Women and war*. London and New Jersey: Zed Books.

Vojna enciklopedija (1977). Istorija srednjevekovne bosanske države (A history of the medieval Bosnian state). Belgrade.

Vukov, M., and N. Baba Milkić (1993). *Osećajni život savremenog čoveka i droge* (Drugs and the emotional life of contemporary man). Niš: Prosveta.

Wiesenthal, S. (1991). *Maks i Helen* (Max and Helen). Novi Sad: Dnevnik.

Zajovic, S. (1994). Zloupotreba žrtava (Abuse of the victims). In *Žene za mir.* Belgrade: Žene u crnom.

Žarkov, D. (1995). Gender, orientalism and the history of ethnic hatred in the former Yugoslavia. In *Crossfires: nationalism, racism and gender in Europe*, eds. H. Lutz, A. Phoenix, and N. Yuval-Davis. London: Pluto Press.

List of contributors

Slobodanka Konstantinović-Vilić is a professor of criminology at the Law School in Niš. She is the author of *Women Murderers* and one of the co-authors of *The Criminality of Adolescent Girls* and *Women of Krajina: War, Exodus and Refuge*. She is one of the founders of the SOS Telephone for Women and Children Victims of Violence (in Niš and Leskovac) and the Female Research, Education and Communication Center (in Niš).

Vesna Nikolić-Ristanović is a senior researcher at the Institute for Criminological and Sociological Research and a lecturer at the Center for Women's Studies in Belgrade. She is the author of *Women Victims of Crime* and *Social Control and Criminality of Women* and a co-author of *Women of Krajina: War, Exodus and Refuge*. She has published a number of criminological and victimological papers on the topic of violence against women. She is also the co-ordinator of the Group for Women's Rights (the European Movement in Serbia), and the president of the Victimological Society of Serbia.

Nataša Mrvić-Petrović is a senior researcher at the Institute for Criminological and Sociological Research in Belgrade. She is the author of a number of works dealing with violence against women and co-author of *Social Control and Criminality of Women* and *Women of Krajina: War, Exodus and Refuge*.

Ivana Stevanović is a research assistant at the Institute for Criminological and Sociological Research in Belgrade. She co-authored *Women of Krajina: War, Exodus and Refuge* and is currently the vice-president of the Victimological Society of Serbia.

The authors are members of the Group for Women's Rights (the European Movement in Serbia), under whose auspices this research on violence against women in the war in the former Yugoslavia was carried out.

Index

Also Available from CEU Press

Recently Published

Voices in the Shadows
Women and Verbal Art in Serbia and Bosnia

Celia Hawkesworth, School of Slavonic and
East European Studies, University of London

"A standard reference book for everyone dealing with the history of the region." **Zdenko Lešić,** Hankuk University of Foreign Studies, Seoul

Women are conspicuously absent from traditional cultural histories of South-East Europe. This book addresses that imbalance by describing the contribution of women to literary culture in the Orthodox/Ottoman areas of Serbia and Bosnia.

The author provides a broad chronological account of this contribution, dividing the book into two main parts; the earlier period up until the eighteenth century concentrates on the projections of gender through the medium of oral tradition and the lives of a handful of educated women in medieval Serbia and the few works of literature they left. Hawkesworth also looks at the written literature produced by women, first in the mid-nineteenth century and then at the turn of the century. The second part focuses on the trials and tribulations that affected feminism and women's literature throughout the twentieth century. The author finishes by highlighting the new women's movement, 1975–1990, a great period for women in Yugoslavia which created a stimulating atmosphere for outstanding pieces of women's journalism, prose and verse, culminating in the creation of new women's studies courses in many universities.

Voices in the Shadows is the first complete literary history in relation to women's writing in South-East Europe.

2000
281 pages
963-9116-62-9 cloth $49.95 / Ł31.95

AVAILABLE TO ORDER AT ALL GOOD BOOKSHOPS
OR CHECK OUT OUR WEBSITE WWW.CEUPRESS.COM
FOR FULL ORDERING DETAILS.